BEYOND SITCOM

BEYOND SITCOM

New Directions in American Television Comedy

Antonio Savorelli

McFarland & Company, Inc., Publishers
Jefferson, North Carolina, and London

The present work is a revised and expanded edition of a book published in Milan, Italy, by FrancoAngeli in 2008 titled *Oltre la sitcom: Indagine sulle nuove forme comiche della televisione americana*

LIBRARY OF CONGRESS CATALOGUING-IN-PUBLICATION DATA

Savorelli, Antonio.
    Beyond sitcom : new directions in American television comedy / Antonio Savorelli.
    p.   cm.
    Includes bibliographical references and index.

    ISBN 978-0-7864-5843-1
    softcover : 50# alkaline paper ∞

    1. Situation comedies (Television programs)— United States. I. Title.
    PN1992.8.C66S38   2010
    791.45′617 — dc22   2010008705

British Library cataloguing data are available

©2010 Antonio Savorelli. All rights reserved

No part of this book may be reproduced or transmitted in any form or by any means, electronic or mechanical, including photocopying or recording, or by any information storage and retrieval system, without permission in writing from the publisher.

Cover image: Lisa Kudrow as Valerie Cherish in *The Comeback*, 2005 (photograph by John P. Johnson, HBO/Photofest)

Manufactured in the United States of America

McFarland & Company, Inc., Publishers
  Box 611, Jefferson, North Carolina 28640
    www.mcfarlandpub.com

Table of Contents

Acknowledgments vi
Preface 1
Introduction 3

1. Situation Comedy 21
2. *Scrubs* 35
3. *The Office* 65
4. *The Comeback* 85
5. *Ugly Betty* 107
6. Genre Dynamics 132
7. Comedy, Misplaced 152
8. Comedy and Reality 167

Glossary 185
Chapter Notes 191
Bibliography 197
Index 205

Acknowledgments

I am not exactly a fan of long tearful lists of helpers, but I must thank my very good friend and copyeditor Erin Wilcox for her courage and patience in helping me make my work become an actual book in English. Also, thanks for those happy old times as stand partners in the second violins of the UC Berkeley Symphony Orchestra — that is when I realized there might be hope for my Italian humor in a foreign place.

Time to thank the parents now — what kind of son would I be otherwise? She may have been spared from this edition, but I must thank my mom for helping me proofread all the different versions in Italian, and I swear the (very, very few) mistakes left are all on me. And my dad for sitting through hours of *Friends* and, back in the early '80s, when I had no idea comedy would become this important, through reruns of *Alice*, *The Mary Tyler Moore Show* and, above all, *Three's Company*.

Finally, I must thank all the friends, on two continents and various coasts, whom I have coerced into becoming television addicts, or who have, at one time or another, shared a couch and a TV set with me. Thank you all for the time, the talking, the suggestions, the endless quotes, and that pair of navy scrubs.

Preface

This book is the culmination of almost five years' worth of work and thousands of hours of television watching. It originally appeared in Italy (FrancoAngeli, 2008) as a modified version of my doctoral dissertation. Publishing it in the United States has given me the opportunity to go beyond a simple translation and consider my new audience — a readership potentially much wider than my original one, and with a much more diverse range of cultural and theoretical backgrounds.

I acknowledge that semiotics might not be every American's most familiar subject — whereas Italian communication and media students find it a core subject in their early curriculum. Therefore, I have attempted to ease the reader's way into the issues at hand, as much as possible without becoming too didactic for the more informed. This is, after all, a book on a particular kind of televisual text, and semiotics is the key I use to unlock the example texts and understand how they work. The semiotic practice, and specifically the structural analysis, is only one of the many possible scientific approaches to these texts, and, while this study does not aim to be comprehensive, it strives to be accurate within its chosen frame.

Although I am not dealing with history per se, I always confront the perishability of the objects of my research. Television is a quickly produced, quickly consumed medium — in the United States even more than in Italy, where production and broadcasting practices allow for slightly more relaxed pacing. One of the shows I analyzed in this research, *The Comeback*, was canceled even before I started writing about it for the first time, back in 2005. However, that does not mean it is outdated or that it has lost its relevance: I like to think it was aired ahead of its time. I also like to think that, thanks to the endless possibilities for televisual texts to be enjoyed out of their original medium (what a head-scratcher for classic media theories, and perhaps for semiotics, too!), my readers will still appreciate its role in the evolution of the narrative languages of television comedy.

Preface

In order to provide a broader understanding of the scope and significance of contemporary comedy, I have added a chapter on the uses of comedy in non-comic shows. The crossing and mixing of genres is moving from being the exception that confirms certain predefined textual boundaries to becoming a new rule, or a diffused practice in television making. This new chapter also underscores comedy's cultural role in processing reality and making sense of the world.

The conclusions of my study have not changed in the past two years. The more television I watch, and the more I re-watch old shows, the more I can confirm that an evolution is under way. American televisual comedy has reached a more mature, complex stage of its existence, and the same can be said, more generally, about television as a narrative medium. Whether the evolution of expressive forms is cause or effect — or simply an indication — of changes in their cultural and social context is beyond the scope of this analysis, but I hope my research will be a solid basis on which to build future studies not only of texts, but also of their audiences and the cultures in which they are produced.

This edition has also gained a glossary that will provide insight into those terms readers may find unfamiliar or even controversial.

Introduction

For the past decade, the production of comic series on American television has revealed a new tendency, which, even at an uninformed glance, clashes with the situation-comedy genre's well-known tradition. With this research I have departed from the established path of television studies based on socio-psycho-economic paradigms, which seem to be better regarded in both American and European academia. Although I do not underestimate the significance, the importance or the results of such approaches, I prefer to turn my gaze onto other aspects of televisual fiction, particularly those aspects related to the texts' structures of meaning production.

To this effect, I chose to explore the matter by following the established structuralist methods of semiotic textual analysis, which have been developed not only as studies of utterance and narrativity, but also as tools to investigate the field of enunciation and the pragmatic aspects of texts.

Regardless of its dominance on the economic level (and, consequently, on the cultural one), American television production has been widely neglected by semiotic research, for different orders of reasons. One is the current lack of a strong semiotic culture in the United States — and more generally in the field of English-language television studies. Even those who have practiced semiotic approaches within the framework of cultural studies still overlook the field's importance. This results in its dismissal as an almost play-like intellectual activity performed on "texts," rather than a discipline with rigorous scientific foundations.[1]

Second, and the reason why in the line above I chose to put the word *texts* between quotes, I have noticed a more and more frequent tendency to underestimate the epistemological weight of the concept of text, which gets deprived of the necessary autonomy to produce meaning *independent* of an audience's presence. This is not to say that a text does not need a receiver, or that the audience is totally irrelevant in the process of televisual communication. It means, rather, that I would like to avoid

Introduction

complying with a centrifugal tendency to consider the text as a signifier whose signified is idiosyncratic in nature, residing chiefly on the receiving end of communication, hence outside the text itself.[2]

While I do understand the reasons behind this kind of criticism, which structural semiotics has often not been able to prevent or oppose, I continue to believe that texts are autonomous to a certain degree, not simply as glass-enclosed worlds, but as relatively open systems necessarily in touch with the cultures that foster their production. Some might consider this point of view rather conservative, but I want to keep believing in this autonomy: perhaps the text will not be the only source of salvation, as maintained by what is probably the best known (and most often misquoted) of Algirdas Julien Greimas's precepts, yet the text's capacity to predict the ways audiences will comprehend it remains vital. Therefore, the text plays a key role in the choice of appropriate analytical tools. As much as the act of reception is most certainly indispensable for bringing texts back to their source cultures, I have deemed it necessary to leave such process outside the scope of this inquiry.

The boundaries of the text (both the general concept of it and the actual object of analysis) need to be redefined and softened when approaching TV production — be it live shows, largely more spontaneous, or ones that are scripted and recorded. Yet, I have chosen not to make such boundaries wider than the texts themselves would allow. The objects of this research have not turned out to be lazy machines, as Umberto Eco would call them,[3] but rather the opposite: they are dynamic and flexible. While they could not in themselves determine which tools to use in their analysis, these texts have assisted from within, due to their own nature, my choice of the most appropriate analytical tools. It has been fulfilling, during and at the end of this research, to realize not only that some initial hypotheses were confirmed, but also that some others were not — an indication that while a text may lend itself to being opened, it will show resistance to forcible misuse.

A third limitation imposed on the study of American TV fiction in my home country is a cultural one, linked to the need for a text to be taken into account as close as possible to its context of origin. This limitation is particularly evident in the texts I considered, whose comic disposition is lost in most attempts to translate their verbal component. In

Introduction

Italy, all foreign audiovisual productions are dubbed before reaching the audience for the first time, usually with mixed results. Even when conducted within semiotic paradigms, recent studies of non–Italian television have been more often than not based on the dubbed versions, which necessarily imposes a bias on any conclusions that may have been reached. Sitcom has, for years, suffered from the effects of dubbing, since many jokes, whose translations fail to reproduce both their humorous and their comedic intentions, clash with the presence of a laugh track. Consequently, foreign series based more on physical comedy have recorded higher success rates than foreign series based more on verbal comedy. Avoiding this inconvenience has been one of the conditions of my research, which I have met through the use of the original versions as the only texts suitable for semiotic analysis, and through my knowledge — not unlimited, but as extensive and accurate as possible — of the cultural context in which the chosen shows were produced.

One further order of issues relates to the kinds of texts on which this inquiry focuses. The difficulties comedy raises stem from the need to overcome definitions of the genre that are no more than truisms, and which end up conditioning the analysis itself. The idea of comedy as something that "makes one laugh" is not only reductive but not necessarily true. The term *comedy,* even in the stricter sense of television series, shelters a number of texts very different in nature. This research focuses on four comedy series that bear, to different extents and for various reasons, links to the realm of situation comedy, and, more generally, show a higher degree of awareness of their televisual nature.

The interest of this inquiry is not whether comedy "makes one laugh." On the contrary, closer inspection reveals that the euphorizing effect is not always the ultimate goal of the series here examined. My aim is to understand which mechanisms lie at the core of the comic text — at least of *these* comic texts, as opposed to the most established comic tradition of television on the one hand, and non-comic televisual productions on the other. My research aims in two primary directions: one is a critique of those definitions of comedy articulated on a strictly thymic basis (that is, in particular, regarding its euphoric and euphorizing functions), while the other explores issues of veridiction and the relationship between comedy and televisual realism.

Introduction

Without anticipating too much of the next chapters, those last two points must be further explained. First, the series I have examined show that comedy does not necessarily have a euphoric content, thus does not always stage worlds ruled by jokes and stories with happy endings. The laughter comedy provokes, as will be seen, is not always immediately euphoric in nature.

Second, due to comedy's postulated inclination to cause laughter, many critics and viewers consider it a scarcely realistic genre, one whose veridictive pact would entail an adherence to worlds that almost never work like the real world works. Or, alternatively, they justify comedy as a veil that, once lifted, reveals the real tragedies of human existence. As I will demonstrate, veridiction in comedy is quite a different issue, and its connection to reality does not necessarily lie on the axis of comedy's willingness or ability to represent that reality. On the other hand, the link to tragedy and the possible presence of tragedy in contemporary American television pertain to a separate order of problems that would need to be investigated through dedicated research.

Lexical Ambiguities and Theoretical Lacks

I will not spend too many words on the misunderstandings generated in Italy by the use of the term *fiction* to refer to something that it is not — a genre — when it is actually a class of genres, or better, a heterogeneous class of texts produced for television. The word *fiction* is used in English very differently, to indicate literary narratives — not including texts of a biographical nature, which are classified as nonfiction.

The use of *fiction* constitutes a fairly new terminology trickled into everyday language from Italian television-production lingo, which — like many corporate environments — is known to like, overuse and misuse English words, especially of American origin. Previously — particularly in the 1980s, when the newborn Italian commercial networks started importing massive amounts of foreign productions — the term used to indicate television series and serials, specifically American ones, was *telefilm*. This term constitutes an impropriety of a different sort, as it more correctly indicates films made for television. While *telefilm* is still

Introduction

in use in informal language, it seems to be deprecated in the official vocabulary of television in favor of the more modern, more inclusive *fiction*.

From a certain point of view, any scripted text is fictional — it's the destiny of performing arts as two-stage arts. A literary biography and a filmic one are deemed to make, for some reason, different veridictive statements, as if the former could be a faithful account of reality (showing what has been), while the latter were nothing more than a representation, a staging (interpreting what has been). This is a reason why there is no concept of documentary in literature, while it exists on both film and television.

It is true, in a way, that the issue of the shifting boundaries between fiction and nonfiction exists only in an intercultural perspective, being that in either of the languages I'm comparing, the term *fiction* is used only in one medium and not the other. On the Italian side, though, the problem remains because this term, once used only in the restricted milieu of television producers, has now spread to the public and covers, without further specifications, a range of very different textual genres.

One consequence is the lack of precise genre indications on Italian television guides, a situation so far gone that almost any pre-recorded, strictly scripted show is considered "fiction," from the two-part biopic to the American teen drama, all the way to soap opera. This lack is reflected in the academic discourse on televisual narratives, which often cannot see beyond the pseudo-genre of "fiction." In so doing, it flattens all actual genre distinctions instead of taking them into account, a research condition which would be fundamental to in-depth analysis.

On the other hand, to completely avoid this lexical ambiguity, some consideration could be given to what author and screenwriter Andrea Camilleri proposed during his talk at the Roma Fiction Fest 2007, namely to resume the usage of the term *sceneggiato,* literally "scripted": after all, the one common element among fictional televisual products is their being scripted. At the same time, though, this word still carries connotations dating back to an unripe stage of the history of Italian television, when it used to stage well-known stories, transposing them from other media — that is, from other semiotic systems.

The limitations of this class of genres in Italy partially explains the lack of properly conducted semiotic studies applied to televisual narratives in general,[4] not to mention a substantial absence of studies specifically regarding comedy. On the other hand, newscasts and reality shows have caught the attention of semioticians,[5] perhaps because of the idea that they are somewhat more genuinely televisual than narrative series — which I maintain is only a false impression.

The lexical ambiguity is maintained in a recent Italian publication, the collection of the proceedings from a conference on televisual narratives held at the University of San Marino in 2007,[6] whose title can be translated as *Serial Worlds: Semiotic Paths in Fiction*. Despite being the only semiotically strong approach to televisual narrative texts published in Italy in recent times, by not explicitly mentioning television in its title this collection perpetuates the lack of genre definition that affects both the production and the understanding of television in Italy. Unfortunately, this indeterminacy is reflected at the theoretical level in a couple of contributions to the collection, both of which deal, in part or in whole, with comic texts. These contributions either fail to appropriately recognize comedy as pertinent in the analysis or approach the idea of comedy laterally, considering comedy not as a structural property of the text but as a possible interpretation.

One contribution, whose title translates to "Why didn't *The O.C.* work?: Triumphs and failures of teen fiction,"[7] studies teen drama (called "teen fiction" in the original) "in order to see how it had developed since the times of *Happy Days*." By considering *Happy Days* (ABC: 1974–1984) as a historical antecedent of *The O.C.* (Fox: 2003–2007) and *Dawson's Creek* (The WB: 1998–2003), hence failing to recognize it as a situation comedy, the analysis assumes a double fallacy as one of its premises: it wrongly identifies the show's genre and, consequently, misjudges its target audience. Not once does the article mention comedy or the presence of a laugh track in the show. The failure to acknowledge genre — especially one so complex as comedy — as pertinent to the analysis endangers whatever results the article reaches, not only about the meaning of *Happy Days* in and of itself, but also particularly when comparing the cultural relevance of the three shows.

The second contribution, "Looking across Italian fiction: The case of *Boris*,"[8] considers a contemporary Italian comedy series, *Boris* (Fox Italia:

Introduction

2007–present), which was remarkably similar — both in terms of the way it was produced and in its particular thematic approach — to newer American shows. The article correctly assigns the show to the genre of comedy and identifies its satirical goals, which are targeted at a certain way of making television. However, the pertinence of comedy is often treated as secondary. The focus seems to be on the term *fiction* as central to the analysis: "*Boris* is a meta-fiction: it tells the story of how an Italian fiction is made."[9] This is not entirely accurate. *Boris* is a *comedy show* about the making of a low-grade Italian *soap opera,* and it lacks the descriptive, almost prescriptive quality emerging from the article. The article seems to consider comedy not a structural property of the text but the result of an act of interpretation obtained with the aid of paratextual cues, such as the opening theme — as if the text itself were not offering enough evidence. The insistence on the concepts of parody and satire, while certainly appropriate, results in a marginalization of comedy as a stand-alone genre and the identification of the comic effect as secondary to a somewhat nobler, less mundane intent of criticizing a certain state of affairs (deemed as real, that is empirically verifiable), with an ultimate ethical goal.

That a lexical ambiguity originating in Italian television production is carried over to television studies indicates a lower level of interest in televisual narratives as forms of expression. Semiotic approaches should never take any kind of status quo for granted, yet even the few existing ones do not clarify the ambiguity. On the other hand, the lack of semiotic studies of television contrasts with a historical abundance of studies on cinematic narratives. The formal resemblance between the two semiotic systems, however, should not fool anyone, as the conclusions drawn — as well as the methods used — in the study of cinema cannot be lightly applied to a different medium. With my research I would like to take a few more steps toward a more autonomous and legitimized consideration of television's fictional narratives, and comedy in particular.

I built my initial approach to televisual text from Christian Metz's film theory, with regard to both the mechanics of discourse (such as text segmentation) and other thorny aspects yet crucial to my analysis, such as the theory of enunciation. It seemed natural to adapt Metz's theory to a medium and a class of texts it did not originally include, but whose diversity from cinematic text had not necessarily been taken into account.

Despite its similarities to film, televisual narrative text can be studied independently of it, since it is *by its own nature* destined to television. By nature, that is not only because it was produced for television broadcasting, but also because it contains textual markers, both discursive and narrative, of a sort of televisual form imposed on a common material origin, which makes film and television substantially different, albeit not radically so.[10] The semiotic tools most effective to film analysis served as an excellent base for this research, but it has been necessary to bend some of their assumptions to adapt them, as required by the texts, to a medium that follows textual logics different from cinema's, in spite of a common audiovisual appearance.

The Intervention of Semiotics

To convey how semiotics can shed some light on texts and reach the ultimate goal of this research, I must first eliminate a common ambiguity on the role of semiotics and its operative function, that is, the idea that the purpose of structural analysis is only that of taking texts apart layer by layer, like onions, to reveal their deep structures. Actually, the primary criticism stems from the fact that, in many cases, texts similar in genre or cultural origins are based on similar deep structures — with the limit often attained by reality shows, commonly regarded as being "all the same" deep within, which would invalidate the effectiveness of the semiotic approach.

One response to this kind of analysis is that the generative approach is a semiotic method at all levels, and that different texts will make different levels of the generative trajectory relevant to their comprehension, without the process becoming any less semiotical. Secondly, one might say the structural analysis of an isolated text, without premises and goals specific to a certain research, is nothing but a scholastic exercise, which cannot but lead to results of limited interest. Even stronger, then, is the need to compare texts as a way of revealing the levels pertinent to the analysis itself.

Introduction

I would have never thought of conducting this research simply by comparing the results of a deep-structure analysis of the chosen texts. On the contrary, I will show that these texts may often deploy the pertinence of other levels in the production of meaning. The generative model, as well as the theories of enunciation, was developed originally for verbal texts, and particularly for literature, and only later extended to visual texts. Its further extension to the moving image happened first with classic film, and now tends to fail again when approaching evenemential texts (that is, those that happen in the moment, and can be planned only to a certain extent), such as those of live, mostly unscripted television.

One more issue I must clarify regards the multiplicity and variety of television's semiotic systems. First of all, television is, like film, a syncretism of various semiotic systems contributing to the creation of a complex system whose capacity for meaning is, arguably, greater than that of the sum of its parts. In addition, just as verbal languages require different approaches depending on the medium that carries them and whether they are oral or written, likewise television does not consist of a uniform language. Failing to evaluate television's specificities would generate an error similar to a very common one in musical semiotics, which occurs whenever music is considered as a solid system that can be approached indiscriminately with the same set of tools. It is not so, and the required tools are not necessarily the same ones used in classic semiotics, tools more oriented to verbal languages. This has been only one obstacle in the way of a sensible development of musical semiotics.

Studying televisual narratives could then be, to semiotics, a way to sharpen its tools and approach a class of languages unfamiliar and neglected by definition. Classic film theories can help only in part, and I will show how they can be transported to a medium in constant evolution, which is emerging more and more as a new art form.

Rupturing the scholastic frames of generative analysis means daring to break out of the utterance and tackle enunciation mechanisms that are less and less abstract, less presupposed, more present and almost tangible. It is necessary to revise the theories of enunciation in order to understand the dynamics that hold together narrative televisual texts, and particularly contemporary American comedy, whose funny side can often be counterintuitive.

Introduction

One last confirmation that semiotics is not ready to approach televisual texts — but, for the same reason, also cinematic and theatrical ones — is the enormous lexical ambiguity generated by the term *actor*. In televisual texts, an actor is not only a discursive configuration, but also the person (physical, real, empirical, whatever the term might be) who plays a certain role on stage or set. In my analysis, I will avoid both the capitalization of terms of the semiotic realm (Actors, Subject), which I consider pompous and distracting, and the use of disambiguating periphrases such as *actor of the utterance*. Consequently, I cannot but resume using the term *character*, a term deprecated by Greimas himself, who considered it not as semiotically rich as the term *actor*, but one that will in this case remove any ambiguity.[11] In other words, to the purpose of this discussion's simplicity, I hereby assign to the term *character* all semiotic properties attributed to the concept of *actor* in classic greimasian theory. I am sure also the purists will understand the urgency of the matter. (However, derivatives such as *actorial* and *actorialization*, hardly confusing, will be kept.)

The Choice of Texts

For my research I have considered four comedy series produced over the past decade (starting in 2001), which even at first glance appear to be breaking off from the typical features of classic American comedy. I will demonstrate that this fracture is accompanied by an increased self-awareness of the comic genre (or the version thereof embodied by each series) and by an open and continuous dialog with the genre itself and its expressive foundations.

The chosen series, whose details I will introduce in their dedicated chapters, are *Scrubs* (NBC: 2001–2008; ABC: 2009–present); *The Office* (NBC: spring 2005–present); *The Comeback* (HBO: summer 2005); and *Ugly Betty* (ABC: 2006–2010).

Among these, *The Office* and *Ugly Betty* are somewhat special cases. The former is an adaptation of a two-season British series aired by the BBC from 2001. This adaptation does not raise obstacles to the analysis, since the whole series, despite the initial similarities, was recreated

Introduction

to fully adhere to American culture, and, in a way, to represent it. *Ugly Betty* is the adaptation of the 1999 Colombian telenovela *Yo soy Betty, la fea,* reproduced in several other countries before finally landing in the United States. My interest in the American production stems from the particular tone and scope of the adaptation, which has wholly become an expression of the new generation of comedy.

My claim is not that these series are based on new or unique discursive elements. The *mise en abyme,* the embedding of a secondary enunciative level into the main utterance performed by *The Office* and *The Comeback,* has now become a cinematic and televisual topos, while the narrator's voice-over found in *Scrubs* is nothing new, as it can be found in various shows such as *Sex and the City* (HBO: 1998–2004). I have considered these particular series to highlight their specific enunciative strategies and the way they adhere to these strategies without necessarily making them transparent. While the narrator in *Sex and the City* is a discursive device linked to a strong thematic component of the main character (she is a journalist who writes a new article in each episode, which becomes in a way the ideal source of the voice), her voice is used in an almost literary fashion, as if the televisual medium were only a visualization of what might otherwise be read in a book, while the story could be mostly enjoyed also in its absence.[12]

On the other hand, I will show that the narrator's voice in *Scrubs* has no neutral role, but is inextricable from the visual (filmic) portion of the text. Likewise, the multiplication of enunciative levels in *The Office* and *The Comeback* is not simply a rhetorical game, but a definite strategy of enunciation — thus, of communication — that helps in *founding* the two texts' comic natures, instead of being nothing more than an accident.

What is at stake here is not just a definition of *text,* but a definition of *the* texts serving as objects of this particular investigation. Not only in terms of how to motivate the choice of a certain corpus (which texts will be chosen and in what measure — not only number, but mainly duration, in the case of a time-based medium), but also in the definition of what constitutes *text* in the analysis. It is a delicate issue, but not an insurmountable one, and sometimes even quite intuitive, when dealing with the televisual flow, where the text coexists — sharing time, and often even space — with whatever surrounds it, which, if included in the definition, would radically change the object, scope and purpose of the analysis.

Given the presence of a televisual flow — especially for series aired on NBC and ABC, which show commercials not only between programs but also within single episodes — it bears clarifying what I have considered to be text in this work. In particular, I have decided to analyze whatever has actually been used in producing the DVD version of each series, for reasons of practicality and coherence, since part of the task was performed on the DVDs, while more recent seasons were analyzed on the recordings of aired episodes. Hence, I have left out all possible graphic overlays, including network logos, even when they made direct references to the texts. More specifically, working on *The Office*, I have analyzed only the episodes produced for television, thus excluding the webisodes and deleted scenes published on NBC's website starting in the summer of 2006. Similarly, I have not considered, with *Ugly Betty*, the episodes of the telenovela *Vidas de fuego* or any other special content published on ABC's website.

A discourse on new forms of comedy and on the possibilities offered by the links between different media, particularly between television and web, could be expanded well beyond the boundaries of this research. My goals, though, do not require such an expansion, but favor a more restricting definition of text, within the limits traced by the medium and the languages of television.

Metatextual Nature of New Comedy

One common element among these texts is the metatextual and metasemiotic inclination, which is explicit and constant, albeit different in each series, at both the enunciative and the utterative levels. Classic comedy also has metatextual tendencies, but they are usually expressed as intertextual references, aimed at mutual confirmation and validation among texts of the same genre; a second, important function of metatextual tendencies in classic comedy is to strengthen, starting from a single utterance, the communication strategies of a television network.

Introduction

These are mostly isolated occurrences that do not constitute the core of these series' discursive and narrative strategies, and thus do not alter, with any substantial variations, the solidity of the original model. Intertextual references become an occasional form of play, which reinforces the texts' comic foundations without that play becoming their main source.

Several newer comic series, whose details I will not consider here, but which I will refer to from time to time, use metatextuality as one of their main discursive elements. I am going to outline the different levels at which this process occurs.

First, we find a purely utterative level of quotations and citations — usually verbal, in the characters' discourses — alluding to other televisual texts, which are a necessary reference for the construction of the shows' identities and the consolidation of a collective imagery. This is the simplest level, inherited from classic sitcom; despite not being anything new (quoting is allowed and widespread in all media and art forms), it becomes an integral part of new comedy's metatextual system.

A second kind of intertextual quotation, also placed within the utterance, exploits the characters' thematic construction, particularly in the choice of actors who play certain roles. Some actors' professional histories become not only objects of allusion, but often also grounds for discursive and narrative elaboration. In a first-season episode of *Arrested Development* (Fox: 2003–2006), Barry Zuckerhorn, the Bluth family's inept lawyer played by Henry Winkler (well known as Fonzie on *Happy Days*), is about to comb his hair in front of a bathroom mirror, but stops and raises his arms in Fonzie-like self-satisfaction — the only occasion on which the lawyer shows some confidence. In season three, a new lawyer, Bob Loblaw, played by Scott Baio, claims that it would not be the first time he has been called to replace Zuckerhorn; this is one more reference to *Happy Days,* where Scott Baio's character, Fonzie's younger cousin Chachi, was reportedly introduced to give support to an aging Henry Winkler.

This second kind of metatextual reference becomes extreme when one of the actors plays himself, even though not in a biographically accurate way. It's the case of the main character in *Curb Your Enthusiasm* (HBO: 2000–present, in noncontinuous seasons), Larry David, in real life the co-creator and producer of *Seinfeld* (NBC: 1989–1998). What is peculiar in this series is the blending of fictional traits — that is, generally, the episodes' premises and narrative developments — with others that refer to a certain "reality," both extratextual and metatextual. The external references can be considered textual objects, since the general public rarely has direct access to and first-hand experience of news and knowledge about celebrities' lives; rather, these are most often based on media texts of different kinds and genres. *Curb Your Enthusiasm* builds on the fact that Larry David has been prone to episodes of intolerance and hot temper (both on the job and in his private life), which serves the show as a great source of credibility and narrative development.

These first two levels of metatextual references — also intertextual because they are linked to the existence of *other* texts beside the main one — are widespread in comedy, and become even more prominent in newer comic forms of televisual narrative. They are employed in the series analyzed here, but these series take some further steps. A third kind of metatextual behavior is the frequent insertion, within the utterance, of other fictional texts functional to the existence of the primary text. This occurs in *Ugly Betty,* and also, in a lesser form, in *The Comeback.* A telenovela and a newscast in the former, a sitcom and a reality show in the latter become an integral part of the primary text, with notable consequences on the enunciative level.

A fourth kind of metatextual behavior involves a further shift of the metatextual mechanism toward the realm of the enunciation, with the *mise en abyme* of uttered enunciative devices, consistent in form with the primary enunciation, yet mostly transparent in its regard. This happens in *The Office* and *The Comeback,* which imitate respectively the documentary genre and a form of reality show.

This fourth level is a short step away from a more generally metasemiotic inclination. If intertextuality is a reference to texts that actually exist outside the main text's boundaries, and pure metatextuality is the existence, in different forms, of fictional yet embedded texts, a metasemiotic function is achieved when a discourse is explicitly built *about* the semiotic system used to produce the main text. Even so, the reference can be established to empiric, external texts; to fictional, embedded texts; or, in a self-referential act, to the main text itself. All three cases occur, specifically, in *Scrubs* and *The Comeback,* but I will show how all the chosen texts eventually perform some metasemiotic activity and tend to discursivize self-referential acts. This can occur both within verbal utterances (in the characters' discourses), and, more subtly, wherever the enunciative device plays with the visual component to build discourses on the languages of television (as in *The Office*).

Opening of the Serial Model

Confirming a progressive distancing from the narrative standards of traditional situation comedy, the shows I have analyzed can also be differentiated from each other by the degree of opening of their serial models. Two of them (*The Comeback*, *Ugly Betty*) are built from the beginning as open series, featuring long-running narrative frameworks. This implies, especially in *Ugly Betty,* a more complex story that overflows the boundaries of each single episode so far as to possibly cover the entire span of the series. I will show that each of them adheres to this model in varying degrees, according also to the textual genres of reference (reality show in one case, and especially telenovela in the other).

In contrast, the other two series are originally more closed, which means that actions developed in each episode hardly condition other episodes. This is true both in a narrative sense and, as a direct consequence, from the point of view of fruition: a closed series is more suitable for casual viewing, whereas an open one requires dedication and is more likely to build a solid, constant viewership. However, *Scrubs* and *The Office* do not deploy the same kind of closing. Even though it usually closes story lines within one episode's span, *Scrubs* maintains a long-run time progression, which allows for the characters to grow beyond their original design; on the other hand, the first season of *The Office* features episodes that seem temporally disengaged from one another and can easily be watched at random without any effect on one's understanding of the story. Despite this difference, both series' repetition models are built on the constancy of basic discursive structures (particularly the characters' definitions and the relationship among them) and, symmetrically, of the shows' underlying value systems.

The model of serial closing is limited, nonetheless, because it keeps working only as long as the series' premises keep constant. More specifically, it works only as long as the relationships between discursive elements (in series with discursive constancy) and between narrative elements (in series with narrative constancy) stay the same. When this identity fails — and often even when it is later restored — the serial model undergoes a process of opening, which is frequent when a closed American series survives its first season. That is what happens, for instance, with *Friends* (NBC: 1994–2004), where the cliffhanger that ends the first season starts the troubled story of Ross and Rachel, which had previously been little more than an inside joke, just a hint of future developments. It is definitely the destiny of *Scrubs,* which opens its serial model when the relationships among characters change more radically (particularly with Jordan's speech at the end of season one and her comeback in season two, when she decides she wants Dr. Cox back). It is even more the case with *The Office,* whose second season starts several long-term narrative lines (the ambiguous relationship between Jim and Pam, Michael and Jan's story, but also Dwight and Angela's).

It often happens that one of the main motives for serial opening of an originally closed series is the evolution of the characters' passional investments, which are deployed as the emergence and recurrence of themes of love and sexual engagement. Despite any apparent similarities — and possible comments by fans or critics — this phenomenon has very little to do with the way soap operas feature such themes as serial mechanisms.

Plan of the Work

The next chapter will consist of a brief overview on classic-form situation comedy, which will better highlight its borders with new comedy and provide more detailed reasons for the choice of analyzed texts.

The four following chapters will then conduct the structural analysis of each series. It will not be a detailed account of the analysis, which would be fatal to any reader, but a more concise version, functional to the goals of this research. Quoting audiovisual texts raises, as can be imagined, issues in any written account of the analysis. Thus, for prac-

Introduction

tical reasons, I have chosen to quote excerpts as transcriptions of dialogs, accompanied, when necessary, by descriptions of scenes and actions, which should provide readers with the appropriate amount of detail. If this cannot replace the viewing of the texts themselves, I have at least tried to integrate as many elements as could favor the reader's imagination. As with all textual analyses, I still recommend that the reader be familiar with the texts under scrutiny — if not with the whole series, at least with the general concepts and, specifically, with the cited episodes.

The sixth chapter, "Genre Dynamics," will cover the relationship between the analyzed texts and the wider panorama of classic American sitcoms. Based on the performed analysis, this chapter's main point of view follows the strategies employed by each text in order to "find its genre," that is, to place itself in opposition to situation comedy. I will also show how this placement lends these shows an important metadiscursive function that is anything but occasional, and in fact vital to their existence. As opposed to what happens in situation comedy, as revealed in chapter one, I will also show the different strategies each series employs in the management of dysphoria.

The seventh chapter, "Comedy, Misplaced," will elaborate on the issue of genre dynamics by giving a few significant examples of a phenomenon that seems quite frequent in recent television, that is, the introduction of comic elements in shows that are, by definition, non-comic. These might be called odd episodes, interrupting as they do the normal flow of a series, dismantling its regular enunciative mechanisms, even though only for a moment within the show's entire span. In that moment, comedy seems to have its way, but does it really? Far from being exhaustive of all possible cases (only a whole book might explore them in more depth), the chapter explains the function of such incursions of comedy into serious drama.

The final chapter, "Comedy and reality," focuses on another key point in the definition of comedy as a fictional genre, namely the veridictive status of televisual texts — not only comic texts, but fictional ones in general. This chapter benefits from the analyses conducted in previous chapters and helps further reframe them in the broader context of narrative television. The results are anything but predictable.

1

Situation Comedy

Definitions

The American Heritage Dictionary[1] defines *situation comedy* as "a humorous television series having a regular cast of characters." This definition, quite useless in itself, stresses the regularity of the actorial structure, which does not shed much light on the concept, considering that any television series is based on a regular cast of actors.

A more adequate definition may be achieved by splitting the concept into its two core terms. The *American Heritage* defines *situation* as "position; location," but also "a state of affairs." While the latter definition could easily stand as a metaphoric extension of the former, both come in handy for better understanding the concept of sitcom.

The following paragraphs will consider sitcom's spatial component, its peculiarities and its relevance not only on the utterative but also on the enunciative level. I will also show how these spatial features contrast with those of the new comic series, and how this distinction is anything but accidental.

The *Encyclopædia Britannica* is slightly more informative in its definition of situation comedy, and it adds some of the thematic and technical features I have mentioned in the introduction:

> Radio or television comedy series that involves a continuing cast of characters in a succession of episodes.
> Often the characters are markedly different types thrown together by circumstance and occupying a shared environment such as an apartment building or workplace. Typically half an hour in length and either taped in front of a studio audience or employing canned applause, they are marked by verbal sparring and rapidly resolved conflict.[2]

Both definitions mostly overlook one of the fundamental elements, namely that of comedy: the former dismisses it with a quick reference to the humorous aspects of the texts, while the latter takes it completely for granted. Neither provide a univocal set of definitions, or standards that would allow one to recognize comedy and to analyze the comedic act.

Traditional sitcom solves the issues of belonging and recognition with the use of a laugh track, which marks the difference between comedy shows and every other televisual narrative genre; as Brett Mills notes, "It underlines the artificial, theatrical nature of the genre, and the fact that sitcom requires an audience for its existence to be at all meaningful."[3] The laugh track highlights comic moments, fulfilling the meta-comic function of positively sanctioning their effectiveness and, at the same time, the pragmatic function of "educating" the possible television audience to recognize the show's comic style.

Depending on whether the laugh track is original, prerecorded or sweetened (mixing original and prerecorded laughter), the proportion between sanctioning and educational effect changes. Sitcom's fictional status makes it a sensible idea for viewers to accept the further narrative pact the laugh track offers. Consequently, the laughter — no matter if natural or artificial — will be considered not as part of the paratext, but as a product of the primary enunciative device.

A more effective definition of comedy can be obtained going back to Aristotle's, certainly the most classic definition of all. It does not really matter that Aristotle did not particularly respect comedy (as opposed to tragedy); what counts is that the definition he gave, despite its age, highlights better than others not just the effects of comedy, but some of its structural features:

> Comedy is, as we said, imitation of more loathsome things, albeit not in regard to all that is evil, yet it is the ridiculous side of what is ugly. It is indeed ridiculous whatever error and vice that is painless and harmless, like the comic mask is ridiculous, deformed but cause of no pain.[4]

This definition refers to a kind of comedy formally quite different from the kind here analyzed; yet the basic principles are, as I will show, still applicable. It delves deeper than any dictionary-based definitions, which revolve around the content's humorous features and happy ending.[5] While important, these elements restrict the concept of comedy to euphorically oriented content, rather than trying to capture the specificity of comic texts. Despite historical and formal differences between con-

1. Situation Comedy

temporary American televisual comedy and classic theatrical comedy, Aristotle's definition remains useful to my analysis.

From a semiotic point of view, the absence of explicit laughter makes grasping the essence of comedy a harder task. On the one hand, the laugh track serves as a natural help to semiotics, as it textualizes the comic effect and makes it explicit; on the other hand, considering the laugh track as little more than background noise allows the possibility for the viewer to enjoy the text directly and to evaluate the places, times and intensity of its comic style.

The lack of laughter in the shows here examined, which veer from a well-beaten path, leaves semiotics wrong-footed, but only for a moment. It becomes necessary, first of all, to address the validity and applicability of two basic semiotic concepts inevitably summoned in an analysis of comic texts: the thymic category and the issue of veridiction. Second, the very concept of comic effect must be reconsidered, especially its validity within a properly semiotic approach, which maintains the text as object and primary source of information.

Situation: A Matter of Space

Space is a core component of situation comedy. While the use of three or four cameras creates a dynamic effect of openness, in reality the scenes are confined to enclosed, repetitive places, with a strong sense of orientation. In every represented space, one wall is never shown, and for obvious reasons: it is the proverbial fourth wall that separates the scene from the audience, and which can never be shot because it is not physically present. One of the most common space-defining elements in American sitcom — consequently, one used by anyone who has ever tried to produce sitcoms in other countries — is the couch, usually placed centrally in the room and the shot. In workplace comedies the couch is normally replaced with a desk (as in *The Mary Tyler Moore Show* [CBS: 1970–1977], *Murphy Brown* [CBS: 1988–1998], or *Suddenly Susan* [NBC: 1996–2000]), which is a flexible figurative element that can be easily multiplied, or sometimes by the counter of a bar or diner (as in *Cheers* [NBC: 1982–1993] or *Alice* [CBS: 1976–1985]). Even in workplace comedies, though, as soon as the scene leaves the workplace (sometimes just by moving to the next room, as in *Cheers*), the couch immediately regains its central placement.

The couch surely represents the comfort of home, but more than this — and more interesting to a semiotic approach — it is remarkable for its ability to accommodate more than one person, whose look and posture it sets in a privileged direction, perpendicular to the rows of the audience, albeit not without admissible alternatives. In any room containing a couch, the main shot is the frontal one, with a slightly diagonal variant that allows those sitting on the sides (usually on an armchair) to be shot at an angle similar to those sitting on the couch, thus eliminating or diminishing any possible hierarchies among actors.

Space is not only dominated by the couch, it is also defined and designed by it. The area directly in front of the couch is largely static, where actors limit their movements to those needed to reach or leave a certain sitting position; in the area behind it movements can be wider, directly feeding the action and supporting scene changes. In *Friends,* the couch in Monica Geller's apartment separates the living room from the kitchen, and the space behind it becomes a passage from the entrance door, on the left of the frontal shot, to the bathroom and balcony on the right. Strangely enough, though, the invisible wall is placed slightly to the left of the couch, which makes the lateral or diagonal shot the privileged one for a total shot of the apartment. This also makes Monica's couch hierarchically secondary to the one at Central Perk, the coffee house where the show begins and where, at the end of the series finale, the characters say they are going. In other shows, such as *Three's Company* (ABC: 1977–1984), *Will & Grace* (NBC: 1998–2006), *Mork & Mindy* (ABC: 1978–1982), *The Cosby Show* (NBC: 1984–1992), and also the much less fortunate *Joey* (NBC: 2004–2006), the space behind the couch is where almost all the room's doors open (often including the main entrance to the apartment), and becomes one of the main action spots.

Speaking of *Joey,* part of the reason for its failure might be found in the asphyxiating excess of sitcom's typical features, from the couch to the extremely stereotypical characters, to the continuous presence on the scene of the character Joey Tribbiani, apparently not able, after ten years of teamwork in *Friends,* to sustain the whole narrative load. The show was canceled in 2005 before the end of its second season, despite the fact that all episodes had already been shot. Its failure could be interpreted as a sign of the times, ripe not only for the emergence of newer comic models, but also for classic sitcom to progressively leave the stage.

I definitely do not want to reduce all differences between sitcom and new comedy to the presence of a couch, or lack thereof, but this figurative element highlights some broader conceptual distinctions. Whereas sitcom spaces are more strictly organized, which inevitably constrains the narration, new comedies' reduction of technical constraints allows for some looser hierarchies. The first constraint to fall is the use of more than one camera. On the one hand, using multiple cameras facilitates some aspects of the production (shooting more than one angle at once makes episode filming shorter and the action less prone to continuity errors), while on the other it prevents cameras from performing movements that would end up showing other cameras on the set, and revealing part of the enunciative device. Consequently, the next constraint in line to fall is the presence of a live audience, which does not fit in a highly fragmented, not necessarily sequential production, one in which a camera can orient itself in virtually any direction.

The need to shoot in a soundstage is the last constraint to fall, although in some cases setting up scenes in a studio may contribute to the reality effect, if the scene itself is coherent with a certain reality. *The Office* is the perfect example of this: its first season was filmed in a real office building, which was then reproduced in a studio for the following seasons. What gives a hint that a constraint has fallen is the fact that, contrary to sitcom, new comedies are usually able to use all available space, so that all walls (including, if needed, the ceilings) are potentially visible, opening up the possibilities of shot orientation.

Sitcom's spatial hierarchy involves a sort of interrelation between certain kinds of actions and the spaces in which they take place. For instance, actions with a more inchoative or terminative aspect are usually placed in higher-rank spaces, while collateral actions (such as the episode tag, the last sequence running during the closing credits, usually preceded by a commercial break, whose temporal and spatial placement are mostly irrelevant) can take place in lower-rank spaces. In new comedies, spatial ranking is usually determined by character hierarchies, and it is never given by default. *The Comeback* represents an extreme situation in which no space is privileged per se, yet any space where the main character is present is the only one worthy of being shot. Moreover, *The Comeback* escapes sitcom's usual topology more easily, thanks to the improvised shooting style.[6] *The Office,* seemingly more refined and carefully designed, uses more classic shooting angles, somewhat similar to sitcom's, where natural framing elements affect the way each scene is framed and edited. In *Scrubs,* whose utterance does not include cameras, spatial management is not necessarily linked to a specific character or the continuity of an action (whose independence from the shot is particularly relevant here). Rather, spatial management is subject to rules encoded within the text itself. In *Ugly Betty,* the variety of characters and their rotation as active subjects allow for a broader use of space, with frequent and extensive outdoor shots (whether actually filmed outside or, more often the case, in a studio in front of a green screen). Nonetheless, as I will consider, the characterization of spaces in *Ugly Betty* is notable for its relevance in more general thematic and axiological oppositions.

Situation: A Matter of Events

Just as sitcom exploits spatial hierarchies, it also thrives on highly stereotyped characters. Such stereotypization manifests itself in basic and extreme thematic contrasts between actors, or, better, in the discursivization, through every single actor, of contrasts present in the empiric world. The higher the number of characters, the more evident and combinable the conflict, not only as an opposition between polarized thematic investments, but also as a modulation of similar investments. The higher the number of possible combinations, the higher the possibility, throughout the series, to downplay some of them while favoring others, in order to restrict the déjà vu effect quite typical in sitcom. Déjà vu is not a danger in itself, since it is in part a desired meaning effect, necessary for the text to function; nonetheless, some series use it to their own advantage more successfully than others. One example can be found in *The Nanny* (CBS: 1993–1999), whose six seasons were little more than a long succession of variations on the same theme, which did not detract from the show's comic power.

What matters, in the end, is maintaining a certain order that was established at the beginning of the series, often in the pilot episode. The relative immutability of the characters' features is a guarantee of this kind of stability, and also of a certain continuity in positive audience response. Even in sitcoms experiencing actor replacements, the replacing character maintains some, if not all, of the original character's features. This was the case in *Three's Company*, where the character of Chrissy Snow, the sexy, ditzy blonde, was replaced twice,[7] first with a similarly ditzy blonde, then with a nurse who was definitely smarter than Chrissy but still blonde and sexy.

Consequently, no matter how well defined they may be, sitcom's characters often suffer from a lack of depth that usually manifests as a lack of detail in aspects of their lives that are secondary to the story line. This lack of detail is quite naturally necessary and desired, as it is functional — or at least not detrimental — to the comic development of a series. Ross Geller (*Friends*) is a paleontologist, but while he does reference more or less real theories and is even seen teaching a few times, only once in ten years does he actually go on a dig, at the end of season one. Frasier Crane (*Frasier* [NBC: 1993–2004]) is a psychoanalyst, but he hardly becomes more professional than during his radio show, where he gives some pretty basic advice to callers. Grace Adler (*Will & Grace*) is an interior designer, but is mostly seen handling fabric swatches on her desk — which in turn is so untidy as to make any kind of work impossible. A further, more emblematic example is the case of Chandler Bing in *Friends*, whose job is "data reconfiguration" — a vocation so boring and unlikely that none of the other characters ever knows or seems to remember what it is.[8]

This lack of memory consistency is an integral part of a show's narrative structure; it is the reason why the protagonists of *Friends* can spend way too much time at the coffee house, even at odd hours (which is also motive for several jokes throughout the series), while in workplace comedy characters are constantly at work, even though they rarely seem to get any work done. In the end, the place itself dominates the scene and the action. Space, as well as the characters' defining traits, works as a grid within which the sitcom genre develops its (almost) infinite possibilities. But instead of being a limitation, this grid becomes a condition of existence.

Without reaching the extremes of certain animated series (not only classic cinematic series such as *Tom and Jerry*, but also contemporary televisual ones like *The Simpsons* (Fox: 1989–present), where erasing the results of actions within a single episode and restoring any starting conditions is necessary to the show's existence, sitcom maintains a certain degree of fixity — thematic, figurative and, ultimately, axiological — in order to keep its narrative structure working. On the contrary, as will be shown, new comedy series go one step further, testing the very structures on which they stand, in a constant, yet not always obvious confrontation with traditional sitcom.

Avoiding Dysphoria in Classic Sitcom

The most evident mechanism by which classic sitcoms preserve their euphoric value involves actively avoiding or eliminating dysphoria. This, however, does not mean that dysphoria is never represented; on the contrary, dysphoric elements exist as initial imbalances (often amplified, with grotesque effects), which will supercharge any euphoric narrative resolutions. On the other hand, when dysphoria is inevitable, its effects are erased by the accumulation of contextual euphoric elements, or by the use of rhetorical devices typical of the genre — running gags, physical comedy, inside jokes — that provide unexpected turns within dysphoric moments.

Insisting on the characters' stereotypical traits and on the predictability of behaviors reinforces isotopic networks within the texts, calling attention away from the representation of dysphoria. The resulting meaning effects aim, instead, at giving more relevance to the circumstances of dysphoria and its resolution.

Death is the most exemplary case of avoided dysphoria: avoided first of all by pretending it does not exist; second, by considering it something that concerns "anyone but us"; third, by recounting instead of representing it. During its ten years on the air, *Friends* featured several deaths

1. Situation Comedy

(grandparents, neighbors, even a psychic), and all of them, no matter how painful, were always sources of immediate euphoric release — for both the characters and the audience in the laugh track. One of the show's premises is Phoebe's mother's suicide, which took place more than ten years before the beginning of the story, and which is the source of comic exchanges throughout the whole series. Only the death of Ross and Monica's maternal grandmother is directly represented, but even in this case the attention shifts from death itself to its unusual circumstances,[9] which makes the characters' behaviors less dysphoric than they would have otherwise been.

Season finales are special cases, and even more so series finales in which the detachment between a show and its audience is textualized with some form of detachment within the utterance. A similar highly dysphoric situation must be managed according not only to the genre's but also to show-specific expressive modes. The series finale of *Friends* represents not only a detachment between actors of the utterance (Monica and Chandler moving out of the city) but also between the whole group of characters and the past they shared (figurativized by Monica's apartment, to which everyone has a key). Almost as a way to counterbalance this detachment — which is ultimately only symbolic — the reunion as a couple between Ross and Rachel stands as a guarantee that, despite being different, things will not really change. At the end of the episode, the six characters decide to go get a cup of coffee before saying goodbye:

> (Friends, *1020, final sequence. Monica and Chandler's apartment.*)
> RACHEL (*weeping*): Do you guys have to go to the new house right away, or do you have some time?
> MONICA: We got some time.
> RACHEL: Okay, should we get some coffee?
> CHANDLER: Sure. Where?

Obviously, no one but the studio audience's laughter answers Chandler's question: it's certainly paradoxical that anyone should ask where to go get coffee after ten years occupying a couch at Central Perk. This is a further confirmation, Chandler style, that not everything will change.

Similar in some aspects is the series finale of *Will & Grace*, where the conditions for detachment arise quite suddenly and are textualized with a double temporal prolepsis ("two years later" and "twenty years later"), which moves away from sitcom's usual "realistic" link between enunciation and utterance. Will's voluntary detachment from Grace is compensated when the four main characters meet again for a drink, "twenty years later," while a zoom out from a detail of their glasses shows them again — in a surreal way — "as they were" before the detachment. Once again, a confirmation that the world (in the utterance, but not only there) can change, but what's important stays the same. Any generated dysphoria is explored and each time eluded and erased not only at the utterative level but through direct actions of the enunciative device.

In a league of its own is the series finale of *Seinfeld,* accurately described and analyzed in its cultural implications by Joanne Morreale.[10] Not only does the episode signal a detachment of the series from its audience via a story that detached the characters from their original, natural setting, but it also constitutes a sort of self-referential concentrate absolutely in tune with the history of the show.

Situated Realities

The laugh track, one of sitcom's more prominent expressive elements, is more than a quirk of style that contributes to a definition of genre. If that were the case, there would be little sense in the practice, typical of the 1960s, of adding laughter to shows not filmed in front of a live audience. The laugh track is, more than anything else, an unmistakable marker of the installation, within the text, of a second-level enunciation. Better yet, it is an index of the presence of a receiver inscribed in the text itself, which betrays the corresponding enunciative instance — of which, by the way, no other explicit markers exist. Certainly, this receiver is not congruent with the televisual one, considering that the circumstances of the uttered enunciation are very different from those of the primary enunciation; at the same time, however, the laugh track stands as measure and control system of the comic effect.

The enunciative action sitcom operates is quite different from that of the majority of drama shows, whose main utterance is a direct product of the primary enunciation. Nonetheless, there are exceptions of drama series whose enunciative structures are not as linear. One such exception is *Desperate Housewives* (ABC: 2004–present), whose filmic utterance is accompanied by a verbal utterance, similar to *Scrubs*. But one must notice the main difference: in *Desperate Housewives,* the subject of verbal enunciation continues narrating the whole series, despite the fact that she has committed suicide at the beginning of the pilot episode. Far from being a novelty, this discrepancy has the main meaning effect of pushing the series away from a realistic representation of the empiric world. Moreover, *Desperate Housewives* combines various traits typical of different televisual genres, including comedy and soap opera.

While hiding the markers of an uttered enunciation, sitcom clearly gives hints of it. It's a typical case of transitional genre, almost a fossil of an era when television still had to develop a language of its own, but sitcom nonetheless became, thanks to its peculiarities, a central genre in American television.

Sitcom can serve as a clear example of the difference between enunciation as a logical device and the physical modes of textual production. The latter involve the idea of the existence of cameras, on a set built inside a large soundstage, filming a theatrical scene taking place in front of an audience able to react to the scene itself. As such, sitcom would seem like an evolution of theatrical performances that television often broadcast at the dawn of its history. In a way, it is in fact an evolution of this non-genre, a borrowed language, but in sitcom the presence of cameras on stage is anything but accidental: the theatrical action exists only because the cameras are there, part of the device that will produce the final text. Thus the enunciation as a logical instance turns the "physical container" into part of the textual content: those elements that are to the audience in the soundstage nothing but a glimpse of the productive machine are, within the televisual text, premises of the enunciation — the device that is never seen because it is responsible for the production of the utterance itself. Moreover, the enunciative device absorbs the audience, which is just an external observer of the theatrical action, and places it *within* the text, albeit only the aural component of its presence.

Sitcom becomes, inevitably, a composite genre, which cannot completely separate from its theatrical origins. It needs an audience to function properly, even when the audience is nothing but a recording. Not only does sitcom have its own timing, it also thrives and is conditioned by the audience's timings, just like theatrical action. The split enunciative level is often forgotten, too often considered nothing but a nuisance, which has fostered negative judgments of sitcom. Such judgments underestimate the importance of the distance introduced between the intended or empiric receiver of the text and the main utterance.[11] Contrary to most other televisual genres, sitcom does not want to either *cause belief* or *show to believe* in its own story. Rather, it reveals its nature of fiction, in Greek known as μίμησις [*mímēsis*]: imitation not of reality but of other forms of expression. The sanctioning and moralizing function of the Greek chorus is here replaced by the function of an audience reacting exactly as Aristotle's definition suggests: with laughter.

What is left of reality is, in turn, a representation — no matter whether or not it conforms to the rules of the natural world. Often enough, in order to remain faithful to its own mission, it drops all attempts at making the represented reality credible. What is left are stereotypes and models of behavior that make the machine work, aiming to provoke a positive reaction from the audience *within* the text, a verification of the comic effect.

Breaking Out

In the end, sitcom presents itself as an established reference model, backed by a history of several decades rooted in a pre-televisual world, in radio and theater. References to sitcom remain in new comedy at different interrelated levels. Sitcom is a touchstone, a source of textual allusions, a negative model that *cannot but be* cited and quoted, and whose gravitational field must eventually be faced through successive attempts.

Despite its history, the model of situation comedy has proven less solid than expected. Experimentation has led to the development of new narrative languages of televisual comedy, which, far from being revolutionary (by subverting existing canons), constitute its natural evolution. By merging and appropriating languages that were once the prerogative of other narrative genres, new comedy is building fresh models, thus making more elastic and permeable the boundaries between various genres.

1. Situation Comedy

At the end of the 1990s, a new series like *Sex and the City* seemed unusual and experimental, so much that, in spite of its usually light tone, it never really became a comedy show — one of its premises being the employment of internal use of humor and sarcasm more often than full-fledged comedy.

Until recently — even just a few seasons back — the new forms of televisual comedy seemed to be sharing time with classic sitcom, which did not seem destined to fall out of fashion, whether resulting from a sort of due respect or from historical strength. By the end of 2007, things had changed very rapidly. A look at television schedules clearly shows a shift in trend. NBC's Thursday night can serve as an example. The night that during the "Must See TV"[12] era accommodated *Friends, Frasier, Will & Grace* and before them *Cheers, Seinfeld, The Cosby Show* and *Golden Girls* (NBC: 1985–1992) has been entirely occupied by new-generation comedy series in recent years — *My Name Is Earl* (NBC: 2005–2009), *30 Rock* (NBC: 2006–present), *The Office, Scrubs* (before it moved to ABC in its eighth season), as well as the more recent *Parks and Recreation* and *Community* (respectively started in the spring and fall of 2009). As if to mark this difference, in 2006 NBC coined a new slogan for its Thursday nights: "Comedy Night Done Right."

What was once the cohabitation of new comedy with the old sitcom is becoming a progressive substitution. At the same time, the only remaining ABC show in situation-comedy format was *According to Jim* (ABC: 2001–2009), starring James Belushi. ABC opened its 2007-2008 season very aggressively, disseminating its schedule with brand-new half-hour comedy shows such as *Samantha Who?, Carpoolers, Cavemen* (only the first of which actually survived the 2008 writers' strike and was picked up for a second and final season), in addition to producing comedies for other networks — including *Scrubs*. ABC's cutting-edge predilection for genre crossing has given birth to such hour-long series as *Desperate Housewives* (which is usually categorized as comedy in television awards), the newer (yet short-lived) *Pushing Daisies* (ABC: 2007–2009) and, in a particularly more comic direction, *Ugly Betty*. At the start of the 2009-2010 season, CBS seems to be the only national network still solidly committed to traditional studio sitcoms, with *The Big Bang Theory* (2007–present) and the longer-running *Two and a Half Men* (2003–

present), both co-created by Chuck Lorre, as well as the new *Accidentally on Purpose*.

It would be impossible to give a detailed account of all the nuances televisual comedy has developed over the past few years in its struggle to attain a new genre stability. Thus, I will limit the in-depth analysis to the four series presented in the introduction. These shows highlight some of the traits — technical, discursive and narrative — that distinguish new comedy. Their examination paves the way to a broader discussion of the comic genre and its links with both empiric reality and the televisual context.

2

Scrubs

NBC launched *Scrubs* in the fall of 2001, scheduling it in its Thursday-night lineup, along with *Frasier, Friends* and *Will & Grace,* some of the most beloved situation comedies of the day. But *Scrubs* was different, as it broke the consolidated format of the sitcom, bringing to network television what cable producers had already been experimenting with the previous few years. The eighth season of the show, which started in January 2009, moved to ABC, primarily due to NBC losing interest and canceling it in the aftermath of the Writers Guild of America strike of 2007-2008. Season eight was the last of the show's original run: the ninth season, beginning in December 2009, completely retooled the initial concept, constituting something closer to a spin-off than an evolution. For this reason, the following analysis of *Scrubs* will be limited to the show's first eight seasons.

Scrubs is set in a hospital, where the characters spend most of their waking time. The main character, John "JD" Dorian, is joined by Dr. Chris Turk (his best friend roommate from college until Turk's wedding), Dr. Elliot Reid (a woman), nurse Carla Espinosa (Turk's girlfriend, then wife), Dr. Perry Cox (involuntary mentor to JD, whom he usually calls by girls' names), Dr. Bob Kelso (the chief of medicine) and the Janitor (JD's nemesis, always left unnamed).

The episodes share some of sitcom's features, particularly the length (usually around twenty-one minutes) and the use of a cold open, which precedes the opening credits by a few minutes. However, contrary to the production of most situation comedies, the show is filmed using a single Super 16 film camera, and is set not in a sound stage but in an actual unused hospital (the North Hollywood Medical Center, in California). These details explain the lack of a laugh track.

The series' structure reflects what has become the genre standard, comprising twenty-two to twenty-four episodes per season, with the exception of seasons seven and eight, which count fewer than twenty episodes; moreover, despite seasons five and onward all starting midseason, the story lines still reflect the fall-to-spring time span, as if the show had started regularly in the fall schedule.

One more element distinguishing *Scrubs* from classic sitcom is the long span of the story arc, which gives the show an open serial structure. While sitcom — with eminent exceptions, such as *Friends*— tends to make every episode a closed, isolated unit, *Scrubs* not only frequently concatenates episodes, but also proceeds by longer narrative blocks, which frequently coincide with an entire season or even overflow its boundaries.

Textual Complexity

The Visual Component

Scrubs's repertoire of shots, angles and camera movements is very broad. Due to the dynamism of the environment in which the stories take place, shots range from close-ups of people standing at the nurses' station or the operating table to three-quarter and medium shots during motion scenes in the hallways. Contrary to sitcom, usually confined to narrow spaces, *Scrubs* features frequent outdoor scenes, which allow for long shots as well.

Static scenes, such as those in patients' rooms, almost constantly use shot/countershot techniques, while motion scenes tend to be or look like long takes, which amplify the appearance of the space actually available on the set.

Scrubs often features shots that are unusual or unconventional in comedy, such as very low angles or bird's-eye shots, which are used both in fantasy sequences and when required for physical comedy. The frequent runs, slips and falls lend themselves to being seen from the point of view of the subject involved, thus showing the world from down below — or, on the contrary, from up above, when the camera focuses down on the fallen character.

The most commonly used transition is definitely the fake wipe, obtained by panning horizontally or vertically from one scene to the next, as if the scenes were taking place in adjoining spaces. This effect

2. Scrubs

takes advantage of the presence in the hospital of many curtains, doors, walls and screens. Not infrequently, sequences are connected by cross-dissolving between two identical or similar subjects: for example, the same character at different times, two characters in similar poses or close-ups of two objects of similar shape.

The Sound Component

The most noticeable element in the soundtrack is the narrator's voice, which will be later discussed in detail, in the context of analyzing the enunciative device.

No less important is the non-verbal component of the soundtrack. Whether extra- or intra-diegetic and whether proper music or sound effects, this component plays a prominent role in further defining the enunciative domain and the highly metatextual character of the utterance.

Extra-Diegetic Soundtrack

The series uses more or less known music pieces throughout the episodes, especially to underscore crucial moments. It is made clear in the early episodes that the show gives special attention not only to the story itself and its visual aspect, but also to the expressive possibilities of the text's sound component. The main musical sources are the classics of rock and pop, but sources also include contemporary productions, including independent ones.

The coupling of songs with particular scenes is so intentional that in some cases the lyrics serve as commentary to the action, and some sequences are even edited based on the internal articulation of the accompanying song. One of the most prominent examples can be found in the final sequence of "My Sex Buddy" (211), where Elliot decides not to continue her sexual relationship with JD because she is afraid she will not be able to keep her feelings out of it. The whole scene is accompanied by Del Amitri's song, "Tell Her This," whose lyrics are thematically connected to the situation and even provide JD with possible responses to Elliot's decision ("Tell her not to go"). The parallel articulation of the extra-diegetic song and the images in the filmic utterance goes so far as to make specific words match the action, as in the synchronization between the word *kiss* and Elliot giving JD a peck on the cheek.

The show employs imported music as well as original music composed specifically for the show, usually consisting of short drum cues (or music in which drums have a central role, but which can also feature other instruments, mostly guitars or piano), similar to those used in stand-up comedy to mark jokes, with which the show's drum cues often establish a symbolic relationship. Seeking out and unmasking comic clichés is also self-reflected, so much that at the start of the fourth season, in one of the typical moments of confusion between the realms of enunciation and utterance, JD directly refers to one of these musical phrases as a product of his imagination. The phrase is a two-element descending progression on the piano, always used in moments characterized by particular emotional involvement, although not necessarily dysphoria.

> (*401, 10:15. JD follows Dr. Cox out of a patient's room, begging for his attention. Dr. Cox responds sharply.*)
> JD: Please, you know you love it. Now, come on, one more time for nostalgia's sake: you come see my patient, you teach me a lesson, and then the music plays, right? In my head, it sounds like this: ba-ba-bah-ba-ba-bah-bah-bah, ba-ba-bah-ba-ba-bah-bah-bahhh.
> (*Dr. Cox looks at him, bewildered.*)
> (*Carla passes by.*)
> CARLA: Dr. Cox, can I borrow you for a minute?
> DR. COX: Borrow me? Dear heart, you'd be rescuing me. (*To JD.*) Newbie, you're on your own. Get used to it. (*Leaves, following Carla.*)
> (*Piano cue.*)
> JD (*sings, softly*): ba-ba-bah-ba-ba-bah-bah-bahhh.

INTRA-DIEGETIC SOUNDTRACK

The participation of reasonably well-known musicians as actors highlights once more that the boundaries between enunciation and utterance are not insurmountable. One of the most notable appearances is that of Colin Hay, from the band Men at Work, who, in "My Overkill" (201), plays a troubadour, a figure bordering between reality and JD's fantasy. He always carries and plays a guitar (until Dr. Cox breaks it against a wall), and sings Men at Work's "Overkill," which reconnects to the episode title.

2. Scrubs

The characters themselves are often seen in different musical performances, both in reality and in fantasy sequences — from JD and Turk's love for singing to Elliot's weird relationship with karaoke.

In "My Heavy Meddle" (116), Carla and Ted sing Poison's "Talk Dirty to Me" to grant a coma patient's wish.[1] Ted himself is in an a cappella quartet called The Worthless Peons that appears in several episodes.[2] In "My Philosophy" (213), a patient awaiting a transplant claims she is not afraid of death, and hopes it is like a Broadway musical; when the patient actually dies, in JD's fantasy the whole cast performs Colin Hay's "Waiting for My Real Life to Begin."

These few examples show how intra-diegetic music is not only frequent and rooted in the show's structure, but how it is entwined with the story itself to the point of becoming an integral part of it, not just a staging element. Although in several cases this tends to create reality effects, it frequently attains the opposite result, thus contributing to shifts onto different planes of surrealism or fantasy.

In other circumstances, even when diegetic music seems to be featured in a more innocent and neutral way, it can in fact have a referential role, thus pointing to certain extratextual elements. The most striking example can be found at the beginning of "My Way Home" (507, the show's one hundredth episode), whose first shot shows an iPod playing "Africa" by Toto. Such reference is very subtle, and can be understood only backwards, later, since the theme of the whole episode pays homage to *The Wizard of Oz*. The band itself is named after Dorothy's dog, Toto. Not unexpectedly, Dorothy is also the name by which Dr. Cox decides to call JD in the episode, which ends with The Worthless Peons standing on the hospital rooftop singing "Over the Rainbow."

Another special case of intra-diegetic soundtrack can be found in "My Musical" (606), which follows a certain trend — almost a topos of contemporary television — of inserting a musical episode that breaks the normal flow of the show. "My Musical" breaks from the established discursive and enunciative patterns by making the characters sing and dance, thus giving the impression that the music is, paradoxically, both intra- and extra-diegetic: the characters are aware of its presence — so much that they sing to it — yet the music has no actual source within the utterance. If left unresolved, this issue would make the episode an enunciative oddity. It is, instead, solved within the utterance, by pointing to a patient's aneurysm as the reason why she hears everyone else sing and sees them dance (not much different from what happens to the eponymous character in *Eli Stone* [ABC: 2008-2009]). This effectively deploys an enunciative disengagement, and, in a way, installs an extra embedded enunciation, which changes the perspective from which events are framed whenever the patient is in the scene, while JD correspondingly loses his narrating voice. The normal order of things is reestablished at the end of the episode with the removal of the aneurysm, while JD reacquires his voice, perspective and point of view.

Intra-diegetic music, along with environmental sounds, is accompanied by yet another category of sound effects, namely all those artificial sounds, such as whistles, rolls of thunder, tire squeals, and more out-of-context sounds, which are not strictly environmental — that is, they are not produced by anything present on the scene, whether or not within the shot. Despite the fact that nothing physically motivates these sounds, they cannot be considered extra-diegetic, since their production directly correlates to specific elements of the utterance. These sound effects accompany not only fantasy sequences, where logic would suggest a more ideal placement, but also events in the main utterance outside JD's fantasy, such as rapid head movements, impending anger and even more often the high fives given by Todd, the womanizing surgeon. Todd's high fives, whose sounds are exaggerated beyond natural, are the only events that are given a sound effect consistently throughout the series.

Most of these effects are limited to the first season, since the production thought they were making the show sound too much like a cartoon, which might have ended up becoming yet another cliché, thus damaging *Scrubs*'s peculiar style of reality representation.

Paratextual Elements

Opening Theme

The opening theme is a sequence of approximately fifteen seconds during which the camera pans steadily right to left on the hospital ward, while one character walks in the same direction, carrying a patient's chart, and exits on the right side of the frame; a second character, seen at first on the left side of the frame, starts walking to the left, grabs an X-ray from a patient's bed, then exits on the right; a third character stands beside the patient's bed, receives the X-ray, hangs it in the light box, then exits the frame. Once the screen is turned on, the X-ray reveals the show's title, which turns into the wording, "created by Bill Lawrence." The actual duration of this sequence is variable, as its speed changes according to each episode's time needs. As one might imagine, such differences affect the pitch of the musical theme, with consequences on how natural the singer's voice might sound. The show's credits are shown for a few minutes at the bottom left corner of the screen following the opening theme.

The characters who populate the opening sequence have not been better identified for a good reason: despite its being a continuous sequence, the opening sequence is in fact more of a "multiple exposure," where each character of the show appears only for a split second, then fades into another one. The appearances behave as follows:

- chart-bearing characters: JD, Cox, Turk, Elliot, Kelso, Carla (twice), Turk (exits);
- X-ray-grabbing characters: Elliot, Turk, Carla, Kelso, JD, Cox, JD, Carla, Cox (puts his stethoscope around his neck), Elliot, Kelso (grabs the X-ray), Turk, Elliot, Carla, Elliot, Cox (exits);
- X-ray-receiving characters: Kelso, Cox, Carla, Kelso, Cox, Kelso, Turk (receives the X-ray), JD (hangs the X-ray, then exits).

A very significant soundtrack accompanies this dynamic series of visual effects, a fragment of Lazlo Bane's song "Superman" (usually introduced by brief drumming a few moments before the start of the opening theme visuals): "I can't do this on my own, no I know I'm no Superman."

The combination of visuals and music discursivizes the theme of collaboration and of the single person's smallness in the face of the medical profession's required tasks. This does not necessarily mean that every character can be easily substituted, but rather that a certain narrative program cannot be realized without a collective effort — whether the actors involved are the program's subjects or helpers. As such, the choice of song is highly appropriate, and fully adheres to the meanings carried on by the text's filmic component.

It must be noted that for a few episodes at the beginning of season two the show attempted a longer opening sequence, which included the Janitor on account of Neil Flynn becoming a star of the show. The new sequence did not meet the audience's favor and was soon replaced by the original one, which was used for the rest of the series' run.

Episode Titles

Scrubs follows the standard behavior of many American TV shows and does not broadcast episode titles as part of the opening sequence. Titles are part of a broader paratext, which includes information found in television guides and dedicated websites. Not even the DVD editions show the episode titles on-screen, but only printed on the included leaflet.[3]

All but eight titles start with the possessive "my," which refers to JD: the first person reflects the voice-over narration, almost as if the title were part of it. The titles usually focus on the main theme or on a narrative detail: the first season starts with "My First Day" and ends with "My Last Day." This category of titles also includes "My Mentor" (102, with reference to Dr. Cox), "My Old Lady" (104, where an elderly patient has a lot to teach JD), "My T.C.W." (218, where the acronym means "Tasty Coma Wife," with reference to the attractive wife of a coma patient). Examples abound.

Very frequently, though, titles involve puns and double meanings, often played on common expressions of the English language, such as "My Bad" (106) or "My Way or the Highway" (120). One of the most prominent medically derived titles is, without a doubt, "My Ocardial Infarction" (413). References to the cultural context are very numerous, among these: "My Bed Banter & Beyond" (115, with clear reference to the chain store Bed Bath & Beyond), "My Big Brother" (206. This title can be taken literally, since the episode introduces JD's older brother, but the pop-culture reference cannot go unnoticed in times of reality shows),[4] "My Brother, My Keeper" (214. The expression "my brother's keeper," used by Cain in Genesis, is systematically exploited in television), "My Brother, Where Art Thou?" (305, echoing the Coen brothers),[5] not to mention "My Best Friend's Wedding" (322), which, for once, is a literal reprise of a movie title.[6]

In eight cases, the initial first-person possessive is replaced by third-person possessives, masculine or feminine, and in two instances plural. This represents a shift in perspective that reflects a replacement of JD as narrator by a different character. I will delve deeper into this issue in the section dedicated to JD's voice.

Season Eight

The eighth season of *Scrubs* is notable for a few subtle changes in appearance that accompanied the network transition. First of all, the picture format changes from the previous 4:3 aspect ratio to 16:9, and the show is broadcast in high definition. The episodes also gain a tag, that is a short sequence during end credits, which in previous seasons were displayed over still images taken from the episode. Instead of providing, as is generally the case in classic sitcom, an off-theme closure, these tags generally feature outtakes, bloopers and improvised sketches. More generally, the visual impact of the show seems to be more cinematic, with a more intense — and, in a way, less obviously comedic — use of colors and light.

Due to budget restrictions, each actor in the main cast was forced not to appear in two episodes, which leads to two anomalous episodes. In "My Absence" (809), as the title suggests, JD is not visually present, but still gets to do most of his usual recap while Elliot is on the phone with him; in "My Full Moon" (813), JD is simply not present, making this episode the only one without a narrator.

Characters

Main Characters

Apparently light-hearted and optimistic, John Dorian (Zach Braff) is admittedly pessimistic, narcissistic, and with a tendency to find himself in embarrassing situations, not always for selfish reasons. He lives in symbiosis with Chris Turk, his roommate of twelve years until season five, so much so that they can often understand each other without speaking. JD has an almost morbid admiration for Dr. Cox, who in turn categorically refuses the idea of being his mentor.

Despite his efforts, JD is not able to carry on a steady sentimental relationship, not even with Kim Briggs (Elizabeth Banks), the doctor with whom he has a son in season seven — although in this case the instability rests largely on her and her behavior. For example, she at one point fakes a miscarriage.

Chris Turk (Donald Faison) is, as per Dr. Cox's brilliant definition, JD's "blacker half," and he exhibits all the self-possession that JD lacks. He usually presents himself like his own man, but is often unable to express his emotional side — although he does when JD is involved, to the extent that he appreciates and reciprocates the affectionate nicknames JD gives him, but only thanks to the long friendship they share.

Elliot Reid (Sarah Chalke), an upper-class woman from Connecticut, is burdened by her father, also a doctor, and his expectations, and by her disturbed mother, a drinker and nymphomaniac. Nonetheless, in time she is able to overcome her own insecurities and the clashes with her superiors (Dr. Kelso often targets her and tries to convince her to change careers, although he later starts appreciating her as a doctor), and fully take charge of her role. She and JD have an on-again, off-again relationship, which often evokes that between Ross and Rachel in *Friends* — a fact that leads to several running jokes throughout the series. Just like the reference model, the two of them will become a couple again at the end of season eight.

Perry Cox (John C. McGinley), an attending doctor not afraid to speak up, also a disturbed narcissist and scotch drinker, is, he admits, in love with a woman he hates, Jordan Sullivan (Christa Miller Lawrence), whom he divorced in a time before the series. During season two, he and Jordan have a son (then a daughter in season six) and move in together again, reestablishing a relationship that is as solid as it is unlikely. His efforts to keep JD at a distance seem to be, after all, aimed at teaching him well: Cox's total commitment to the medical profession puts him in constant conflict with Bob Kelso, the chief of medicine, whom he never spares from his personal and professional attacks. He likes giving people demeaning nicknames, including the feminine names he usually gives JD, whom he often also calls "Newbie."

In season eight, after Kelso retires, Dr. Cox becomes chief of medicine and begins to understand some of Kelso's behaviors, even starting a "secret friendship" with his old enemy.

Carla Espinosa (Judy Reyes), is of Dominican origin, a very competent nurse, fond of hospital gossip and of the advisor's role she often assumes. During season one, she starts dating Turk; in spite of some difficulties, the two of them get married at the end of season three, and, after a few failed attempts, have a daughter at the beginning of season six. She is able to establish sincere and direct relationships with all the other characters, even the tougher ones, but she is not without insecurities herself, which only Turk is able to soothe, often in goofy ways. She has a younger brother she cares about very much and two beautiful sisters, whose friendship she forsakes for Elliot's, despite a rough start between them.

Bob Kelso (Ken Jenkins), the seemingly cold-hearted chief of medicine, is married to Enid, who is never shown and whom he loves in strange ways, while still keeping a soft spot for younger Asian women. He is a competent doctor, but usually shows himself more interested in the hospital's well-being than the patients'. He claims to hate everybody else, and particularly Dr. Cox, who reciprocates, and often shows it; he loves to pronounce and hear his own name and is passionate about any kind of food—from soup to peanut butter to muffins. He is an old-fashioned doctor, politically incorrect, who never spares anyone a verbal beating and whose mood changes are swift as his tongue.

The Janitor (Neil Flynn) starts off not as one of the main characters, but as JD's nemesis, almost a product of his imagination. In time, the Janitor starts interacting with other characters, who continue to know nothing about him but whatever he likes to make them believe (including his name). His main occupation, beside cleaning floors, is tormenting JD with insults, pranks and threats. Carla is usually the only one who can intimidate him. Later, he establishes more civilized relationships with others, and he even has a brief crush on Elliot, because, he says, she's the only one who treats him like a person (episode 419, "My Best Laid Plans"). In the season-eight finale, the Janitor says he has never told JD his name, which may or may not be Glenn Matthews, because JD has never asked him.

Secondary Characters

The hospital environment requires the utterance to be populated by different orders of secondary characters, from those played by the so-called "B cast" (those actors whose presence in episodes is not continuous, but who often play key roles and whose characters can evolve in ways similar to those played by the main cast), to the nonspeaking extras, to the one-time characters. This last category includes most patients, who, apart from isolated cases (such as that of Ms. Wilk, Ben Sullivan, Jordan's brothers or the hypochondriac, Mr. Corman) do not appear more than once. It may also include characters who are not patients but who still appear in one or very few episodes, such as Dr. Kevin Casey, Julie Keaton (the sexy pharmaceutical representative) and the lawyer Neena Broderick.[7]

The nonspeaking extras include all those characters — doctors, nurses, patients — that populate the hospital on a daily basis. For reasons relating to the production process they are played by the same group of about twenty people, who end up appearing on-screen scene after scene — which is not implausible in a busy hospital. Some of these characters have such peculiar features that the audience, particularly on Internet forums, has given them appropriate nicknames. The production actually ended up using some of these nicknames, thus giving these characters unexpected moments of notoriety — and sometimes even a voice. This happened to a stern-looking bearded doctor nicknamed "Dr. Beardface," who gets upset when characters mispronounce his name, which, he says, should sound like "Beardfacé," almost as if it were French. Another doctor, who bears a striking resemblance to Colonel Harland Sanders, founder of Kentucky Fried Chicken, is usually called "Colonel Doctor" by other characters, to the point that in "My Jiggly Ball" (504), Dr. Kelso, who apparently doesn't know his real name, calls him the epithet to his face. "Colonel Doctor" does not seem upset by that and responds with a smile and a thumbs-up.

Occasional characters are those with speaking roles who do not appear unless the story specifically requires it, and who are often played by more or less well-known or emerging actors. Among them: the anxious dermatologist; the swinger oncologist; the Janitor's shady friends; and Lloyd, the frustrated and drug-addicted delivery guy (played by Mike Schwartz, writer, story editor and producer on the show), who may actually be Colonel Doctor's son. Relatives of the main characters can easily fit in this category: JD's brother, Carla's brother (played by Freddy Rodríguez, at the time in the main cast of *Six Feet Under*), Turk's mother, Elliot's parents.

The B-cast characters constitute a separate category, in that they are always ready to use in interactions with the main characters as their backup, or as setups or payoffs for jokes. In some cases, they may have their own secondary story lines, which cross and enrich the primary ones. These include: nurse Laverne Roberts (Aloma Wright), a big African American woman, very religious, gossip-loving, hypercritical yet good-natured; Todd "the Todd" Quinlan (Robert Maschio), the dumb, sex-maniac surgeon, always prone to making dirty jokes; Ted Buckland (Sam Lloyd), the hospital's attorney, always covered in nervous sweat, Dr. Kelso's own personal punching bag; Doug Murphy (Johnny Kastl), an incompetent doctor who will find his calling as a pathologist; and Jordan Sullivan, who starts off as mean, unlikable character but in time becomes more sociable, ready to fight for her new/old relationship with Dr. Cox.

Time and Space

The utterance's main space, the hospital, is anything but a unitary entity. Several subspaces can be identified within it, and categorized according to the kinds of actions they host:

1. workspaces:
   a. wards and patients' rooms (with or without windows on the ward or in hallways)
   b. laboratories
2. recreational spaces:
   a. the cafeteria

      b. the basketball court by the parking lot
      c. the roofs
  3. hybrid or connecting spaces:
      a. the nurses' stations
      b. the hallways
      c. the entrances and the parking lot
      d. the surgical scrubbing room
      e. the offices (Dr. Kelso's, Ted's)

Among the spaces outside the hospital, the highest-ranked is JD and Turk's apartment. Its relevance is highlighted by its internal fragmentation, similar — albeit on a smaller scale — to the hospital's. Its different focal points (the living room and kitchen, JD's room, Turk's room, even the bathrooms) are mostly treated as autonomous spaces, not simply as portions of a wider space.

The same cannot be said about all secondary spaces, such as other people's apartments, the diner or the bar, all of which are represented without internal functional distinctions. The only exceptions are the sporadic peeks inside Dr. Cox's or Elliot's bedrooms. When, in season five, JD lives in Elliot's apartment, his (almost) private space is not his bedroom anymore, but a deck he had built on a half acre of land he bought with former girlfriend Julie (Mandy Moore).

From a temporal point of view, the show (as originally aired) follows the typical behavior of sitcoms, which is to make every season run synchronized with the viewers' calendar, so that the holidays within the show coincide more or less with those the audience experiences. Thus, the twenty-four-episode span covers about nine months. Discrepancies can occur, however, at either end of a season, with diegetic time stretched or contracted in regard to empiric time, to cover the months during which the show is not produced. The normal flow of the series compared to the empiric calendar is usually restored within the first episode of the starting season.

To this end, the narrator's role is fundamental. Even more so than usual, his position lies on the thin line between enunciation and utterance: while still not an instance of paratext, JD's voice seems to know very well of the existence of a time outside both the utterance to which it belongs and the filmic utterance about which it speaks. Such knowledge of enunciative time is not explicitly stated, but is usually revealed by either the narrator's recapitulations of events that (supposedly) occurred during the summer hiatus or the need to patch at the utterative level time variations not consistent with those of the enunciation.

This does not mean that the utterative time is always clearly determined, either through its flow or the relations between different actions. In episode 515, "My Extra Mile," JD shaves his head to express solidarity with a chemo patient, but at the beginning of the next episode he has a full head of hair, as usual. In other circumstances, such a detail could have been dismissed as a surreal or episodic element of no consequence, similar to what happens in closed series.[8] In this case the detail of the shaved head is picked up again in "My Chopped Liver" (517), where JD's voice clarifies the utterance's temporal articulation by saying that the events of "My Extra Mile" happened a month before.

This reference, along with the unlikely growth of JD's hair (which was already long in episode 516), might challenge the solidity of the show's temporal structure. What it actually does, instead, is stress the autonomy of the single episode and the elements of serial closure that allow *Scrubs* to be not an indistinct flow of events, but an organic sequence of linked episodes.

The episodes' different narrative lines are always fragmented, with frequent breaks in the timeline of each, which effectively makes every story progress parallel to the others. Such parallelisms can be not only temporal, but also thematic (characters involved in similar situations), plastic (characters shot in similar poses) or lexical (characters pronouncing the same words). They are often emphasized visually (for example, by a division of the screen into vertical subframes) or aurally (by a unification of ambient sounds).

Parallel narrations imply seizing not only the durative aspect of actions, but also their iterative aspect, which serves to point out the similarities between the characters' experiences, even when the stories might at first seem different. A recurring theme in *Scrubs* is, indeed, the replication of experience, due to both the physical and emotional closeness among the characters, and, on a more existential level, to the degree of repetition and recursiveness in life. Episode 522, "My Déjà Vu, My Déjà

Vu," makes exactly this point, right from the title: hospital work entails repetition, which is not necessarily negative, as thematized in the first-season finale. Rather, repetition is a fundamental trait of existence that should teach people how to live — although that's not always the case, and we often end up making the same mistakes over and over again:

> (522, 20:33. *Hospital's back door. JD walks toward the camera.*)
> JD (*narrator*): Of course sometimes things are gonna repeat themselves in the exact same way.
> JD: What the hell?
> (*Cut to JD's wrecked bike. Pan to the Janitor holding a softball bat and Troy holding a crowbar.*)
> THE JANITOR: It's a riddle: two guys destroyed your bike with a softball bat and a crowbar. One of them wasn't me.
> JD: Oh, *that's* what happened to my old bike. Hah! Good day, fellas.
> (*Passes between the two men and walks away.*)

This scene is almost identical to the penultimate sequence of "My Lucky Night" (304), where JD's bike was destroyed exactly the same way. In both cases, the Janitor and Troy (a cafeteria worker who looks and acts like a jailbird) destroyed the bike to get revenge over JD tricking them with a riddle: "Two coins add up to thirty cents, and one of them isn't a nickel." The two thugs feel deceived when they hear what the solution is: one quarter and one nickel.

Parallel Enunciations

Ever since the beginning of the pilot episode, the events of *Scrubs* have been accompanied by the voice of a narrator, a voice-over through which the main character, JD, introduces, narrates and commentates on the events shown on-screen.

According to Gérard Genette's terminology,[9] in its normal form this voice oscillates around an extra-homodiegetic status, since JD is a character of the narrated action, despite the fact that his voice-over does not belong to this level of utterance. A shift away from extra-homodiegetic status occurs frequently, in cases of temporal discrepancies between the narrating and the narrated JD. Even when the time of the enunciation and that of the utterance coincide, a form of autobiographic

2. Scrubs

lie[10] contributes to an amplification of the distance between voice-over and images. The narrating JD is often caught lying to justify his behavior or for other idiosyncratic reasons, which are often left unclear.

Albeit accurate in itself, Genette's terminology cannot completely cover all nuances of JD's position as a narrator, which at times becomes almost intra-diegetic, especially in the rare cases in which the voice-over migrates from one character to another, explainable only by admitting a certain subordination of voice to images. More often, though, the voice-over becomes extra-heterodiegetic, when JD narrates events of which, according to the images, he simply cannot have any knowledge. This happens during recapitulations (always at the end of episodes and often halfway through them, at the end of the first act) and marks a change in the relationship between images and voice: the latter is no longer subordinated, but links to the former through a referential process.

As is often the case with definition, one cannot define and understand the complex structure of enunciation in *Scrubs* by examining the rule only, but must take into account the exceptions as well. The use of a narrator other than JD is one such exception, along with any situation in which the primary enunciation plays with secondary enunciations, or with the conditions and boundaries of its own existence. As will be further explored, such *divertissements* are more frequent at a more mature stage of the series, particularly from season five, and lend extra consistency to the metatextual nature of several of its narrative elements.

The Normal Form

As I have mentioned, a narrator's voice drives the episodes, and this narrator describes and commentates each scene as if it were part of the same utterance as his own. If *Scrubs* were a purely verbal text, such as a literary story, this would be not only plausible, but also semiotically feasible. Contrary to what occurs in literary texts, in televisual texts a verbal enunciation — that is, one based only on linguistic matter — can hardly produce, by way of disengagement, a filmic utterance naturally syncretic and comprising types of purport not available to a verbal enunciation.

The foundation of such observation is chiefly logical, even before finding an empiric confirmation: the narrator's voice is, by nature, not able to disengage into an utterance made of filmic substance. The subject of enunciation can say "I" in reference to the image of JD that appears on-screen, but the fact that the voice comes from outside the scene makes it impossible to link this image to an act of engagement that assimilates the voice to the image. Consequently, the corresponding disengagements are equally unlikely. If the voice says "I" and recounts present or past events, it produces an utterance flowing parallel to the filmic utterance, which is, in turn, produced by a higher-level enunciative instance also responsible for the discursivization of the narrator's voice.

The voice is often mixed up—and not by chance—with another voice-over that is technically identical, yet semiotically different, and identifiable as JD's thoughts. The main difference between these two voices lies in the fact that JD's thoughts are always uttered when JD is in the shot, or at least in the scene. In this case, the voice is directly attributable to JD as actor of the utterance, with whom it shares an existence in the temporal dimension. In terms of space, the actor and the voice-thought share at least a cognitive space, if not a physical one. While the ability to carry on a narration remains always anchored to JD—except in the following cases, which are very well marked—it is not uncommon to hear the thoughts of other characters, always only for the duration of their permanence in the shot. Such a phenomenon usually accompanies effects of parallel flow, either temporal or thematic (such as recap sequences).

Replacing the Narrator's Voice

In a few episodes, JD relinquishes the role of narrator to different characters. Such events are reflected in the corresponding episode titles, which become "His Story," "Her Story" or "Their Story," followed by a Roman numeral if necessary, to indicate how many times the title has been used. The switches happen eight times, in episodes 215 ("His Story," with Dr. Cox as the narrator), 318 ("His Story II," with Turk), 405 ("Her Story," with Elliot), 510 ("Her Story II," with Carla), 519 ("His Story III," with the Janitor), 607 ("His Story IV," with Dr. Kelso), 617 ("Their

Story," with Ted, the Todd and Jordan) and 812 ("Their Story II," with the new interns).

The moment in which the switch happens is usually visualized by a form of physical contact between JD and his replacement, or by a very prominent camera movement that refocuses the attention on the new narrator.

Episodes 318, 405 and 519 feature the physical-contact technique. In the first case, JD and Turk are sitting on the couch in their apartment; JD is sealing Turk and Carla's wedding invitations. JD is upset with Dr. Cox and ends up snapping at Turk for no real reason. His narrator voice admits to not having any stories to tell, while JD stands up, walks behind the couch and gives Turk a friendly slap on the head.

When Turk finally finds the courage to mail the invitations at the end of the episode, a symmetrical contact restores JD as the narrator:

> (*318, 17:35. On the street. Mailbox. Turk is holding a bunch of invitations.*)
> TURK (*narrator*): It's weird. Just by the simple act of pushing me to do the right thing, I remembered why Carla's the woman I want to spend the rest of my life with.
> (*He drops the bundle into the slot.*)
> TURK (*narrator*): End of story.
> (*JD arrives.*)
> JD: You did it!
> (*JD congratulates Turk, hugs him and hits him lightly on the back of the head. They walk to the car together.*)
> JD (*narrator*): Oh, man, what a long day.

In 405, the switch happens when JD bumps into Elliot's shoulder, a moment that is shown in slow motion and accompanied by a sound effect. At the end of the episode, JD gets his voice back in a very similar manner.

In episode 519, the effect of replacement is enhanced by a physical replacement (or, rather, a disappearance) within the utterance: the Janitor sees JD napping on a bench, puts a bag over his head and locks him in the water tower, effectively rendering him unavailable for the whole episode.

In the episode's finale, JD regains his voice when the Janitor helps him back to his feet. The moment is marked by JD repeating, with a twist in meaning, words just uttered by the Janitor's voice:

(*519, 20:03. Hospital roof.*)
THE JANITOR (*narrator*): Now help him up, so he thinks there's hope for our relationship yet. (*Helps JD back on his feet.*)
JD (*narrator*): Even though the Janitor had basically kidnapped me, when he helped me up I couldn't help but feel there was hope for our relationship yet.

The voice replacement is not the only violation of the show's canon in episode 519. As I have established, JD's voice is semiotically incapable of performing a disengagement toward a further level of filmic enunciation. To overcome this limitation, in this episode JD wears a camera on his head (he wants to show his mother a typical day of his life), thus turning himself into a filmic-enunciation device. Once again, the boundaries thin between different levels of enunciation: the primary enunciation succeeds at bending the constraints it had cast upon itself, while the filmic utterance incorporates a subordinate device that mimics the main enunciation.

The text finds yet a new way to play with the premises of its own existence, to the point of almost denying their basic principles, such as the impossibility for JD to produce filmic utterances. In reality, however, such assumption is still confirmed by the immediate replacement of JD by the Janitor, which marks once more the separation between the various levels: the enunciation JD embodies has no power over and remains confined within the main utterance, with no chance of escaping.

In episodes 215 and 510, the focus is no longer on the utterance (as was the case in instances of physical contact) but on the enunciation, and a camera movement shifting the focus from JD to the substitute narrator signals the voice replacement. Typically in *Scrubs*, subsequent scenes are fused into a single sequence shot entirely in the same space. The scene's boundaries are marked by major camera movements and, usually, by movements of the actors within the shot (including entrances and exits). The nonphysical voice-replacing mode exploits this behavior, yet its effects fall outside the filmic utterance, influencing the behavior of the verbal enunciation.

The Narrator's Voice-In

All the cases just considered make it clear that the verbal and the filmic levels may become intertwined more often than not. One further example can be found in those uncommon situations in which JD's voice becomes intra-diegetic in regard to the filmic utterance, thus violating the show's cardinal rule. Such a phenomenon can present itself as a plain deception, immediately revealed, or as a sort of wink to the audience, at times even accompanied by the actor's looking straight into the eye of the camera. A running gag in "My New Suit" (518) leads to JD repeatedly addressing the camera as if in an attempt to break the fourth wall and speak directly to the audience, but at each turn the montage reveals the presence of a receiver within the utterance, virtually placed on the audience's side of the camera. Thus, the enunciative device acts under the pretense of its own transparency and provides a shot of JD from the (falsely) subjective point of view of its intended interlocutors.

In "Her Story II" (510), Elliot reproaches JD for being too much "inside his head," and the narration switches over to Carla. Nonetheless, while JD and Turk are sitting in the cafeteria, JD's voice is suddenly heard narrating and speaking of Turk in the third person. A cut to JD's face reveals that this recap is not uttered by JD's usual narrator voice — as the modalities of its enunciation would make one think — but by JD himself. When Turk asks for explanations to this behavior, JD tells him about his decision to be less inside his head and, consequently, to narrate and elaborate on events aloud.

In "My Big Bird" (508), during a morbidity and mortality conference following a patient's death, JD, Turk, Elliot and Carla must give public accounts of the past day's events. At the end of a flashback, JD's voice provides the usual recapitulation, until the montage reveals, once again, that it is JD himself speaking as the voice-over becomes a regular on-screen voice. Dr. Kelso stops him and assumes his right to be delivering the recap.

Interaction of Narrative Trajectories

While it positions itself at a fair distance from traditional workplace comedy, *Scrubs* takes on one of its fundamental thematic oppositions, between *work life* and *personal life*. This opposition is aggravated by the fact that working in a hospital forces people to keep unusual hours, thus unbalancing the opposition in favor of work time over personal time. Even those who do not hold a medical position end up spending nights in the hospital, as in Ted's case — one can only reckon it happens on Dr. Kelso's orders, or just because, as everyone knows, Ted has no life.

The preponderance of work time is so strong that, often enough, the younger doctors are not able to either manage their time outside the hospital or to effectively separate the two main areas of their lives. Many personal relationships fail because of the hours of overtime spent in the hospital, while it is not unusual for work performance to be less than appropriate due to the subject's personal issues.

The action of characters' cognitive processing of their life conditions is continuous. The more the two thematic trajectories of *work life* and *personal life* proceed on a collision course, the more necessary it becomes to perform a sort of self-analysis, and with increasing frequency, in order to optimize what is in the end nothing but one's own narrative trajectories.

This basic opposition is reflected, at the level of narrative semantics, in two main classes of trajectories of which all characters, eventually, become subjects. Such classes are not necessarily in conflict with one another; rather, by acquiring the right competence in managing their separation, anyone can successfully fulfill both.

The work-life trajectory is undoubtedly the more relevant one, at least because of its discursive predominance. Throughout the series, the younger characters are seen growing from interns to attending doctors, in constant dialog — often conflictive — with the senior doctors. What emerges clearly is yet another opposition, in this case a modal one, relating to the two main ways in which the medical profession is performed. On the one hand, we have a modality that sees medicine as an almost mechanical activity, which will be called *medical doing*; on the other hand, we have medicine as vocational commitment, as a role and an identity, which will be called *medical being*.

While the *medical-doing* modality is always present in the utterance through the showing of patients and diseases, of surgery, and even more through the lexicon, it is systematically eclipsed, especially by a certain excess in some discursive manifestations: the actual possibility of following any medical activity in the story is limited first of all by the high temporal and spatial fragmentation; secondly by the dissemination of surreal moments, which produce an alienation effect; and finally by the quick pace of speech, which makes any scientific conversation barely intelligible. These three elements tend, ultimately, to shift the attention from the medical activity to the human processes that surround it.

It would come naturally to think that such *medical doing* affects each character's thematic trajectories, since the result of any narrative program related to this *doing* cannot but affect future performances. The *doing* in itself is, however, limited to a very few almost archetypal figures of the medical activity: the placement of an IV line, a hand holding a scalpel, a defibrillator; anything else is usually lexicalized, hence not irrelevant, yet not fundamental to the construction of meaning.

If the *medical doing* is conditioned to a previously acquired competence — that is the achievement of a certain academic career — the modality of *medical being* is linked to a progressive competence acquired daily on the field, a process that is virtually endless. Then, if interns face an opposition between a *medical doing* (as the only possible modality underlying the narrative trajectories and thematic roles on the workplace) and a *being* or *being able to be* something else (narrative trajectories and thematic roles of the private life), through the consolidation and practice of their operative competence, they progressively replace the *medical doing* with a *medical being*. Through various characters, the text often voices the possibility that a doctor, despite years of study, might not be cut out for the profession. Dr. Kelso repeatedly advises Elliot to rethink her career choice:

> (*119. Hallway.*)
> DR. KELSO: I've seen lots of doctors who got into this for the wrong reasons. You know what happens to them?
> ELLIOT: No...
> DR. KELSO: They quit and get their real estate license. You look upset, sweetheart. You shouldn't be. I think you'd look super in a gold blazer.

When Doug asks her to tell him, sincerely, if she thinks he should be a doctor, Elliot ends up giving him a negative answer — only to subsequently witness his professional renaissance as a pathologist ("My Malpractical Decision," 409). In "My Cabbage" (512), JD is forced to suspend an intern who makes repeated mistakes, and he advises the intern to reconsider his choices. The intern will not come back — except later, as a barista in the new hospital café.

The splitting and isolation of the roles become prerequisites, in the form of narrative programs of use, for the *medical doing* to become *medical being*, which contributes to increasing the competence necessary to perform well in the medical profession. The separation between the two modalities is also a prerequisite for a happy fulfillment of any narrative trajectories related to the private sphere.

The Value System

The narrative trajectories pertaining to the *medical-being* modality are not based on a universally shared axiology. The texts' most evident conflict, between Dr. Cox and Dr. Kelso, can be summarized by the opposition between the medical profession's *human ends* and its *economic ends*. To determine whether such opposition can be further simplified as *altruism* vs. *egoism*, it is necessary to consider the nature of Dr. Kelso's narrative programs.

His economic purpose is not strictly personal — sure, his professional actions have positive effects on his financial situation, but this is also true of Dr. Cox and whoever else embraces this career.

> (*115, flash. Dr. Cox, standing, talks to a psychologist hidden "behind" the camera.*)
> Dr. Cox: Well gosh, I guess I became a doctor because, ever since I was a little boy, I just wanted to help people. I don't ... tell this story very often, but, I remember when I was seven years old, one time I found a bird that had fallen out of its nest. And so, I picked him up, and I brought him home, and I made him a house out of an empty shoebox, and —(*starts laughing*) Oh my God! (*sighs and recomposes himself*) I became a doctor for the same four reasons everybody does: Chicks, money, power, and chicks.

As openly stated by Dr. Kelso in season one, the meaning of everything lies in "what's best for the hospital," following the often cruel rules of the American health system, which frequently means not taking care of those who can't afford treatments.

> (*105. During a game of golf.*)
> Dr. Cox: You know that before medicine ever became a business, the only rule was to do your best to help the patient.

2. Scrubs

(*Cut: JD tries to hit a ball that's stuck in the sand. Kelso is at his side.*)
DR. KELSO: Like it or not, medicine is a business. If the hospital shuts down, who are we helping then?
...
(*Cut: trees. Kelso is speaking while JD, hidden in the trees, hits the ball and scatters foliage around.*)
DR. KELSO: It's about what's best for the hospital.
...
(*Cut: pond. Cox is standing on the edge while JD, knee-deep in the water, tries to hit the ball, which has sunk.*)
DR. COX: It's about what's best for the patient.

Naturally enough, the narrative program that consists of "doing what's best for the hospital" is, according to his statements, one of Dr. Kelso's main programs; to him, carrying out a medical activity in the best way would only function as a narrative program of use. His position, albeit merciless, can be explained by his role not only as a doctor but also as a hospital administrator, whose tasks and purposes are *by definition* not merely medical.

Dr. Cox's situation is quite different, since his role has no further purpose than that of performing as honestly as possible in his profession. His narrative program, openly stated, is "doing what's best for the patients."

There is, nonetheless, a second level of narrative trajectories based on the same opposition, which works reflexively on the level just considered. One of the reasons for which Dr. Kelso is always in contrast with Dr. Cox is the latter's apparent lack of career ambition. According to Kelso, doing what's best for the hospital *must* have a positive return on the subject, in the direction of a personal realization beyond a psychological and moral aspect. It is not only a matter of financial satisfaction, but also of social status (outside the hospital) and ultimately of power (within the hospital, but not only there). This results in a circle (virtuous, according to Kelso) of narrative programs aimed at making sense not only out of the profession, but, in the end, out of the subject himself.

Dr. Cox stands in direct contrast to this worldview. His not being keen on conforming to Dr. Kelso's directives — and his frequent violations of these directives — have brought him, despite the obvious economic benefits he derives from his profession, a substantial lack of career advancement. At the start of the series, Cox antagonizes Kelso as part of his broader strategy of annihilation of any private narrative programs that might have objects of positive value. Career (as intended by Kelso), family, health are always put aside, and not only because he has already suffered a failed marriage: his marriage failed because of his *not being able* or *not wanting* to make it work. Self-annihilation is one of Dr. Cox's typical traits, and is, almost paradoxically, a necessary condition of his success as a doctor — a success that can be measured strictly in terms of *medical being,* and not in Dr. Kelso's economic terms. His tendency never to compromise allows him to achieve his own professional goals and deliberately sabotage his private ones.

It must be considered that a positive sanction of the medical activity cannot simply be defined in terms of whether a patient recovers and lives. That is, simple competence is not a sufficient condition of successful performance. There is always a rate of *not being able,* related to both the limitations of scientific progress and the possibility of human error — including the possible failures in other people's performances. Medical competence is also represented as a knowledge of this intrinsic constraint, and the performance always implies acting at the best of one's possibilities. Thanks to such awareness, doctors should be able to effectively separate the results of their professional narrative trajectories from their private spheres. Naturally, this is not always possible.

Consequently, the relationship between the professional and private sphere is ambivalent. On the one hand, a separation is required for a successful performance; on the other, at the stage of sanction, the outcome of a professional trajectory might affect the private one either in a positive sense, as intended by Dr. Kelso (or by Jordan, when she decides to get back together with Dr. Cox), or negative, as with Dr. Cox's voluntary atrophy of private self in the early seasons — a tendency that remains in varying degrees throughout later seasons, despite the character's evolution.

Just as Dr. Kelso's position has an egoistic end, which may have positive, albeit totally circumstantial effects on others, Dr. Cox's actions cannot be called completely altruistic. Dr. Cox's prevailing trait is a tendency toward the annihilation of his private self, that is, a position of *non-egoism,* the altruistic results of which are mere side effects.

A more direct altruistic inclination can be found in Dr. Cox's discourses on his profession and its relationship with the private sphere. The main receiver of such discourses is usually JD, although Elliot sometimes benefits from such positive outbursts, which Dr. Cox usually denies as soon as he utters them. As a rule, he avoids positive, euphorizing discourses because they do not fit his communication strategies. Such discourses, and the circumstances of their production, highlight the younger doctors' positions in regard to the more general value system just considered.

Complying with the System

Even after the doctors complete their residencies, their narrative trajectories are not aimed at finding placement within the system, but at showing the kinds of doctors they are — that is, the basic ideologies they are willing to accept and perpetuate. Under these circumstances, the conflict between Dr. Kelso and Dr. Cox revives. JD has always been prone to becoming a Cox-style doctor, though possibly without the latter's self-destructive inclinations. While Cox educates JD away from a position of *non-egoism*, JD tries to grasp the positive aspects of Kelso's ideology, while still recognizing its frequently inhuman aspects. JD's narrative trajectories commingle purely altruistic values — Cox's position, minus the self-destructive tendencies — and a state of *non-altruism* achieved via the displacement of Dr. Kelso's egoistic values he deems necessary for a correct balance between professional and private life.

In a way, JD reciprocates with Dr. Cox, offering a sort of re-education regarding personal relationships in exchange for the education Cox has given him. Especially in the realm of friendship (less in that of love), JD shows a higher competence than others do, although he cannot claim mastery of that realm. JD's balance between professional and private life is expressed in a series-long narrative program aimed at obtaining from Dr. Cox a recognition of the existence of a deeper connection between them than the simple work relationship. Just as Kelso does, JD needs his job to reflect positively on the subject, but to him such reflection is merely human: the mentor he sees in Dr. Cox is nothing but the affirmation on a personal level of values otherwise confined to the professional sphere. A mentor is someone who not only teaches, but is also able to radically influence other aspects of the subject's life.

Likewise, JD is hungry for signs of gratitude from patients. This is not a form of narcissism, as it would be in Dr. Cox, but rather an affirmation of his *medical being*. He is bothered by the idea that a patient may consider his job such a mechanical transaction ("I get sick, you treat me") that it does not deserve mention in the case of positive outcome.

Elliot's is a case of positive relation between professional and private trajectories. She starts out a clumsy intern, insecure and subject to her superiors' wrath, but she progressively becomes a competent and confident doctor.

Contrary to other characters, Turk and Carla seem to know from the start how to successfully separate the two fundamental aspects of life: Turk does so thanks to his confidence when it comes to women (although Carla's determination makes him commit to a relationship that becomes a marriage), Carla thanks to her extreme competence in any kind of interpersonal relationship. (Even in her case, it is possible that a positive feedback of work onto the private sphere is at play: Carla is a few years older than Turk, and at the series' start she has already been working in the hospital for eight years.)

One Step Back

An analysis of the utterance cannot neglect the results of the analysis of the enunciation. Until now, I have mainly discussed the narrative trajectories pertaining to the filmic utterance, hence leaving behind a whole block of meaning production, namely the narrator's voice. This is not a simple utterance, wherein certain actors perform certain actions. Rather, it is a discourse that has as its primary object the narration produced by the filmic enunciation.

Given its extended and constant presence, the narrator's voice is the fundamental aspect of differentiation between *Scrubs* and classic sitcom. It is also different from other cases in which a voice-over was used as a narrative or rhetorical device to obtain results otherwise impossible or unattainable using only a filmic utterance. The discourse it produces is intimately linked to the abundant use of fantasy sequences within the filmic utterance. The use of first-person narration allows the narrative point of view to zoom in on the story enough to provide a better grasp of its mechanisms; however, being substantially extraneous to the story itself, the narration creates a detachment that is indispensable to the production — and, consequently, to the comprehension — of meaning effects not necessarily inferred from the structure of the filmic utterance.

The enunciative engagement marks JD-narrator — subject of both the enunciation and the utterance — as distinct from a "copy" of the JD present on-screen. The almost totally subjective point of view of this verbal narration makes it possible to go into the details of the actorial construction, which cannot always emerge in the assumed objectivity of stand-alone film language.

Consequently, JD-narrator's main narrative program is to provide explanations, not only of stories that would otherwise still be understandable, but above all of himself, and to himself. This voice operates with different narrative modes, and the modulation from one to another happens in almost imperceptible shifts.

First of all, there is a sort of classic inner monolog, in which JD is subject and sender of an act of communication directed to himself. In a way, it is the least dangerous form of autobiography for the subject, in that any form of lie remains, theoretically, completely free of negative sanction; yet it is at the same time functional to the subject's own coherence. As his own sender, the subject has the power to justify himself and glorify his actions or, on the contrary, to take responsibility, feel guilty, and so on.

The existence of an inner monolog is also inscribed within the filmic utterance as one of JD's typical traits. Often enough, however, it betrays a superior awareness and installs a possible receiver of JD-narrator's communication, an unidentified *you*, which the English language allows to remain unnumbered. It's an incomplete communication process, where not only is the identity of the receiver unclear (always a simulacrum of an entity external to the utterance, an entity of which no one but the subject himself ever takes the place, thus becoming also the receiver of his own discourse), but where any details about the communication medium are also lacking.

It is distinct from, for instance, the narrator in *Sex and the City*, who in a way gives a voice to the articles the main character writes and publishes within the show. This makes both the channel and the receiver explicit (albeit fictional), as well as the circumstances of enunciation, and often clarifies the temporal relationship between voice-over and images.

The filmic enunciation in *Scrubs,* thanks to its syncretic nature, often plays with the possibility of installing within itself different levels of uttered enunciation, and even more so plays with constructing secondary instances substantially different from the main enunciative device (there are just a couple of cases of substantial similarity in the first five season, in episodes 417 and 519). On the contrary, except in the variations already considered, the narrator always keeps his hands on the wheel, and leaves it to the filmic enunciation to discursivize any voice not belonging to the subject. The narrator's knowledge of the existence of a filmic utterance is, thus, presupposed but masked: on the one hand, the subject *cannot know* of the existence of such utterance (it is still pure fiction, and not a fictional rendition of a certain reality), but on the other hand, whenever the monolog is more externalized his behavior presupposes he *cannot but know.*

As I have already explained, the relationship between the two enunciations is very solid: ideally, the utterances they produce flow parallel to one another, yet one of the goals of the primary enunciation seems to be to deliberately confuse the different planes — both enunciative and existential — in which the subjects operate.

By the time *Scrubs* reaches its eighth season, the characters have undergone a substantial evolution, to the point that the show is able to comfortably challenge the solidity of its premises. From a show that, at its inception, bordered on experimental, *Scrubs* has consolidated its own mature language. The possibility of further transition — specifically, into a ninth season without JD, where the main characters will be, once again, new doctors, interns and students — is anticipated by calculated glitches in the enunciative structure, such as the absence of JD and his narrating voice. Yet these anomalies are accompanied, throughout the eighth season, by a confirmation that the struggle to affirm values is over, only to start again: those characters who used to be the newbies are now responsible doctors taking on the task of passing down their knowledge — and, possibly, their wisdom — to the next generation.

3

The Office

In 2005, NBC started airing *The Office*, a remake of the British series created for the BBC by Ricky Gervais and Stephen Merchant, originally aired in the United Kingdom from 2001 to 2003. Contrary to other cases of imported TV programs,[1] *The Office*'s creators completely re-adapted the BBC version to better fit American culture and its stereotypes. After the pilot episode, which maintained the original script's key scenes by adapting them on the linguistic level, the show starts following a path of its own, with only a few narrative ideas taken from the original.

The Office, just like the British version, is a typical example of genre embedding: it is presented as a documentary about the Scranton, Pennsylvania, regional office of Dunder Mifflin, a fictional paper company. In contemporary television jargon, it is a case of *mockumentary*, a neologism that conveys the concepts of imitation and derision. As will be seen, the object of derision is not the documentary genre itself, but more likely the characters it portrays, framed as they are with an appearance of realism.

Breaking the fourth wall, usually considered a taboo and a boundary of televisual narratives, becomes not only an accepted practice, but also a mark of the show's style. Hence, the actors often gaze straight into the camera, and many situations rise and develop on account and to the benefit of the camera itself.

Nonetheless, the camera never appears in the shot, not even by mistake, and the characters show a certain level of restraint in talking about it (in a form of documentary, it would be too overt a violation of established rules of objectivity). Although the presence of the camera in the office can be assumed as transparent, its role often becomes anything but that of a casual or passive observer.

The circumstances of enunciation carry notable weight, also, when one compares *The Office* with the British version. The first six episodes produced by NBC constitute, alone, a single season (aired in the spring schedule, often used for experiments), almost as an imitation of the original show, whose two seasons — as is customary in British television — counted six episodes each. The following seasons were programmed with a more regular number of episodes, between twenty-two and twenty-five. Due to the Writers Guild of America strike of 2007-2008, which some of the show's writers and actors were actively involved in, the fourth season of *The Office* counts seventeen effective episodes, two of which (the first and last) double in length.

This analysis will pay particular attention to the way in which the first two seasons might, only superficially, appear as a single, homogeneous suite of episodes. A closer look reveals a fracture between two separate blocks, which, does not, however, correspond to the given seasonal division. The most notable element that differentiates the second block of episodes is the introduction of a cold open, typical of traditional sitcom, starting with the third episode of season two.

One might infer that season one should have been longer than it actually was, counting eight episodes instead of six, yet additional clues point to only episode 201 being part of an extended first season. Among them is the opening credits showing fragments taken from season one and episode 201, but none from 202; also, the music at the end of episode 201 being extra-diegetic, which never happens anywhere else in the series, an exception that could perfectly fit a season finale. Nonetheless, stronger elements of consistency allowed me to include episode 202 as part of an extended season one, and it will be considered as such throughout this chapter.

Though some might dismiss the introduction of the cold open as a simple stylistic variation, it is, in fact, an indication of a mutation in the show's narrative structure and, more generally, a subtle shift in its genre placement. The way each episode works internally changes little, but this fracture makes it necessary to treat the two episode blocks as separate. While I will not change the given episode numbering, from now on any generic reference to the first season should be understood to include the first two episodes of the second.

3. The Office

Discursive Complexity

The Visual Component

The Office features a high degree of fragmentation of the narrative flow, with a large number of rapid shots that are often difficult to group in defined sequences, and which tend to challenge the criteria of Christian Metz's great syntagmatics.[2] The soundtrack's specific role must also be considered, in that it often regulates, quite autonomously, the narrative rhythm, which makes it even more difficult to perform an episode segmentation in traditional terms.

Even the unsophisticated glance can distinguish two basic kinds of sequences: action/dialog sequences featuring two or more characters, and talking-head sequences, in which a single character (or, very seldom, two or more) is shot in close-up and talks looking directly at the camera, commenting on previous actions or recounting new ones. For simplicity's sake, I will refer to the former kind as action sequences and to the latter as interview sequences.

Interview-style sequences are a recurring trait of documentaries, but the modalities in which they are used in *The Office* are far more similar to the way they are used in reality shows: the single interviewees are isolated from the rest of the group, so that they can speak freely. Violating the rules of impersonal documentary, the subjects not only speak directly into the camera, but also often refer or speak to an interviewer behind the camera, who remains implied and unidentified.

The show uses classic camera shots, with preference for mid shots, close-ups and full shots of the whole office or smaller rooms. Full shots of the office are most often taken from the reception area, or from the area in front of the boss's door.

Particularly remarkable is the frequent use of what could be called a candid shot, with the camera peeking through a window or behind venetian blinds onto an action taking place inside a closed room. The show often uses this technique to capture an outdoor scene from inside the office, zooming in on the characters outside the building. Even though the windows or blinds do not make the camera invisible to the characters, they normally do not notice it and behave as if they were unseen.

Most action sequences consist of dialog between characters, who sit or stand, one on each side of a desk. Thus, the camera must correctly frame all actors on their speaking turns. In the frequent case of narrower shots, two main techniques achieve this result: a shot/countershot montage, or the rapid panning from one character to the next, following the flow of the dialog. The use of one technique over the other is anything but casual. As I will explain later, this choice creates very specific meaning effects that reflect on the role of the camera and, more generally, on the show's enunciative structure.

Often enough, interview sequences are interrupted (even while the interviewee is still talking) by fragments of office scenes, short flashbacks or even anticipations of future scenes. This is not so different from what happens normally in film, where clean cuts between shots or sequences are usually compensated by the reuse of thematic and figurative elements (not only in the visuals but also in speech), and, more generally, by the logic of diegetic implication.[3]

While transitions between sequences are very sudden and may happen in the middle of dialog, the very tight montage and the effect of sequence superposition provide narrative continuity, even in cases where adjacent scenes are conceptually and temporally distinct.

The Sound Component

A peculiar trait of *The Office* is the absence of extra-diegetic musical soundtrack, which strongly contrasts with the opening theme. The only two exceptions are the final sequence of the pilot episode, which simply reprises the opening theme, and that of "The Dundies" (201), in which the soundtrack plays one of the songs Michael Scott (Steve Carell) has sung during the episode. Starting with "The Dundies," intra-diegetic music becomes more present during parties, meals at restaurants, dates — any time the action takes place in spaces other than the office or its immediate surroundings.

Predominant in the soundtrack, in the absence of dialog, are the typical noises of the office. Keyboards, calculators, chairs and telephones are the background of a setting in which sounds as much as visuals contribute to confirming the characters' hierarchy.

3. The Office

Not only are the main characters seen on screen more often, not only are they physically placed to the camera's benefit, but they also enjoy privileged speaking turns. On the one hand, this may sound obvious, since whoever is seen more often is also more likely to speak; on the other hand, even in collective scenes, traits of each character's speech underscore the power structure: volume, tone, continuity of enunciation — all this independent of whatever is being said or its perlocutionary effects. It is, consequently, a way to spotlight not only the actual power relations within the office, but also the desired, unrealized ones.

The camera usually frames the speaking character, with possibility of brief off-screen moments during cuts or camera movements. However, during interview sequences the character's speech often becomes a voice-over for extraneous shots, linked only thematically (if at all) to the words of the interviewee.

Opening Credits and Theme

The opening credits consist of a twenty-shot sequence, which runs for about thirty-two seconds. All shots are taken from first-season episodes, except the first three and the last two. This is the order of the shots:

1. industrial building (paper company) in Scranton, Pennsylvania
2. Scranton street traffic
3. Scranton-city-limits sign
4. Dunder Mifflin office building, with logo
5. Michael sitting in the conference room, talking to the employees (Oscar and Meredith can be spotted from behind). Starting in "Office Olympics" (203), this shot is replaced by one of Michael standing in the middle of the office, talking to the employees
6. photocopier functioning
7. Kevin's calculator functioning
8. Dwight destroying documents with an electric shredder (Stanley and Phyllis can be seen behind him)
9. Pam's hand brushing correction fluid over parts of a document

10. the copier producing copies
11. Jim on the phone
12. a hand highlighting a document
13. Pam at the reception desk
14. water cooler
15. Ryan on the phone (other employees visible on the background, through the conference-room windows)
16. Dwight throwing his tie over his shoulder
17. Ryan, at his desk, picking up a full plastic bag
18. Jim and Pam at the reception desk
19. Michael, in his office, placing a "Dundie" trophy on his desk[4]
20. sign bearing the word "Office" in boldface sans serif font. The article "The" is superimposed right above it, with identical font, to form the series title.

The opening credits perform two important metatextual functions: to introduce the characters (and the actors who play them) and to establish their internal hierarchy from the start. In a negative sense, it also establishes that all characters not directly introduced in these thirty-two seconds will be considered secondary.

The music theme is lively, with a warm, homely, almost rustic character. Its melody, in a 4/4 tempo, is introduced by solo piano, followed by an accordion sustained by a single drum. The melody then repeats in a more pop style, with accompanying drums and guitars.

Space and Time

The space of the action is mostly confined within the office. The characters rarely leave the premises, and when they do, they do not go far — usually to the parking lot or the warehouse on the ground floor. After season two, *The Office* expands its territory beyond Scranton, with frequent road trips, including several to other Dunder Mifflin branches or to the New York corporate headquarters.

On a temporal level, one must distinguish between series, episode and sequence time. The third, microscopic level is chiefly a product of

3. The Office

the combined actions of camera movements and montage, which privilege discontinuities and the mixing of different or undefined time placements. Despite referencing other sequences that immediately precede or follow them, interview sequences are particularly atemporal, in that their precise temporal placement within the narrative flow is not pertinent. Such peculiarity is evident in what could otherwise be considered continuity errors and appear as discrepancies not only within the scene (such as a nighttime action mixed with a daytime interview) but also between the interviewees' discourses and the actions that are the objects of their comments. This alienation effect is produced by the continuous engagements and disengagements between the two main enunciative devices, and by the camera's consequent functional shift.

(103. Office. Michael unsuccessfully tries to come up with a surprise for his employees, who look furious.)
(Cut to Michael in his office.)
MICHAEL: When I am backed into a corner, that is when I come alive. See, I learned improv from the greats, like, um, Drew Carey and Ryan Stiles.
(Cut to the area in front of Michael's office.)
MICHAEL: *(claps hands)* God, yeah ... Ahh! *(tries to think)* This ... *(suddenly shuts up)*
(Kevin looks around and then leaves, followed by Kelly.)

Notably, actions and dialog are often captured in their durative aspect, as if the camera (or the fictional documentary editor) wanted to select only the most relevant moments and leave out anything that would hinder the narrative's fluidity and swift progression. Something similar happens in cases that might seem opposite in nature, that is when the action in progress is not only unrelated to its context, but also favored over a temporally adjacent action that in turn gets omitted. This is what happens in one of the initial sequences of "Health Care" (103), which depicts a short exchange between Pam Beesly (Jenna Fischer) and Jim Halpert (John Krasinski), who are discussing a television show. Michael interrupts them with a very loud entrance, despite not having anything to say besides calling Jim "Jimbo"—thus showing a camaraderie that he and Jim do not actually share. The dialog between Jim and Pam will never be resumed.

This sequence's goal is to introduce Jim and his familiar relationship with Pam, who was already shown in the episode's first sequence, through a light-hearted exchange that culminates with a sarcastic joke by Pam at Jim's expense, to which Jim himself contributes. The primary enunciation places here the first explicitly comedic moment of the episode, which in season two would probably be moved to the cold open, right before the opening theme.

Interview sequences are cued in a similar manner, as if in the middle of a conversation between the interviewee and the interviewer, who is never shown or heard. The interviewees sometimes act as if they were answering questions that were never explicitly asked on-camera, and were left for the subjects to "repeat" rhetorically:

(*101. Jim's interview.*)
JIM: Do I think I'll be invited to the wedding?
(*He thinks, scratches his head, then gazes into the camera.*)

At the single-episode level, the whole action takes place during a normal workday, whose precise chronological articulation is provided by seemingly minor thematic elements, such as lunch breaks. Although the time progress is quite obvious, the sequences' temporal ambiguity often makes it unclear — or irrelevant — in what exact moment events take place.

Particularly in season one, episodes are often set on a Friday, naturally favoring the suspension of the action, or the lack of resolution of certain narrative elements, which remain open at the end of the episode. While in season one such suspension is usually permanent, in the following seasons some narrative threads are resumed in later episodes, thus becoming the substance of new and continuous narrative developments.

At the level of the series, the fracture between seasons one and two is very clear, beside the productive considerations seen above, also because of the way episodes relate to one another and to the empiric calendar, that is to the normal flow of time as experienced by the audience. The first season's episodes are substitutable, as there are no explicit elements that would force a certain order in the series' fruition. The themes introduced in the titles are developed within each single episode and never resumed by following episodes. At the same time, there is no significant relationship with the calendar year.

The situation is different in season two, where the episodes' titles can sometimes indicate a precise placement on the calendar ("Halloween," "Christmas Party," "Valentine's Day"). Moreover, the rule of thematic closure is broken by the introduction of narrative cues that link episodes together also on the temporal level, which has an inevitable impact on how the show can or should be enjoyed.

The Characters

Main Characters

In order to better understand the main characters' fundamental traits — and ultimately to outline the series' complex actantial models — I must first highlight the main isotopic networks in which they are involved.

First of all, the most important recurrence — especially in light of the show's appearance as a documentary — is that of *company management*, an isotopy that permeates Michael's and Dwight's discourses. Both in the dialogs with employees and in interview sequences, Michael presents himself as the busy manager, efficient, diligent and, above all, capable. His vision of himself is, however, often distorted by delusions of grandeur.

> (*103. Michael's interview in his office.*)
> MICHAEL: The most sacred thing I do is care and provide for my workers, my family. I give them money. I give them food. Not directly, but through the money. I heal them. Today, I am in charge of picking a great new health care plan. Right? That's what this is all about. Does that make me their doctor? Um ... yes, in a way. Yeah, like a specialist.

His role as regional manager is lexicalized as *being busy*: "lots to do," "an unbelievably busy day," "I have work up to my ears," "I'm just too busy," "I'm swamped," "I am unreachable"; as *providing for the employees*: "[I] care and provide for my workers," "I heal them," "I will have [...] a big surprise"; and also as *delegating*: "I'm going to let you ..."

Dwight Schrute (Rainn Wilson) shows his commitment to managing the company, but his manifestations take a different turn, in the realms of *authoritarianism, hierarchy, command, punishment* (all to his coworkers' disadvantage) and *competition* with his boss, to which Michael is particularly sensitive. Dwight tries to turn any order he receives from Michael into a chance to fire some of his coworkers.

One more isotopy that permeates Michael's discourses and remains linked to his work relations and his activity as a manager can be summarized as *comedy,* but further articulated as *fun, morale boosting* or *maintenance of good spirits*. In particular, Michael claims his ability as a comedian and entertainer are fundamental to guaranteeing good productivity from his employees, who, thanks to having a mood enhancer of a boss, will feel at ease. On the contrary, he who cannot positively manage his employees' mood has no chance of being a good manager. It is important to notice how this thematic isotopy, once manifested in Michael's actual behavior, normally assumes an aspect of attempt (a virtual state, as opposed to one realized in Michael's discourse) that results in the realization of values opposite to those Michael desires.

This includes livening up, so to speak, the work atmosphere through jokes and witty comments directed at employees. Pam is one of his most frequent targets, but anyone whose looks or other personal traits draw Michael's attention may provide him with a setup for his next joke.

Not unusually, such jokes obtain the opposite result of upsetting people. In the pilot, in a sketch almost literally taken from the British original, Michael uses Ryan Howard (B.J. Novak), the new temp, as an involuntary accomplice and pretends to fire Pam, claiming she has stolen Post-It notes from the office. He keeps the joke going despite both Pam and Ryan's disbelief—Ryan can actually be seen shaking his head lightly, as if he wanted to reveal Michael's joke and, at the same time, shows his extraneousness to the charade. Michael's goal is to show Ryan how he governs the office and, ideally, to pull a prank on Pam so everyone will laugh about it later. Not once does he realize how inappropriate his behavior is—not even when Pam starts crying and, upon Michael's revealing the prank, calls him a jerk and leaves the room.

Jim and Pam are the remaining main characters, who, even when they lack a predominant role in the episode, tend and often try to condition the other characters' (particularly Dwight's) behaviors. What Jim and Pam have in common is a substantial extraneousness to the pressure and expectations linked to work and career. Such a trait becomes a sort of negative pressure, that is, an attempt on their part to resize the weight of their work lives on their existences.

While still performing on the job with precision and consciousness, they are able to keep from taking interpersonal dynamics inside the office too seriously, and succeed in making fun of some coworkers' extreme lack of humor. Dwight is their favorite target, whom they strike directly (with words and actions) or indirectly.

Secondary Characters

The Office features a rich set of secondary actors who take turns assuming key roles in each episode's narrative structure. The roles of non-key secondary characters are normally interchangeable, and seem to serve mostly as a collective character, supporting or contrasting the main characters. Secondary characters' spoken lines are consistent with the thematic roles associated with each, roles which remain unaltered throughout the first season.

Stanley Hudson (Leslie David Baker), a heavy middle-aged African American salesman, is characterized as serious and often worried, with very little time to put up with Michael's quirks. Sitting at the accounting desks are Oscar Martinez (Oscar Nuñez), a Hispanic man in his thirties, reserved but friendly, whose being gay is often a target to Michael's awkward comments; Kevin Malone (Brian Baumgartner), an overweight white man of similar age, with a taste for suggestive jokes, which he often tells while looking into the camera; and Angela Martin (Angela Kinsey), a very small white woman, also in her thirties, portrayed as stern and religious, a strict vegetarian with a strong sense of duty who does not seem to be friends with anyone and who does not like Kevin's jokes — or anyone else's, for that matter.

Meredith Palmer (Kate Flannery) is a white woman in her forties, had health issues in the past and shows clear signs of a drinking problem. She is usually the quiet type, but normally more sociable than Angela. Phyllis Lapin (Phyllis Smith) is the same age as Michael, but, due to her outmoded style and her usual shyness, looks older — or at least

Michael thinks she is, to the point of calling her the "grandmother" of the office in "Sexual Harassment" (202).

Other secondary characters include Kelly Kapoor (Mindy Kaling, one of the show's writers), the ditzy customer service representative, perpetually in love with Ryan; Toby Flanderson (Paul Lieberstein), the human resources representative whom Michael hates for no apparent reason; Creed Bratton (Creed Bratton), the hippy and creepy quality assurance director; and Andy Bernard (Ed Helms), a character introduced in season three, and the only salesman left from the Stamford, Connecticut, branch of Dunder Mifflin after the Scranton branch incorporated it.

A further class of secondary characters includes those who are recurring but noncontinuous throughout the series. The most frequently present of these is Jan Levinson (Melora Hardin), Michael's boss, who works at the New York headquarters and comes to Scranton to discuss important matters. She is an attractive woman, around forty years old, who has taken her role as a corporate executive very seriously, and who demands — often without obtaining it — a similar kind of commitment from Michael. She is often featured only as a voice on the phone, on which occasions she appears even more strict and determined than in person. After she starts an affair with Michael, which affects her performance on the job, the company fires her. Consequently, she develops serious psychological issues that will ultimately lead to the end of the relationship.

Narrative Complexity

As anticipated, the primary enunciative device of *The Office* is in charge of the fictional product, within which an enunciative disengagement installs a second device. This secondary enunciation is substantially similar to the primary one on the plane of expression, and accounts for the show being presented as a documentary.

At the same time, the interview technique allows for several more disengagements, which in turn create several parallel enunciations — anything but impersonal, in this case, and strictly linked to each interviewee's personality. This is relevant to the identification of the actantial

3. The Office

model, since the characters' roles change, sometimes radically, according to the enunciation level at which they operate.

In other words, the story the camera mediates accompanies the stories each character tells in the documentary. Far from being objective accounts of or impartial commentaries on what the documentary is showing, such new narratives discursivize new values and new narrative programs that transform the actors' qualities and the modalizations of their given actantial roles.

Michael Scott's narrative trajectory is split into two conflicting levels, albeit both legitimized by Michael in his own discourse. First, we have a class of corporate programs in which Michael is in charge of managing the office, and second, a class of personal ones whose object can be generically identified as *the morale,* that is the well-being, chiefly psychological, of the employees. The morale can be boosted thanks to the comedic competence Michael claims he has, but which, for the most part, is neither recognized by the intended receivers nor positively sanctioned at the corporate level.

The conflict between these two levels is actualized not only in Michael's (or other characters') discourses, but in the actions of the subject himself: Michael constantly chooses the personal level over the corporate one, behaving as if they belonged to one single trajectory, and as if the hierarchy of values were the opposite of what it actually is. Unfortunately for Michael, in everyone else's eyes the only possible level is the corporate one, which catalyzes Michael's actions to inevitable failures of his personal narrative programs, and also most of his corporate ones.

According to Michael, the employees do not accept his narrative program because they are bound by corporate rules, which he portrays as dysphoric, thus wrong for office management. He rarely admits, and only indirectly, to his own difficulties in establishing a real rapport with his intended receivers. His discourse implies a positive sanction of his performance, even when the facts — that is the higher-level utterance — openly contradict his words. One of the few cases in which he speaks lucidly is in one sequence of "Hot Girl" (106), when he is talking to Katy, the handbag saleswoman. He admits to her, as she listens with a mix of astonishment and embarrassment, his difficulties in connecting with his employees, and in tearing down the walls they put up. He goes as far as to say that no one gets him.

This discourse, seemingly sorrowful, does not have the same meta-narrative function of the interviews, where the subject sounds much less sincere. Rather, its function is self-referential, aimed at succeeding in a different kind of narrative program of which Michael is both subject and receiver: the conquest of the hot girl.

At first, the text presents the morale-boosting narrative program as a program of use serving the corporate program — the latter of which has Michael as subject, but whose sender is, generally, the company's executive ranks. Paradoxically, however, in Michael's discourse the corporate program, which should be logically more relevant as it is his primary narrative program, is gradually put aside. In the best of cases, it is neutralized in favor of its program of use; in other cases, in favor of completely unrelated narrative programs.

In the pilot episode, Michael fails right away in the task of not letting the employees know about the possibility of layoffs, while the mission with which he charges himself for the rest of the episode is to introduce everyone to the camera (that is to the documentary's audience). Moreover, in the absence of a real audience, he turns anyone present — and particularly Ryan, to whom he seems almost physically attracted throughout the series, which becomes a running gag — into an involuntary spectator of his comedic performances.

Throughout the course of each episode, Michael tends to present himself more and more as subject and receiver of narrative programs that relate to entertainment and sociability, with whose objects of value (comedy, improvisation skills, the ability to impress women) he deems himself already joined. In such programs the employees become nothing more than extras in his fantasy, possible helpers, unrealized senders whose role is merely that of sanctioning Michael's performance, thus confirming and making sense of his "artistic" abilities. If the helpers do not cooperate, Michael promptly gives them a negative sanction, moralizing their actions as dysphoric.

Within the higher-level utterance, Michael is subject of narrative programs that, despite being quite similar to those he utters, modalize him in a remarkably different way. Despite his *wanting*, Michael is conditioned to a *not being able to do* that ultimately stems from a lack of competence (the same he, on the contrary, believes he has). By relying on the entertainment and morale-boosting narrative programs, which he fails to achieve, Michael also fails to realize his primary narrative program, that of office management. The reasons for this failure can be found in the subject's lack of adhesion to the values he should share with his sender (the company, Jan), in his avoidance of responsibility (his *not wanting* to fulfill the narrative program he was charged with), and, in many cases, in the consequent decision to delegate the program to a different subject.

In "Health Care," Michael becomes sender of a narrative program (choosing the health-care plan for the employees) whose subject is Dwight, who in turn understands and actualizes the program in a different way from Michael's. For him, it is yet one more chance of joining himself with his object of value, that is the expression of power. Even the fact that Michael gave him this task makes Dwight believe he has already reached a position of power, and so he repeatedly tries to confine his coworkers to a status of subordination. Having an office (which is not an office, but the conference room), being able to decide on an issue that everyone (except him) deems essential and the ability to make his coworkers unhappy are the milestones of his performance that, in his view, mark the achievement of his goal.

Dwight is generally aware of the dysphoric character of his behavior, and such dysphoria is functional to the realization of his narrative programs. What matters to him is the complete opposite of what matters to Michael, for whom a euphoric moralization is essential to a successful performance. But while Michael usually fails in his efforts to characterize his actions as euphoric, Dwight reaches his goals in a manner consistent with his value system.

In Dwight's world, personal and professional narrative programs largely coincide. When they do not overlap completely, they are still based on similar axiologies. Moreover, in certain cases the personal trajectory is bound and subordinated to the company's hierarchy and values. In "Hot Girl," Dwight asks Michael's permission to date Katy, and then, once he finds out that Michael will drive her home, Dwight implores him not to try to seduce her. In the conquest of Katy, Dwight-subject's *wanting* seems subordinated to both a *having to do* and a *not being able not to do*, since the girl matches all his selective criteria — not of personal preferences, but functional to a higher end:

> (*106. Dwight's interview.*)
> DWIGHT (*off*): The purse girl hits everything on my check list.
> (*Cut to Dwight.*)
> DWIGHT: Creamy skin, straight teeth, curly hair, amazing breasts. Not for me, for my children. The Schrutes produce very thirsty babies.

If Michael-subject tends to neutralize his professional narrative programs and Dwight tends, on the contrary, to generalize them in other realms of his existence, things are different for Jim and Pam. In their discourses, as well as in the higher-level utterance, their professional programs have already been realized, thanks to lower initial thresholds. The two subjects' passional investments in this category of programs is minimal and mainly dysphoric, and what matters to them is finding a way to escape the logic by which what a person does for a living also defines what he or she is in life.

Jim and Pam's professional narrative programs are not neutralized, and as such they are regularly achieved, although they are largely not represented in the utterance. At most, Pam is shown answering the phone or giving Michael messages, while Jim can be seen typing on the computer or talking to a client on the phone. Their attempts at talking about their jobs are weak; the characters lack motivation and end up attaching dysphoric values to the jobs themselves.

> (*101. Pam's interview.*)
> PAM: I don't think it would be the worst thing if they let me go. Because then, I might ... I just, I don't think it's many little girls' dream to be a receptionist. Um, I like to do illustrations. Um, mostly watercolor.

This excerpt highlights the characters' attempt at giving a positive value to her personal sphere, and to keep the two narrative trajectories as far apart as possible, preventing the two worlds from intersecting. Or, stated another way, the two worlds and the two paths are constantly intersecting, but the subjects define them as separate and try to make sure that their work lives are neither cause nor effect of their personal ones. The separation of the two worlds does not necessarily effect positive results in the personal sphere. While the subjects might not always admit to this, it is clearly discursivized by the secondary enunciation, or in the discourses they make about one another — such as Jim's comments on Pam's relationship with Roy, her fiancé at the start of the series.

Another category of narrative programs to which Jim and Pam are committed is the interference with Dwight's life and work. Such interference is often negative, as when Jim acts as opponent to Dwight. He does not act as an anti-subject because very rarely do Jim and Dwight have the same goals: while they do the same kind of job, they are never competing for the same objects or the same values. While Jim takes this separation as a given, thus acting at a different narrative level, Dwight behaves as if such distinction did not exist. This behavior creates the interference:

> (*101. Jim places a row of pencils pointing up between his desk and Dwight's.*)
> (*Dwight sits at his desk.*)
> DWIGHT: You can't do that.
> JIM: Why not?
> DWIGHT: Safety violation, I could fall and pierce ... an organ.
> JIM: (*Crosses his fingers*) We'll see.
> (*Dwight hits the pencils with his phone's receiver to make them fall.*)

Even when Jim *makes it seem* as if he were acting as a helper to Dwight's programs, in reality this is most often part of a strategy of interference, which Dwight continually fails to see as such. At times, and even more strikingly, Dwight actively seeks Jim's collaboration — often with ultimate intention to undermine him — but ends up falling victim of his own traps.

The Camera's Cardinal Role

As anticipated, the textualization of the camera's presence, that is the recognition of its presence by the utterance's actors, implies and highlights a splitting of enunciative levels. At the highest level, we find the enunciative device in charge of the fictional utterance, which disengages from a secondary device in charge of the documentary utterance. The camera, in its function as an actor of the utterance, is placed at this second level.

The camera's presence, however, is not only assumed by the other actors' gazes and, more generally, by proxemic elements — which would be better considered as devices used to textualize the simulacrum of a receiver, as usually occurs in news programs, and as happens in a documentary, impersonal and objective though the latter may be. Some of the fragments quoted here show how the characters of the utterance make more or less explicit references to the camera and address it directly in the second person. An even more relevant element is that the camera often tends to be dragged back and forth between the realm of the enunciation and that of the utterance, thanks to certain movements that not only follow the action, but, in a way, commentate on it. One might cast montage, firmly anchored to the realm of the enunciative device, in opposition to seamless camera movements, which tend to interfere with the action.

In instances of the latter kind, the presence of the camera, whether or not overtly recognized, questions the truthfulness of what is shown, as well as the characters' credibility.

(*103. Initial sequence. Jim and Michael in Michael's office.*)
MICHAEL: There's a decision that needs to be made, and I'm having an unbelievably busy day.
(*The camera moves to show a solitary Post-It note on Michael's desk, then moves to Jim, who is looking at the note.*)

Within the set of the utterance's characters, the camera has a very subtle role, given the fact that it remains most often undetected and unrevealed by the other actors. This ambiguous actorial presence is opposed to the camera's central position in terms of the actantial roles it assumes and, consequently, in terms of the whole enunciative structure.

The camera's presence is made even more significant by its total absence from the frame. It certainly is there; it is named (albeit rarely and with a sort of modesty, as if talking about it would equate to breaking a taboo), the material existence of the text depends on it, as well as the splitting of enunciative levels and some characters' behaviors in the second-level utterance.

Following a simplistic reading of Metz's concept of impersonal enunciation, it should be impossible to distinguish the two enunciative levels simply on the basis of the mechanical device in charge of the enun-

3. The Office

ciation. Indeed, the substantial similarity between the two devices, their apparent identities and the postulated absence of a subject able to operate an enunciative disengagement might make the whole distinction based merely on contextual clues (the fact that the text is based on a boxing of genres, hence of enunciations) or on phatic and metatextual elements of the narration (the actors' references to the camera).

What becomes determining here is the behavior of the enunciative device itself, discursivized as camera movements and montage: while the device never provides a psychological characterization of the enunciation (for lack of an actual psychologically endowed subject), it does highlight its split identity between the two levels. As noted, a constant shifting of camera movements occurs between a shot/countershot technique and long takes. This shifting takes place not only between different sequences, but also within a single sequence, and its two terms produce substantially different reality effects.

On the one hand, the shot/countershot montage always gives the impression that the scene was shot using more than one camera. This is true both for alternating close-ups, in cases of dialog between characters on opposite sides of a desk, where the camera holds an intermediate point of view between them, and for scenes with distant shooting points, with alternating mid and full shots, or even peeking shots from outside the room, through a window. The multiple-camera impression's illusory nature is revealed by the fact that the second camera is never shown, not even when the spatial arrangement is such that showing it would become inevitable, and by the physical impossibility for two cameras of a certain size to exist on the same point in space (in cases of alternating close-ups).

On the other hand, camera movements, which follow the action instead of fragmenting it, lend the camera a certain degree of subjectivity (although not, as I said, in a psychological sense), and stress the reality of the documentary—which lies strictly on the level of the uttered enunciation. In such cases, then, the use of long takes makes it possible to identify an actual enunciative disengagement, which allows the secondary level to be not only implied, but also effectively discursivized.

On the contrary, the use of a shot/countershot technique performs the opposite operation, that is an engagement toward the primary enunciative device. The combination of these two techniques, often within the same sequence, should be of no surprise: on the one hand, this combination makes the embedding of levels explicit (where montage, that is the power of breaking and combining shots and camera movements, would by default be placed at a higher level), while on the other it is a behavior very similar — in terms of its meaning effects — to what happens in verbal language with the combination of direct and indirect speech.

Separate consideration should be given to the use of fixed-camera long takes in interview sequences. In such cases, the camera is not only a physical means of narrative production; it becomes the framed character's direct, albeit silent, interlocutor. Consequently, the text discursivizes the camera not only as an enunciative device, but also as a character of the utterance, whose presence reflects on the framed character's actions. This utterative disengagement installs an observing subject, the camera itself, in charge of receiving the discourse of the interview's subject.

4

The Comeback

Between June and September 2005, HBO aired the thirteen episodes of the only season of *The Comeback,* created by former *Friends* star Lisa Kudrow, and producer of *Sex and the City* Michael Patrick King. At a time when reality shows seem to have bored producers more than television audiences, *The Comeback* tells the story of Valerie Cherish, former star of a successful situation comedy, now set to come back to the small screen and regain her lost fame. Valerie lands a secondary role on a new sitcom, *Room and Bored,* while the same network produces a reality show on her everyday life.

Valerie's story is, obviously, fictional, but the format of *The Comeback* is typical of a kind of reality show that features cameras shooting the protagonist twenty-four hours a day. During the day, Valerie is accompanied by a television crew that follows her everywhere, with two more fixed cameras installed in her bedroom and her kitchen.

We could call this a reality show of observation, whose point of view is not unbiased, but on the contrary almost didactic, as the perspective of documentaries can sometimes be. The enunciative device does not simply show an actress's life. Rather, it is motivated by an attention to detail that cannot be separated from the competitive character of the contemporary reality show. Conflict among the characters is what the show seeks, and the question it induces is, "Will Valerie make it?"

Valerie's life constitutes a daily struggle to catch the camera's attention and, paradoxically, a struggle *against* the camera — as I will show. *The Comeback* takes for granted the concept of reality show, but at the same time challenges that concept's meaning at its foundation, that is, at the point of its relationship with empiric reality.

The Comeback is one single title used to denominate two different textual objects: one is, naturally, the series here examined; the other is the reality show of which Valerie is the subject, within the primary utterance that constitutes her reality. The format that shapes the narrative text under examination, however, is not that of a finished product — not one a fictional audience within the utterance would enjoy. Rather, the text is clearly marked as raw footage, that is, a preproduction rough cut of the program.

The Comeback presents itself as an open series, one in which the narrative development of each single episode is functional to that of the show's entire span. Episodes are strictly sequential, predictably, since empiric reality generally proceeds by wide-range narrative developments, while only the intervention of an external narrative design can shape the micro-narrations that constitute single episodes.

Two Enunciative Devices

The Comeback's enunciative structure is very complex. The primary device installs into the utterance a secondary one, responsible for the raw footage and partly coincident with the reality show's productive apparatus. These two devices coincide only in part because the raw footage is actually uttered, and it is understood from the very beginning that the images this raw footage shows are produced (or captured, depending on the chosen philosophical perspective on the nature of the filmic enunciation) by the crew present in the shot. However, according to Metz, the visibility of the crew implies a denial of its role as part of the active enunciative device.[1]

Thus, the device in charge of the raw footage performs an act that is partly self-referential, as it tends to always show a part of itself—although the part it shows cannot be the one actively involved in the enunciation. It is an exemplary case of the device being revealed as a set of functions, in which each individual's subjectivity fades away in favor of the productive process of shaping space and time by capturing slices of a given reality as images. The filmic device is a joint effort of humans and machines, and it normally has no human-like psychological characterization.

While revealing the device is rare in film, it is much less so in contemporary television's reality-based programming,[2] which is never very shy when it comes to showing its technical foundations. It is almost a

4. The Comeback

stylistic cliché of studio shows to have a dolly shoot the floor cameras, or to feature a director's voice-off interacting with the host. Otherwise very similar to fiction, the reality show cannot but show part of the device in charge of its production, discursivizing the very rules that govern it — for example, through the presence within the shot of the show's hosts, extraneous to the action but still internal to the text.

Televisual fiction does not, in fact, go to such extents, except in forms so standard (sitcom's laugh track is an example) that they become almost invisible and remain bound to the expressive canon of more conventional cinema. *The Comeback* plays with this effect by making the primary enunciation transparent. The disengagement the primary device performs, which generates the secondary enunciation, leaves the uttered device in plain view. The expedient of the raw footage is a rhetorical trick, an effective way to justify a device that does nothing but reveal itself and its mechanisms.

The second major element of complexity comes from the fact that the secondary utterance's subject, Valerie Cherish, does not let her story be told in a neutral way — as the rules of reality show would require, and as the producers explicitly ask her to do — but wants to actively contribute to the construction of this discursive level. From her position as subject of the utterance, she imposes herself as the enunciation's co-protagonist (creating a sort of syncretism between the subject of uttered enunciation and part of the secondary device), an imposition that manifests through a constant act of interlocution with the device. Although she accepts being in a reality show, Valerie tries to shift its expressive modes toward those more typical of documentary, denying her role as object of observation and showing herself as an expert subject instead.

Valerie surely does not intend to modify the raw footage's destiny. Rather, she is unaware of the raw footage's existence, which leaves all her attempts at manipulating reality transparent at this level. By showing both the device and its objects, and by revealing, at once, its own production practices and reality show's most consolidated ones, this level tends to show things "as they are." On the contrary, Valerie's discourse aims to show, according to the situation, things as they are not, or not to show things as they are — hence overtly lying or concealing reality. The intentions of a further utterative level can also be inferred from the utterance, though the raw footage leaves that level at a virtual stage. The final cut of the reality show, revealed in the show's finale as one more uttered enunciation, places itself in a paradoxical relationship with the reality it represents. Building on fragments of Valerie's life, the reality show will display a different kind of reality, not always faithful to events as they happened, but which has real effects on the characters' lives.

The Visual Component

Being an HBO production, *The Comeback* is not subject to commercial breaks. Therefore, each episode tends to fill the whole half-hour slot reserved for it. The actual duration varies from the third episode's twenty-seven minutes to the pilot's nearly thirty-two. The episodes feature a total of about fifteen sequences, a number lower than that of both the typical sitcom episode and the two thirty-minute shows already considered — an even more notable difference considering the episodes' longer duration. Each episode counts at least a couple of long takes, usually at least one minute long, but also long shot/countershot sequences featuring more than thirty or forty rapid shots. The simultaneous presence of these two styles of montage can be related to the variety of locations in which the action takes place: long takes are usually employed in car scenes, with the camera riding shotgun while Valerie drives, or in fixed-camera scenes in the kitchen or bedroom, in Valerie's studio interviews or in her personal video diary; the shot/countershot technique is used, as is natural, when two or more characters interact or when shooting wide spaces, such as the interior of the studio or external locations.

One particular use of shot/countershot is in cases when the enunciative levels shift (at least apparently) and the images the reality show's cameras shoot alternate with shots of the crew itself. The paternity of the crew shots is left ambiguous on purpose: while in some cases these shots are nothing more than "mistakes" made by cameras aiming where they should not, other shots are so neatly intentional that it is possible to consider them a direct product of the primary enunciative device — which would consequently break the reality effect created by the raw-footage expedient. Even if it were possible to calculate the precise topography of each scene in order to establish exactly where each cam-

4. The Comeback

era is at any given moment, the paternity issue would probably still remain unsolved.

I must, once again, mention the difference between any devices shown in the shot and those empirically responsible for the primary enunciation. Dramatic actors remain dramatic actors, and the camera people and sound technicians in the frame are not real camera people or sound technicians. Despite the presence of several cameras in the scene, the whole series is shot using a single camera. This technical detail casts a more definite light on the whole enunciative apparatus and highlights even more the purely fictional existence of the devices within the shot.

Using fixed cameras in some locations, on the other hand, constitutes one more visual expedient, common in reality shows, which produces a fusion effect opposite to the visual fragmentation of long shots just considered. A collage of shots taken by the stationary camera in the kitchen at noncontiguous times occupies the eighth sequence of the pilot episode. The common element among these shots is the presence of Valerie, who repeats, quite obsessively, her key line in the pilot episode of *Room and Bored*:

> (*01. Kitchen. Fixed camera. Valerie and Mark.*)
> VALERIE: Alright, so they're all making out in the condo. I come home, see it, and I say, "Note to self: after a long day at work, I don't want to *see* that!"
> MARK (*laughs*): That was funny.
> [...]
> VALERIE (*quite relieved*): Hah! (*Eats a bite.*) Alright. "Note to self: after a long day at work, *I-don't-want-to-see-that*!" Well, works too.
> (*Cut. Valerie takes a chocolate cake out of the fridge.*)
> VALERIE: Note to self: after a long day at work, I don't want to see that!
> (*And so on, for a few more cuts.*)

The element of image quality is tightly linked to the reality effect the complex enunciative apparatus of *The Comeback* is aiming at. The images have a feel of immediacy typical of digital recording, as if to reflect the adhesion to reality show as a nonfictional televisual genre by definition. Apart from a few exceptions, the cinematography appears to be very limited, almost unplanned, consistently with an effect of unpredictability of the characters' actions. Once again, the lack of cinematography is nothing more than a reality effect, and not the empiric operative condition of the primary device, which naturally has all the ordinary tools of televisual production to its avail. An even more pronounced grain can be seen in the personal video diary sequences, during which Valerie performs a confession in front of a camera which she herself operates; during such sequences, the progression of the tape's time code is also displayed, imitating the viewfinder display of a digital camera.

The Sound Component

In agreement with the raw-footage principle, all sounds in *The Comeback* are intra-diegetic. The ending sequences of most episodes are the only exception to this rule, as they pair images and end credits with songs that pertain to the extra-diegetic soundtrack, which is directly uttered by the primary enunciative device. The raw-footage enunciation, given its unfinished nature, would have no business adding extra-diegetic music. The function of such extra-diegetic songs is most often paratextual, as a sort of commentary to the images or to the whole episode. Even when episodes end with songs that are part of the intra-diegetic soundtrack, these still tend to maintain a thematic link with the episode itself.

Due to the presence of characters who are not supposed to be shown on camera, but who often are, off-screen voices are often heard. Similarly, focalization discrepancies between sound and visuals often occur, due to the fact that the utterance's main actors wear wireless microphones, which record their voices even when the camera is, for various reasons, focusing somewhere else. The narrative developments of the show often involve sound as theme, manifested in the technical devices used in its production and the human characters involved in producing it.

The Paratextual Component

The Comeback features a minimal amount of paratext, which is confined to the extremities of each episode. Each of these moments belongs to one of the main enunciative devices operating within the text.

Each episode is introduced by what looks and sounds like a standard digital test screen: a test pattern (three orders of colored and black-and-white bars) on the background, accompanied by a 1000-Hz audio reference tone. Superimposed on the text screen, which lasts two or three seconds, are the title of the show and the note "-raw footage-" indispensable for correct access to the second enunciative level.

This intro screen exists within the realm of the secondary enunciation, first of all to describe the utterance as raw, and also because it establishes a correlation between the utterance's lack of finish and the intro screen's lack of refinement on the plane of expression (the use of a generic text pattern; a grainy, inelegant font; and, not least, the lack of an opening theme, replaced by the reference tone). The primary device performs an enunciative disengagement and assumes this paratextual element as the only opening sequence, and in so doing it makes itself transparent in favor of the secondary device, thus enhancing the reality effect.

At the end of each episode, when the song — different in every episode — starts, the show's actual end credits also start and usually continue on a black background after the episode's final images have faded out. With the end credits, the primary enunciation gets back behind the wheel and reveals the rules of the game, once and for all, with a more traditional closing sequence. Not only does this sequence feature music, often extra-diegetic, but the plastic organization of the verbal component is much more dignified than that of the intro screen. The overlaid credits list appears in the same font as that of the opening title (a sans serif font, like Helvetica, appropriate for on-screen viewing), but its smaller size gives it a more refined look. The credits sequence is organized in the standard production hierarchy and provides the show with the customary official marks the raw footage lacks. Thanks to the possibility of managing the space of representation not only on different dimensions (including temporal) but also on several levels (a superposition of layers that gives the television screen a sort of third dimension, which is actually a meta-dimension), the primary enunciative device performs a final engagement, which allows it to reaffirm paternity of the utterance, and, ultimately, of the text's complex nature.

The Characters

When she was about thirty, in the early '90s, Valerie Cherish (Lisa Kudrow) was the star of *I'm It,* a situation comedy that lasted ninety-seven episodes, three less than the necessary quota to enter syndication. For the last thirteen years, Valerie has be unable to find roles that would put her back in the spotlight. Consequently, she has remained stuck outside show business and married a lawyer, Mark Berman (Damian Young). Valerie appears very thoughtful, to the point of becoming condescending, but only if this thoughtfulness works to her advantage. Because of the cameras' presence, she tries to avoid any topics that might cast her in a bad light, or that she might deem irrelevant. Even in her real life, she appropriates her line from the pilot of *Room and Bored,* the indignant "I don't want to see that!" — a line perfectly in tune with her unwillingness to understand the world objectively. Another of her typical expressions is "Put a pin in that," which she uses when she wants to fake being interested in things she will never bring up again. She tends to forget the names of people she is not interested in, until she realizes that getting to know them may actually become useful to her.

Always at Valerie's side is Mickey (Robert Michael Morris), her hair stylist since the times of *I'm It.* He follows her everywhere, ready to fix her hairdo, but he often also assumes the role of confidant and moral supporter, just like in old times. Despite the way his behavior betrays him in everyone's eyes, he wonders why everyone should take for granted that he is gay — until he reveals it during the series.

Valerie's main interlocutor is the crew shooting the reality show. She often gazes into the camera, and, in a more properly metatextual way, speaks to Jane (Laura Silverman), the show's producer, the only one in the crew with whom she has any kind of direct relationship or whose name and presence she can remember. Jane, on the other hand, for productive reasons prefers not to appear in the shot, but when she decides to initiate interaction with Valerie (always in a modest way, almost in a whisper), she aims at provoking a spontaneous response. She generally avoids any other kind of dialog and tends to remain silent if asked inadmissible questions. The other crew members constitute an indistinct collective character whose single members assume a name and an identity only in rare cases.

Valerie's husband, Mark, is not used to dealing with show business, and while he supports Valerie's choices, he is often intolerant of the way they negatively affect his life, especially when he feels his privacy threatened more than it should be. He has a twelve-year-old daughter, Francesca (Vanessa Marano), from a previous marriage, about whose education he does not seem to have much say, as opposed to his ex-wife. Francesca fully adheres to the stereotype of the Los Angeles kid: rich, spoiled and blinded by the lights of showbiz, the only reason she shows any interest in spending more time with Valerie. Esperanza (Lillian Hurst) is Valerie and Mark's housekeeper. The presence of the cameras makes her very uncomfortable, and she doesn't seem to understand Valerie's behavior.

Among her coworkers, the only one who seems to sincerely appreciate Valerie is the star of *Room and Bored,* Juna Millken (Malin Åkerman), already publicly known for being the lead vocalist in a rock band. She still feels out of place in the world of television, and because of this she sees Valerie as a confidante and advisor. The remaining three actors in *Room and Bored,* one woman and two men, chosen more for their looks than their acting abilities, seem as stereotypical in their real lives (within the primary utterance) as in the roles they play on the sitcom.

Among the production staff of *Room and Bored* are the show's creators, Tom Peterman (Robert Bagnell) and Paulie G. (Lance Barber), whose main outstanding quality is to have won an Emmy award some years before as writers on an episode of *The Simpsons.* While Tom makes himself available to listen to Valerie and, from a certain point on, even behaves affectionately toward her, Paulie G. almost never speaks to Valerie, looks at her with a superior air and always makes it clear that he does not appreciate her being in the sitcom.

The character of Jimmy, the director of part of the sitcom, textualizes an element of the empiric world: he is played by James Burrows, a well-known television director[3] who has also played small roles, most often that of a director. In this case, through the use of a familiar nickname, he plays "almost" himself, assuming from his empiric self—without need to specify any details—the thematic investment proper of a successful television director. Thanks to his experience, and to having worked with Valerie on *I'm It,* Jimmy can be honest with her, often even blunt, and, within the limits imposed by Valerie's will to understand her own position, he succeeds in taming her ambitions while still reassuring her. In the twelfth episode, conditions of the shoot worry her: Tom, the nicer producer, is absent, and Jimmy isn't directing the episode, which leaves her to contend with Paulie G. She shores her fears with Jimmy, who comforts her while in the middle of a film shoot:

> (*12. External, day. Television studios.*)
> VALERIE: (*Laughs, nervously.*) So. Pretty much on my own. You know, just wanted to be good, show Paulie it's OK, I can be — you know, I can be funny, I can be good. You know —
> JIMMY: Blood from a stone.
> VALERIE: What? He's —
> JIMMY: Blood — from a stone.
> VALERIE: Yeah. Incapable. (Jimmy nods.) Yeah. Yeah. No, I understand. Well still, I want it to be good. So, I'd love to —
> JIMMY: You know, the audience will laugh, and you'll go to that place you go. You'll be fine.
> VALERIE: You think?
> JIMMY: You're a giant cupcake.

Spaces and Times

The action is, for the most part, divided between Valerie's house and the television studios where *Room and Bored* is shot. In the house, the most relevant spaces are the kitchen and the bedroom, where the two fixed cameras are located, framing each room obliquely from above. At the television studios, a distinction can be made between public spaces (the stage and the audience bleachers, the common backstage area), private spaces (the actors' dressing rooms, the writers' lounge) and spaces with an intermediate valence (the wardrobe, the make-up room). The outside space surrounding the studios is also often used.

More action spaces include cars (not only Valerie's), the restaurants and cafés where the actors hang out and, more generally, the city streets. No less important is the virtual space in which Valerie's numerous phone calls take place, especially those with her agent. The fact that she almost always uses her cell phone in hands-free mode, to the benefit of the reality show's microphones, broadens the extension of such improvised virtual space.

Space management is an important element, especially in regard to the relationship between the public and the private spheres, and also

4. The Comeback

because of space's role in defining relationships between characters, as well as developing each individual's self-image and identity. In *The Comeback*, seen as an utterance of which Valerie Cherish is the main subject, there is no real spatial categorization based on the distinction between *personal life* and *work life*: from the instant the cameras enter her life, every personal moment is swallowed by the work sphere. This is also the reason why the opposition *public vs. private* is feeble, due to the high public visibility of almost all private spaces in the utterance.

On the temporal side, notable discrepancies persist between utterative and enunciative time, both in terms of absolute temporal placement and the duration and relative placement of events. This can be seen within the consistency of each episode and in the relationships between episodes, which often feature, also internally, days- or weeks-long ellipses, usually revealed by the characters' discourses. Consequently, the span of narrated time does not correspond to the time span of *The Comeback*'s original airing, which covered the arc of one summer.

The story begins in the spring, during pilot season, that critical time when the pilot episodes of new shows are produced to be evaluated for airing in the following season. As a confirmation of a total projection onto the work sphere, the only calendar the show follows is the one relating to television activity: after the pilot season come the upfronts, when the network presents the new shows to a specialized audience in New York, and the event introduces both *Room and Bored* and *The Comeback*; then follows the sitcom's premiere in the fall; and finally (in the thirteenth episode), the premiere of the reality show in January. Contrary to convention in the majority of American shows, *Room and Bored* (and by extension, *The Comeback*) never refers to a private calendar, articulated by civil and religious holidays. Even Valerie's vacation — a weekend in Palm Springs with her husband — is a forced break after the sitcom has been shut down for retooling, and is still studded with work commitments, among which is the obligation to endorse the car one of the reality show's sponsors has provided for the occasion. Since the sponsoring brand also exists in the empiric world, the reality show's product-placement strategy betrays a product placement directed to the empiric audience of *The Comeback*.

As I have mentioned, the discursivization of time within single episodes is discontinuous and functional to a search for narrative coherence. The often long temporal ellipses are marked and explained, mostly in a marginal way, only in the actors' discourses. When such markers are lacking, the temporal succession becomes ambiguous, usually to the detriment of the actions' durative aspect. The moments whose duration (and, less so, iteration) is most often represented are usually those that define or confirm the characters' thematic investments and clarify their narrative programs—with particular attention to Valerie's. The phone calls, dialog before and after scenes, family interactions and attempts at modifying the progress of the story are all entirely captured, even in their still moments and their silences. On the contrary, the performances more strictly related to the profession, such as table-reads, rehearsals and tapings of the sitcom, are usually seized in their inchoative aspect or, seldom, in the terminative one, hence purged of all elements the reality show's montage deems uninteresting to its audience.

Valerie Cherish's Two Realities

In *The Comeback*, it is possible to differentiate between two main classes of narrative programs, which correspond to two main classes of actors. The first class is embraced by all actors related to some aspect of the reality show's production: above all Valerie, and also Jane, the network, Mickey and other secondary or occasional actors. Such class of programs can be called *manipulation of reality*.

The second class, which can be denominated as *preservation of reality*, involves all those who are extraneous to the reality show (beginning with the cast, crew and production of *Room and Bored*), but also those who suffer from the reality show's side effects. The people who are part of Valerie's domestic sphere, particularly Mark and Esperanza, must be included in the latter subset. I will show that Francesca does not fall into this category, but rather into a particular form of manipulation.

Manipulation of Reality

This denomination includes the set of programs aiming at controlling how reality will be perceived and represented by the cameras. They

4. The Comeback

are often organized into complex narrative trajectories, which include intentional acts of communication oriented to providing visions and interpretations of events not always congruent with the uttered reality. The single subjects' programs are in conflict with one another — a conflict often downplayed, but in some cases open and clear to all characters. The manipulative intention, which should by definition be concealed, is brought up by the conflict between programs that pertain to different subjects. Among these is the secondary enunciative device, which, by overtly entering the utterance it produces, is anything but transparent in its actions. Not only does its presence condition the behavior of other actors, but thanks to its intrusive capacities it can often capture their different degrees of intentionality.

Valerie Cherish's main narrative program aims at succeeding in being once again accepted in show business, which has excluded her for more than ten years. Obtaining a part in a sitcom and, consequently, having a reality show of her own are just intermediate steps, narrative programs of use that already seem to be happily concluded at the end of the pilot episode. As it turns out, though, being followed by cameras since the beginning is not a guarantee of success, but only one of the terms of the deal. The ambiguity of her main sender, to which I will return shortly, makes Valerie's future always uncertain, continually forcing both her and the other characters to test and redefine the situation, thus repeatedly questioning each subject's competence.

Valerie's narrative trajectory includes one more narrative program, which consists of the promotion of a positive self-image and the search for ways to erase any elements that might disturb such image. This is not a simple program of use in regard to the main one just considered (finding acceptance in showbiz), but a parallel strategy that aims to define the modalities of her comeback. Not only does Valerie *want* to be a star once again as a result of her role in a new sitcom, but she also wants her success to be accompanied and motivated by the audience's appreciation of her positive personal qualities. To this end, Valerie establishes a continuous communication process with her audience, whose existence is presupposed and represented in the utterance by the cameras, to which Valerie's gaze is directed even when it is not required. Thanks to the (narrative and business) contract that binds her to the presence of the cameras, she exploits the possibility of having a receiver that *cannot but* listen. Better yet, the main receiver of her communicative acts is, in turn, a subject (collective, and only partly human) whose narrative program is to accept and record Valerie's actions and discourses.

As one might predict in such a case, the discourses Valerie produces are innocent in neither fact nor intention; that is, they always are strongly polarized metanarrations. Similarly to the way Valerie imposes herself as a subject of communication, she does her best to avoid becoming the receiver of other people's communicative acts: she filters and distorts any discourse directed to her through the lens with which she has chosen to filter the world and that she has established her audience should also choose. Unfortunately, she is not legitimized by her sender (the network, and, more practically, Jane) to put herself on the camera's side (that is, using it as a direct interlocutor, thus becoming part of the device in charge of the uttered enunciation), and consequently her intentions become explicit. While her discourses might not be unbiased, the reality show's raw footage is, as much as possible, thus it is able to see through her intentions.

One more diffused practice in Valerie's action, which complements that of avoiding potentially dysphoric or dysphorizing discourses (consistent with her role as a sitcom actress), is an ongoing attempt to make sure the cameras' attention remains focused on her as long as possible. Even when she shows herself interested in knowing details about others' lives, such interest is terminated at the exact moment in which she expresses it, as if its expression were enough to make her agreeable, but did not justify an attention shift onto someone else — not Valerie's attention, and the audience's even less so.

> (*01. Television studios, backstage.*)
> VALERIE: Do you have a boyfriend, Jane?
> [...]
> JANE (*off-screen*): Well, I'm not really looking.
> VALERIE (*smiling*): (*Pause.*) I'm sorry, I wasn't listening. Just got distracted, 'cause there's the set! Here it is! Wow!

Being represented, albeit only as a simulacrum, within the utterance it produces, the secondary enunciative device assumes a position of observing subject, whose narrative program is the reception and recording of Valerie Cherish's life. Although Valerie realizes the manipulation

4. The Comeback

largely as masking and positive-image presentation, the goal of the reality show's producers is to accentuate reality through attention to detail. It is important to highlight a fundamental difference between the device responsible for the raw footage and the one responsible of the actual reality show (in turn object of a *mise en abyme* in episode 13): even though both devices try to assign a narrative form to events that tend not to have one (a typical risk of observational reality shows), the device responsible for the raw footage provides a more distant and rich look on the events the reality show presumes as real (respecting the temporal sequence, cutting off the superfluous and often showing more than necessary), while the device in the *mise en abyme* further manipulates and rebuilds it (recombining the available material and eliminating any more than would be necessary for an understanding of events consistent with the way they actually unfolded).

Jane is part of the device, but also a subject in herself. Charged by a sender — generically referred to as *the network* — with coordinating the crew's work, she is also Valerie's direct interlocutor. Her narrative program is more specific, and does not necessarily coincide with that of the enunciative device as a whole; it has a double and apparently contradictory nature. That is, on the one hand she must limit herself to observing and directing the crew so as not to neglect any relevant details; on the other she must control, as best as she can, the action itself, in order to accentuate and mold the narrative structure of everyday life. Her job is different from that of a television director, who would be in charge of bringing narrative material that already exists to a realized stage, albeit in a different form; Jane's narrative trajectory includes the possibility of providing the action with a narrative and passional structure, making explicit some elements that, without her intervention, would not otherwise surface.

(*01. Valerie's interview after the audition. Jane asks her to repeat her line with more emphasis.*)
VALERIE (*smiling*): Well, I got it. (*Laughs.*) And I think —
JANE (*off-screen*): Could — could you do it again?
VALERIE: (*Clears throat.*) Um, you know, Jane? I'm sorry, I just, I, um, I don't wanna look like an idiot. You know, and this is supposed to be reality.
JANE (*off-screen*): Yeah. Well, I — I — I just think that your reality could be more excited.

In her role as an active producer, Jane assumes different actantial roles in regard to Valerie's narrative trajectory. She is, at times, a helper, although her observing role should forbid her from being one, thus often making her an opponent. In other cases she even becomes a sender, either in a strictly coded and institutional fashion in interview sequences where she provokes and directs Valerie's comments through well-aimed questions, or in a completely improvised way when, trying to achieve similar results, she tries to extract words from Valerie, even when the actress seems to be unwilling to talk.

At times, Jane becomes Valerie's opponent not with harmful intentions, but as an indirect consequence of her *having to* fulfill her own professional obligations, among which is the necessity to *not be able to* report to Valerie details that would interfere with the reality show's natural course. Her ambivalent position is particularly evident in the final episode, where, before an interview, Jane lets Valerie know she just finished interviewing Paulie G.; however she does not reveal any details. This case amplifies the opposition to Valerie's narrative trajectory, always aimed at avoiding anything that might place her in an unfavorable light.

In the previous episode, at the end of a work day during which Paulie G. had been particularly irritating, Valerie, still wearing her cupcake costume, punched him in the stomach. Paulie G., who had been feeding himself pizza and soda throughout the day, threw up, immediately followed by Valerie. This event, catastrophic in Valerie's eyes, would become the highlight of the reality show's initial episode — a single moment of loss of self-control that would actually become the catalyst for the show's success.

In this case, not only does Jane deny Valerie the possibility of obtaining the necessary knowledge for controlling any possible damage, but she does not even stop her when, taking for granted that Paulie G. has said horrible things about her, Valerie embarks on a violent rant against him. It is one of the very few moments in which Valerie Cherish loses her smile and finally says what she really thinks:

(13. *Interview.*)
    VALERIE: I have tried everything I could to be nice to him, but Paulie G. has got it out for me. From the first minute he saw me, he's been nothing but hurtful. He is abusive, he is threatening, he is a monster. And I, I hate to say that about anyone, I really do. But he leaves me no choice.

4. The Comeback

Predictably enough, during the reality show's premiere, it is revealed that Paulie G. had words of admiration for Valerie during his interview. The coupling of the two subjects' discourses, accompanied by the repeated showing of the stomach punch, initially seems to make the protagonist's efforts to maintain her image useless. Valerie holds Jane, as part of the production team, responsible for her apparent failure; she also believes that the production team itself, sender of her narrative programs, has violated the contract's rules, making it impossible for Valerie's goals to be achieved. All this happens, for the most part, in Valerie's discourses. It would be difficult to disagree with her, given her interpretation of the facts — namely, accepting that the text's isotopic network validates a narrative path in which the network is sender of the actress's personal success, which in reality cannot possibly be the case.

What happens in Valerie's discourses is a substitution of the network's narrative programs with her own. Valerie is most definitely risking it all for her dream to rebuild her career, but this keeps her from understanding that the narrative program with which the network is charging her is that of being a good *object* to the reality show — and her having a role in the sitcom is functional to this. On the contrary, Valerie pushes to extreme extents her willingness to be a *subject*, not only of the utterance, but also — and above all — at the enunciative level.

In regard to the reality show's goals, Valerie is completely replaceable: in the pilot episode, it is revealed that two other actresses are up for her part in *Room and Bored*, but their motivations are totally different from hers. They see the reality show as the price they must pay in order to get the sitcom job. On the contrary, Valerie *wants* the reality show, due to the new visibility it cannot but bring her. The sitcom, as Jimmy reminds her, is only a way to obtain it. Valerie's subsequent error is losing sight of this hierarchy, this logical succession, and thinking of the reality show as a gift the network is giving her to honor her glorious past and promote her comeback.

A special case of reality manipulation is that of Francesca, Mark's daughter, who tends to become more and more present in the house, despite the fact that she usually lives with her birth mother. Francesca is definitely fascinated by show business and, just like her girlfriends, is an admirer of Juna. She grabs any opportunity to show herself to the cameras, and to this end she decides to improve her relationship with Valerie. It is clear from the start that Francesca has never gotten along too well with her stepmother, as confirmed in *The Comeback's* finale by Mickey's voice, as his interview appears in the *en-abyme* pilot of the reality show.

Francesca's strategy works in a direction opposite to Valerie's. While the latter manipulates the way the cameras perceive reality (no matter how positive the results are for her) in order to make real what is not necessarily so, Francesca modifies her own reality in order to be visible, whatever her ulterior motives may be. While Valerie sees the reality show as a way to regain success and popularity, Francesca's goal seems to be only that of *being* in front of those cameras.

Preservation of Reality

As I anticipated, those who do not actively take part in the reality show's production process do not have, for the most part, any interest in modifying the way the cameras frame their realities. This is also the case with the network, whose role Valerie keeps failing to understand; she considers it an actor with a unified intention, whose single human components all act in agreement. In actuality, despite being two shows produced by the same network, the reality show and the sitcom are managed by different people, and it is never too clear who has come up with the link between the two series and why. Moreover, those who are working on the sitcom—from the writers to the network executives—are more often embarrassed, irritated or confused at the presence of the reality show's crew, and such feelings necessarily affect Valerie. Thus, the network is surely a sender the moment it decides to hire Valerie as the protagonist of a reality show *and* as a secondary actor in a sitcom, but becomes her anti-sender when her narrative programs—not only those she projects and expects to realize, but also the ones she is actually involved in—collide with hierarchically superior programs. When she's called to audition for the part in *Room and Bored*, the producer tells her that not only are cameras not allowed in the room, but also that the executives in charge do not care that the audition is an important moment in the reality show.

4. The Comeback

That reality stands independent of the reality show is clear from the way the network keeps challenging the existence of the sitcom, and with it, also Valerie, who knows her having a reality show depends on her role on *Room and Bored*, a reason for her to try to gain more relevance, however unsuccessfully. The tests the sitcom must pass are partly predictable (initial rewrites, pilot approval, scheduling), and partly typical of a show with limited success (such as being shut down for retooling). Besides these, Valerie is also involved in similar tests with her reality show. However, thanks to the sitcom's shaky history, her own show has an unexpected success, so much that the network will decide, after only one episode, to pick it up for a second season.

Those who produce the sitcom think the reality show's crew is in their way. The narrative programs of such characters as Jimmy Burrows, Tom Peterman and, more generally, the writers of *Room and Bored* are professionally oriented, and, while Valerie *cannot but be* a helper (being herself part of the production), she often ends up becoming an opponent.

In light of what has already been said about Valerie, one can understand that such an oppositional role is completely involuntary. More precisely, it is the undesired result of voluntary actions: this role sits at the crossroads of the success of one narrative program (being in the spotlight, at least in the reality show) and the failure of another (being well considered and liked by everyone). Valerie's marginal role in the sitcom clashes openly with her attempts at emerging (and with her *believing* she has a more important role than she actually does), which tends to obstruct other people's work.

The sitcom's writers are among those whose work Valerie seems to obstruct most often, which results in more or less open conflicts. While at the beginning of the series Tom Peterman's interest toward Valerie is limited to her performance on stage, in time[4] he becomes more understanding, as if showing her he is on her side might better serve his goals.

Paulie G.'s case is partly different. Instead of complying with Valerie (or pretending to do so) and trying, as others do, to minimize the possible damage she does, he voluntarily becomes her opponent. His primary strategy includes hostility in gaze, gestures and a more general willingness to not communicate — which *should* naturally communicate to Valerie much more than what she would ever admit to understanding. A scene from the second episode is exemplary in this sense, wherein Paulie G. shows up at Valerie's door after she has asked to speak with the sitcom's writers:

> (*02. Hotel room. Personal video diary.*)
> (*Two knocks on the door.*)
> VALERIE: Yes. (*Stands up.*)
> PAULIE G. (*off-screen*): It's Paulie G.
> VALERIE: Oh. Great, alright. (*She opens the door. Paulie G., pouting his lips, hands Valerie a note.*) Hi. Oh, great, yeah, you got my note, yeah. Thanks so much for coming down. I left one for Tom, too.
> (*She waits for an answer that does not come. Paulie G. keeps staring at her, skeptical.*) But that's alright. Um, listen. I know you guys didn't wanna write a bit, or anything, but I'm really thinking the network is gonna expect me to say something. You know, now, I'm not a writer, but, uh, I thought I could say something like, uh, "I am thrilled — to come back — to the network." You know, that way I'm working in my reality show too.
> (*Paulie G. makes the gesture of shooting her in the head, accompanied by the imitation of the sound of a gunshot.*)
> VALERIE: OK, ehhh. Then that happened. Uh. Well, it's late. So. Should probably...
> (*Paulie G. grabs some liquor bottles from a tray and exits, letting the door close behind him.*)

Juna, main actress on *Room and Bored*, also adheres to this class of narrative programs, but with outcomes decidedly more euphoric for Valerie. The relationship between the two women had a rough start, after Juna missed a lunch appointment, about which Valerie has always refused any comments, in order not to publicize a hurried judgment about Juna. Nonetheless, Juna proves to be sincerely interested in Valerie (she was her fan when she was a little girl), and is thus always ready to assume a helper role. She does not seem annoyed by the presence of the reality show's cameras, and she even behaves as if they were part of the landscape and had no effect on her life. The preservation of reality involves, for Juna, not an antagonistic impulse, but a neutrality and lack of prejudice that, in the end, favor Valerie. For her part, though, Valerie still considers Juna to be fearful competition, due to her much younger age, her looks, a certain degree of success she has already gained. For these reasons, she decides it would be preferable to have her as an ally. In this case, her manipulation strategy seems to end up having real effects, with the establishment of an alliance between the two women.

Valerie's domestic environment provides further examples of reality-preservation programs. Mark seems to have a literal understanding of the term *reality show*, and behaves as if the cameras entering the home should guarantee the reality of the events they capture. He does not hesitate to talk to Valerie about domestic matters, react according to different situations and unmask his own thoughts. This obviously contrasts with Valerie's programs and what she deems broadcasting-appropriate reality. Mark is perhaps one of the few people — along with Juna, and possibly also Esperanza, the housekeeper — who face the reality show as if it were indeed a faithful, transparent and innocent recording and representation of reality.

The idea that anyone who enters the realm of the reality show must assume a role functional to it leads Valerie to behave as if this were necessarily true. She does not expect or force others — her husband before anyone else — to adapt to her needs, but simply assumes they want to and will do so. There are clearly times at which she needs to restate priorities (her own, hence everyone else's), but she attributes such out-of-phase incidents to a momentary lack of understanding. In the first episode, her husband calls to remind her of a water leak at home and to tell her she will have to take care of calling the plumbers. Valerie does not even consider the possibility of doing so and explains Mark's attitude as a result of his being unfamiliar with show business. Nonetheless, it's inevitable to catch a hint of resentment in her voice, when — after a phone call with her husband, during which she tried to appear calm — she says that being married to someone who is not in the business can be "a double-edged sword," and that "sometimes, you know, he just — he doesn't get it."

Interests in Conflict

To anticipate some themes that will be developed in the following chapters, I want to underscore that the point of view on the reality of the uttered enunciative device is anything but neutral, in *The Comeback* as well as in other shows. Moreover, the transparency of the primary enunciation in favor of the *en-abyme* enunciation is only presumed — not only because *it is known* that this is narrative fiction, but also because the main mechanism of meaning production consists of the counterposing and attribution of visibility to the various conflicts the text stages at the different levels.

This is really nothing new, considering that conflict sits at the foundation of narrativity itself. However, in *The Comeback*, the different voices at play, which is to say the different levels at which the whole enunciative machine is deployed, highlight conflicts that do not always lie on the same plane. Valerie's struggle does not reside only within the utterance of which she is subject; rather, she is involved chiefly in a conflict against characters that ultimately exist at different levels. Thus, Valerie's conflict is a purely semiotic one, in the sense that it directly attacks the semiotic structures of the text — in other words, of the world in which she exists.

This is, perhaps, the element that represents the show's strength, but also its possible Achilles' heel, not just because it requires from the audience a different kind of competence than that required to appreciate the usual fiction show, but rather because it establishes an unusual veridictive contract: fictional, for sure, for what concerns the utterance's core, but in other ways unexpectedly realistic. As will be seen in the final chapter, though, veridiction might not be the most adequate criterion by which to judge a television show, and reality might not be such an obvious concept as it might seem. Especially not on television.

5

Ugly Betty

Ugly Betty stands out as an anomaly in the corpus of shows I have analyzed because it assumes one of drama's typical traits, namely the duration of episodes, which normally last twice as long as those of comedy shows. Each episode of *Ugly Betty* is given a one-hour slot in the schedule, for an actual duration of about forty-two minutes, not counting commercial breaks.

The show was born as an adaptation of a Colombian telenovela, *Yo soy Betty, la fea,* whose one hundred sixty-five episodes aired between 1999 and 2001. NBC initially developed the idea for the adaptation in 2001, but only starting in 2004 did it actually see the light, thanks to the interest of ABC and the entry of Salma Hayek into the production. In May of 2006, a thirteen-episode season was announced, which ABC then extended for ten more episodes, thanks to the show's success. Consequently, the first season, which premiered in September 2006, is quite clearly partitioned into two half-seasons, as highlighted by the narrative crescendo, the revelations and subsequent cliffhanger at the end of "In or Out" (113), along with substitutions among the cast of characters.

Despite some basic discursive similarities with its Colombian model, soon outnumbered by the differences, I will show that *Ugly Betty* clearly states its distance not only from the discursive model of telenovela, but also from that of soap opera, its American counterpart. At the same time, it dilutes its own comic character using narrative and stylistic elements typical of drama, which may also justify the episodes' duration, unusual for a comedy show.

Besides its admitted derivation from a preexistent text, from which the show immediately distances itself at both the discursive and narrative levels, *Ugly Betty* is rich in strong intertextual links. Most evident, particularly in the initial episodes, is its link with the film *The Devil Wears Prada*,[1] of which the show assumes thematic and figurative elements (foremost those relating to the fashion world), situations, even fragments of dialog, until the reference becomes explicit in the second episode, during an exchange between Betty and her nephew, Justin, when he notices she has brought home the mockup for the next issue of *Mode*:

> (*102, 15:00. Living room of the Suarez house.*)
> JUSTIN (*getting up to grab the Book*): Oh my God! You have — the Book?
> BETTY: Wait, Justin, how do you even know what the Book is?
> JUSTIN: I saw *Prada* like seven times.

The Characters

The protagonist is twenty-three-year-old Betty Suarez (America Ferrera), a young woman of Mexican origins living in Queens, when she is suddenly flung into the illusory world of *Mode*, a fashion magazine where she is hired — for all the wrong reasons — as personal assistant to Daniel Meade (Eric Mabius), the new editor-in-chief, a notorious womanizer and the publisher's son. No one, not even Betty herself, believes she is in the right place. In fact, as she soon learns, Daniel's father has hired her in order to prevent his son from being tempted to sleep with his assistant. Anything but a supermodel, with her huge smile Betty shows her colored braces, while her out-of-style wardrobe provokes disgusted reactions from almost all of her new coworkers. Most prominent among them is creative director Wilhelmina Slater (Vanessa Williams), who has intended to gain control of the magazine since Fey Sommers, longtime editor-in-chief, died in a fiery car crash. Wilhelmina is strong and dangerous, rarely shows any signs of human compassion (barely even toward her daughter, Nico) and often allows her means to cross the boundaries of legality — although she clarifies that she will stop short of murder.

Despite the obstacles the big city raises along her way, Betty succeeds not only in gaining her boss's trust and friendship, but also in solving, day in and day out, all the unlikely situations in which she finds herself involved.

It is difficult to establish a precise, permanent hierarchy of primary and secondary characters, beyond the small pool of protagonists. This is

5. Ugly Betty

mostly due to a generally high number of supporting characters and the broad range of narrative possibilities this situation fosters. While other comedy series often feature recurring characters who have no more than a supporting role (often temporary and in many cases occurring only once), and whose narrative relevance does not exceed the limits of a single episode (often just in the form of sketches), all of the secondary characters in *Ugly Betty* are subject to being used as sources of narrative developments. The common element is, naturally, the possibility for Betty to intervene as a catalyst to their stories. Moreover, the show exhibits a tendency toward re-thematization and re-actorialization, that is, the introduction or elimination of regular characters through sudden minor catastrophes (in the classic sense, not necessarily negative, but passionally charged), which reshape and re-segment the whole show. One of the most prominent examples is the chain of events that leads to the division of season one into two distinct sub-seasons.

Betty lives with her father, Ignacio (Tony Plana); her sister, Hilda (Ana Ortiz); and Hilda's son, Justin (Mark Indelicato). Ignacio is a widower, and in season one it is revealed that he entered the United States illegally thirty years prior, after killing the rich and abusive husband of the woman he loved (who later became Hilda and Betty's mother). At the start of the series, Hilda is thirty years old, and the opposite of Betty in everyone's eyes: thinner and tall, very aware of her looks, flirtatious; she is not stupid, but her ambitions are more modest than Betty's. She became pregnant when she was eighteen, on the night of her prom, but her boyfriend fled, forcing her to raise Justin alone — although not without her family's help. Justin is more into the fashion world than his aunt Betty. He grabs any chance he can get to spend time at *Mode,* and hopes to be able to work there when he grows up. However, by the end of season three his interests seem to have shifted, and he is crushed when his application for a highly selective performing-arts high school is rejected.

One of the characters from Queens, who has a key role in season one, is Santos (Kevin Alejandro), Justin's father, whom Hilda asks for financial help. At first just an occasional guest at the Suarez house — despite Ignacio and Betty's disapproval, and his initial disapproval of the way Hilda has raised Justin — Santos later becomes part of the family and asks Hilda to marry him. He is killed in a robbery in the season-one finale, leaving Hilda and Justin heartbroken, but opening up once again both characters' narrative potential.

At *Mode,* Wilhelmina Slater's assistant is Marc St. James (Michael Urie), a perfect product of the environment: gay, completely devoted to Wilhelmina, whose extreme coldness and inevitable cruelty he does recognize, though not without regret. He is always conspiring with Amanda Tanen (Becki Newton), beautiful receptionist at *Mode,* and less of a ditz than she needs to pretend; at first, Amanda is just one of Daniel's many lovers, but she ends up breaking it off when she realizes she is hopelessly in love with him. In the season-one finale, Amanda discovers she is actually Fey Sommers's secret daughter, and she spends the following year trying to find her real father, albeit unsuccessfully.

Christina McKinney (Ashley Jensen) is *Mode*'s seamstress, who becomes Betty's best friend from the start. Christina is, in a way, a potential Betty. She is Scottish, thus an outsider by definition, and does not follow the unwritten rules of behavior at *Mode,* being, for example, consistently open about what she really thinks of her coworkers. The main difference between her and Betty is her passion for fashion, whose mechanisms she knows and respects very well, even when she finds them absurd.

Besides Daniel, the Meade family includes his father, Bradford (Alan Dale), and his mother, Claire (Judith Light). The former, cold and distant, is, in Daniel's eyes, still mourning the loss of his elder son, Alex, two years before the beginning of the story; Claire, an alcoholic, checks in and out of rehab continually. Bradford will be arrested for the murder of Fey Sommers, prime suspect until Claire clears him by confessing in his place.

Starting in the pilot episode, Wilhelmina often visits a mysterious woman dressed in soft bandages from head to toe, with whom she is plotting to ruin Bradford and conquer Meade Publications. While at first all clues point to this masked woman as being Fey Sommers, who might have somehow survived the accident, in "In or Out" (113) she sheds her bandages and Wilhelmina welcomes, in front of a mirror, a very beautiful blond woman, none other than Alex Meade turned into Alexis (Rebecca Romijn):

5. Ugly Betty

(*113*, 41:20.)
WILHELMINA: Looks like that skiing accident really paid off, Alex Meade.
ALEXIS: Alexis, darling. (*Smiles.*) It's Alexis now!

One of the most evident differences from the Colombian model is the lack of correlation between Betty's supposed ugliness and her love life. This has an obvious impact on the show's actorial configuration. When the series begins, Betty is dating Walter (Kevin Sussman), a neighborhood boy who works in an electronics store, who first leaves her for Gina Gambarro (Ava Gaudet), the local man-eater, then does everything he can to get her back. In "Brothers" (115), Walter accepts a job opportunity and moves to Maryland, knowing very well that his relationship with Betty cannot go on.

Henry Grubstick (Christopher Gorham), who works in the accounting department at Meade Publications, soon develops a sort of camaraderie and friendship with Betty. The friendship, if not the love interest, is complicated at first by Walter's presence, then by the arrival of Charlie (Jayma Mays), Henry's ex-girlfriend, less kind than her looks might suggest, who intends to win Henry back with any means. Despite its failure, for external reasons, Betty's relationship with Henry is the one that affects all the following ones; it is the reason why she cannot reciprocate the love of Giovanni "Gio" Rossi (Freddy Rodríguez) and why Matt Hartley (Daniel Eric Gold) breaks up with her at the end of season three, unleashing a series of events that fuel season four.

Interestingly, the relationship between Betty and Matt is probably the closest to the Colombian Betty's ultimate outcome — that of marrying her rich boss — but in *Ugly Betty* their getting together is by no means the end of the show, an indication of Betty's goals in life or even a willingness on her part to change who she is. Throughout all these relationships, Betty's physical features never change dramatically. Her main thematic investment — what makes Betty herself, and in a way what makes her "ugly" — remains the true constant of her character. The first episode of season four does feature a new, classier hairstyle, and anticipates, via an artsy dream sequence, her braces coming off in a future episode, but this last may be more due to a need for a certain degree of verisimilitude (who wears braces for more than three years in a row?) than to modify the character's core.

The theme of love and romance is, unsurprisingly, one of the main reasons for the appearance and disappearance of characters in the show. Betty is not the only character with love interests. There is also Hilda, who dates Tony Diaz (Eddie Cibrian), Justin's gym coach, then Queens city councilman Archie Rodriguez (Ralph Macchio); Daniel, who finally falls in love with and marries Molly (Sarah Lafleur), only to lose her to cancer in the season-three finale; and Marc, who dates Cliff St. Paul (David Blue), a fashion photographer who is his exact opposite.

Ignacio and Wilhelmina are the two characters least likely to be involved in a love relationship, albeit for very different reasons: Ignacio, as a widower, has always remained devoted to his late wife; Wilhelmina is portrayed as simply incapable of those kinds of feelings, considering her career her only priority. Nonetheless, both of them find love in season three, Ignacio with his nurse, Elena (Lauren Vélez), for which his family gives him some initial grief; Wilhelmina with Connor Owens (Grant Bowler), chief financial officer at Meade, who steals everything from the company and runs away, breaking her heart. (In Connor's defense, he did ask Wilhelmina to run away with him, but that would have meant leaving all her dreams behind, erasing twenty years of work and conspiracy.)

Time and Space of the Series

As per tradition in American television narrative, the utterative times of the episodes follow the general time span of the season's airing — which makes sense in a case such as this, a typical example of open series, whose episodes are chained together and reflect a temporal progression throughout the whole series. Such progression becomes even more relevant, since *Ugly Betty* stages the creation of another serial product, a magazine, whose enunciation is necessarily based not only on an iterative aspect (hence the permanence of certain traits), but also on an adherence to the temporality required by the magazine's production, which varies from season to season (hence implying variability in other traits).

5. Ugly Betty

The time span of each episode does not exceed a small number of days, with temporal ellipses never longer than a few hours. The weekly scheduling of the show leaves room for far wider ellipses between one episode and the next, often even when a cliffhanger at the end of one episode would suggest a possible resolution at the beginning of the next.

While flashbacks are very rare, more frequent is the use of parallel sequences, with scenes taking place at similar times, yet in different locations. Such alternations mark deep narrative oppositions, as I will explain shortly.

There are very few notable exceptions to the linearity of the temporal progression. "Swag" (111) has a very peculiar history, since it was produced as the fourth episode of the season, but the next episode, "Fey's Sleigh Ride," aired in its place. To compensate for the break in linearity and continuity, the episode was re-produced with some scene cuts and the addition of an introductory sequence, along with some inserts and an ending that turned it into Betty's account to Christina of past events. This strategy filled in the gaps that the absence of "Swag" might have left in the overall sequence of episodes, while still forcing a different perspective on the story, mainly centered on Betty, thus limited to her knowledge of the facts.[2]

While the flashback in "Swag" presents itself as a kind of uttered enunciation, by which Betty's voice accompanies another utterance, placed in the past in relation to the primary utterance (in a manner different from that of *Scrubs,* where the narrator's voice is placed in a time and space whose relationships with the filmic utterance are left largely undefined), the temporal disengagement in "Sofia's Choice" (112) is announced in the paratext, via the full-screen sign, "24 hours earlier." Such disengagement remains confined to the realm of enunciation, which is thus able to give a reasonable explanation of the episode's initial sequence, otherwise incomprehensible. The episodes "Odor in the Court" (212) and "Crimes of Fashion" (303) feature a mechanism similar to that used in "Sofia's Choice," with a three-day and six-hour flashback, respectively.

Along with the represented spaces, which I will introduce shortly, the space of representation plays a central role in *Ugly Betty*. Although the text is not based on mechanisms of *mise en abyme,* as happens in *The*

Office and *The Comeback*, the idea of the text's televisual nature is always reinforced through transitions and elements of image composition that are not unusual, but normally discredited by "serious" television. Different sequences are often separated by curtains, rotations and other visual effects that may almost seem amateurish, while parallel sequences (especially when interlinked, such as when they feature phone calls) are grouped by subdividing the screen space into two or more subframes, juxtaposed or bordered in black. Such screen sharing is very similar to that used in *24* (Fox: 2001–present), with the difference that in *24* it is justified by a strict relationship between uttered time and enunciative time, which often makes it necessary to show events that happen simultaneously. Moreover, the enunciative device of *24* shows itself (in a clear example of uttered enunciation), beginning with the elements of paratext (such as the clock showing the progression of seconds), as connoted in a very technological sense. This is not necessarily true in *Ugly Betty*, where the resulting effect is rather that of a certain naïveté, similar to that attributed to Betty's character.

The represented spaces are organized in a strict hierarchy that conditions the characters' behaviors and their relationships with one another. This hierarchy manifests itself first of all as a geographic opposition between Manhattan and Queens, divided by a river yet linked by bridges and tunnels. To Betty, the two boroughs are the respective sites of her public and private worlds, which do not necessarily correspond, as will be shown, to a hostile versus a friendly environment. The space hierarchy is part of a Manhattan-centered view of the world, in which Manhattan dictates the rules, while Queens *cannot but accept* them. The work environment is further hierarchically organized, starting with the topography of the building, whose floors correspond to the relative prestige of their occupants: publisher Bradford Meade's office sits in the penthouse, and, following, the magazines' offices in descending order of importance, with *Mode* on the twenty-eighth floor, the highest.

Whereas in Queens all spaces are externally simple and squared (fenced houses, gates, grid-based streets) and internally redundant (multicolored, rich in information on those who inhabit them), the offices of *Mode* are a maze of elliptically sectioned hallways, round desks, neutral colors, glass walls — providing very few essential details. Wilhelmina seems to be part of the space that contains her, from her impeccably architected hairstyles to her almost always white clothes, a perfect contrast to Betty in skin tone and, above all, body features and clothing style.

Despite the apparent hostility of *Mode*'s environment, Betty is still able to find herself a few safe zones. If not in Daniel's office, where even he does not always feel comfortable, particularly at the beginning, at least in what is called *the Closet,* where Christina works as a seamstress. As is revealed at the end of season one, the Closet used to be a safe spot also for Fey Sommers, whose secret room (also known as Fey's love dungeon) is accessible, with a very classic expedient, through a door hidden behind a movable set of shelves.

The spatial organization mirrors the hierarchy of characters, who acquire privileges not only from their "natural" spaces, but also from what could be called their behavioral competences. Those who belong to a certain space only rarely venture into some extraneous place, and if they do so it is only thanks to some ferrying system that guarantees isolation and safety. Daniel will only go to Queens riding a town car, as Wilhelmina and Marc try to do in "Lose the Boss" (109), only to remain stranded along the way, unable to interact with the environment and the local population. Betty is the only exception to this rule. Despite her appearance and her background, she is often able to tear down the hierarchies that would otherwise tend to limit her actions.

Borrowing Themes

Ugly Betty discursivizes themes typical of longer seriality, drawing particularly from South American telenovela and its closest U.S. counterpart, soap opera. From telenovela, it reprises the theme of the struggle of a single subject (usually a positive heroine) against a hostile environment; from soap opera, it borrows themes of the family saga, sexual promiscuity and an inconsistency of values.

The soap opera-related themes are figurativized in the rich and snotty world of fashion, similar to *The Bold and the Beautiful,* but with a higher level of refinement, since in *Ugly Betty,* fashion is not crafted but conceptualized — a difference that moves it from a purely material level to that of the media, where fashion is only what passes the magazine's aesthetic judgment. From the point of view of *Mode*, designers are nobodies, and their creations have no value until they receive a positive sanction. What makes fashion, and thus the economic and social value of fashion objects and people, is mainly the aesthetic evaluation of people who know fashion (by experience) and who, more generally, can recognize it in the world (by natural gift). Such value seems to be attributed largely arbitrarily — not only because in many cases it bears no relationship with an object's material value, but even more so because it often depends on the willingness and power of a single person, who decides an article's value using inscrutable personal criteria.

> (*101, 22:50. The Closet.*)
> (*Betty is looking at a mannequin, when Christina enters.*)
> CHRISTINA: Feel the fabric on that thing.
> BETTY: It's kind of rough.
> CHRISTINA (*touching the dress*): That's because it's burlap. Basically you're talking seven thousand dollars, for a designer potato sack!
> BETTY: I can't believe people actually buy this stuff.
> CHRISTINA: I can't believe they wear it! And usually just once before they chuck it to make room for next season! But — that's fashion, and I've got to say — I lllove it!

In "In or Out" (113), Christina is hoping to be selected as one of the new designers to watch during Fashion Week. Wilhelmina, who is in charge of making the choice, finds her dressing up a mannequin with one of her latest designs, and surprises her by saying that it is "somewhat interesting" — as opposed to the designs Christina had presented the previous year, which Wilhelmina branded as "hippy hideous." But Wilhelmina, who is planning to use Christina as a pawn in her new scheme against the Meades, has more advice for her:

> (*113, 28:15. The Closet.*)
> WILHELMINA: It's not just about the designs. Christina, it's about the design-*er*.
> CHRISTINA: What d'you mean?
> WILHELMINA: Don't be afraid of office politics.
> (*Cut to Christina, who smiles bitterly, as if she had already understood.*)
> WILHELMINA (*off-screen*): Do favors for the right people. (*On-screen*) You might just get rewarded at the end. Unfortunately, that is the cruel reality in this business.

5. Ugly Betty

Even family relations carry almost completely arbitrary values, starting with the one element that seems to have kept the Meade family together for the two years prior to the story, that is the grief for the loss of Alex in a skiing accident. Despite being closed and reserved, Bradford gives a career opportunity to Daniel, who always felt neglected compared to Alex. It will also be revealed that Claire has eased (or fed) her grief with alcohol. Daniel, as if to meet the family's negative expectations, has spent years squandering his trust fund and going out with a new girl every night.

It can be argued that what instigates the Meade family's soap opera is first a death, then a resurrection. An uncertain, then certain death is that of Fey Sommers, whose place as editor-in-chief at *Mode* is taken by Daniel, and whose twenty-year-long relationship with Bradford is also revealed (a relationship no one knew about except Claire, as a testimony of a certain intrinsic anomaly in family relations). The uncertainty of Fey's death comes from the presence of the masked woman, who starts harassing Daniel on the phone and injects him with doubts about his father. The certainty of her death is then attained when the masked woman loses her bandages and is revealed to be Alexis Meade, that is, Alex resurrected in a feminine body — a perfect body, nonetheless, which (despite the jokes a few characters might make) bears no remaining trace of its masculine origin.

The arbitrariness in family relations is also apparent in the relatively easy way in which Wilhelmina Slater is able to convince Bradford to divorce Claire and marry her at the end of season one. Her interest, far from being based on love, is only for the Meade name, the sole key to controlling *Mode* and getting rid of Daniel once and for all — not because she has anything against him per se, at least not at first, but because he holds the position to which Wilhelmina has aspired for twenty years, and more so since Fey's death. After her presumed friendship with Alexis fails, marrying Bradford becomes the only key to her success.

The Suarez family's Mexican origins provide a fertile ground to (but are not necessarily a guarantee of) the development of telenovela-derived themes. It is actually quite clear that Betty's life bends toward a telenovela when the mechanisms of cultural and social clash with Manhattan are activated. From what can be understood about their life before

Betty entered *Mode*, the Suarez family has at least some of the typical traits of American drama in its story, including a mother who died a few years before; Ignacio, who has remained faithful to his first love and kept taking care of his family; Hilda, who became pregnant the night of her prom and was immediately dumped by the guilty boyfriend (and who was, at the beginning of the story, a salesperson of questionable beauty products, a job she needed to support her son); and the relationship between Betty and Walter.

The equilibrium becomes unstable when Betty finds a job at *Mode*, and the telenovela traits, previously present only in a virtualized state, begin emerging and becoming realized. An element that seemed harmless at first (the HMO denying Ignacio his heart medication) gives way to a series of events and revelations that will shake Betty and her family to their foundations. These events include Ignacio being revealed an illegal immigrant, the understanding of the reasons that forced him to flee Mexico, the legal problems that ensue and his return to Mexico to obtain a visa; these problems force Hilda to ask Santos for money, which leads to a love affair between them, then to a marriage proposal. All of this drama is punctuated by Betty's difficulties with Walter.

Two Anomalies

While the Suarez family's social background is hostile, and Betty is always called on to solve conflicts and difficult situations, only to provoke (unintentionally) further difficulties, the greater form of hostility results, at least at first glance, from the Manhattan environment in which she finds herself newly involved. Betty violates what seems to be an unwritten rule, though the people of Queens often pronounce it in different forms: that is, she who was born in Queens should remain in Queens. This violation differentiates Betty from the typical telenovela heroine, who swims in generally familiar waters, that is, whose social and economic oppositions arise within her natural context. Betty's two worlds, Queens and Manhattan, stand on rules and values that seemingly have nothing in common, and between which Betty becomes the only intermediary. This leads me to highlight a couple of anomalies.

The first is that *Ugly Betty* connects two worlds that usually stand

5. Ugly Betty

well apart. This is not simply a matter of uttered worlds (that is, banally, Manhattan and Queens, which are likely to engage in some form of contact in the empiric world), but of enunciative worlds — that is to say, counterposed, yet analogous textual régimes. The encounter between the two uttered worlds may be solved, so to speak, as a clash of forces and intentions: on the one hand, Manhattan's public world, which has no interest in interacting with anything out of its boundaries, and is thus modalized in a collective *lack of willingness*; on the other, the private world of Queens, which acknowledges its own limitations (active and passive, due to both the diffusion of prejudices and a sort of provincial pride), and thus *knows it cannot* interact.

However, just as the Queensboro Bridge spans Manhattan and Queens in empiric reality, Betty acts as a textual bridge between these locations within the main utterance. Her actions violate all the limitations normally imposed on or accepted by the people of Queens — hence she does not give up, and not only *wants* to interact but *knows she can*. Naturally enough, all this does not happen without resistances on the part of *Mode*'s establishment, a resistance to which all lexicalizations of the theme of ugliness pertain, from the show's title to the different nicknames Betty's coworkers give her, including *grandma*, which is in itself paradoxical, considering she is the youngest worker in the office.

Betty is not ugly when she is in Queens. Better yet, maybe she does not follow the gaudy and often tacky style of local women — another very common stereotype — but her colorful and often slightly antiquated clothing style seems very much in tune with the loud, diverse vivacity of her neighborhood. Her ugliness is relative to Manhattan's standards, and even more so to *Mode*'s. In *Mode*'s terms, ugliness manifests a judgment on Betty's nonconformity rather than a strictly aesthetic evaluation.

Interestingly, descriptions of Betty conveyed by the Italian media (among other sources) when the show was first aired in the country seem to reflect the perspective of *Mode*'s people. These description are misleading in their characterization of Betty as a sort of absolute ugliness, an untidy woman with disheveled hair and thick glasses. At a closer analysis, the only actual elements of distinction are the out-of-style clothes and braces with colored elastic bands — which are more commonly seen in the empiric world than what both *Ugly Betty* and the Italian critics might lead one to believe. It is as if Betty's ugliness were the object of an optical distortion, which amplifies even the most harmless details. Betty's glasses are actually neither thick nor huge, and although her hair is definitely bushy (as are her eyebrows), manifesting a quite anonymous style, it is not really disheveled. In descriptions such as those purveyed by the Italian media, Betty comes off as unaware of and indifferent to her own aesthetics, while, on the contrary, her style is very precise and accurate, no matter how it clashes with the standards of the time and the environment in which she finds herself.

Betty is not the only outsider working at *Mode*. Christina and, in seasons one and two, Henry are the other most evident cases. Christina soon becomes Betty's best friend, while Henry establishes with her a kind of love relationship, which is never fully realized due to Walter's interferences at first, then to the arrival and subsequent pregnancy of Charlie, Henry's ex-girlfriend. Besides Betty's family, Christina and Henry are the only two characters whose geographic origins are thematized as meaningful in regard to their presence at *Mode*: Christina is Scottish, which is very obvious by her accent, whereas Henry grew up in Tucson, Arizona, represented as almost antipodal to New York's climate and cultural environment.

Other characters have more or less vague geographic origins (Marc, for example, has family in Schenectady, close enough to New York City, but he never goes there), which are less relevant to their lives and thus bear a sort of negative pertinence. These characters treat Betty differently than do Christina and Henry. Such characters assume, usually intentionally, the role of opponent, and are perfectly integrated into *Mode*'s environment, so much so that they actually prefer the notion of their geographic origins being lost. The attitude of assuming Manhattan as an adoptive hometown, thus erasing the original sin of having been born anywhere else, might remind one of *Sex and the City*, which makes an explicit value distinction between Manhattan and everything else — not only the other four boroughs of New York City, but also the rest of the country and, often enough, the rest of the world (only Paris can compete with Manhattan, but it is far away and full of French people).

Not only do Christina and Henry assume the roles of Betty's helpers

5. Ugly Betty

(with notable exceptions), but they are also able to maintain a certain degree of extraneousness from *Mode*'s environment. Christina adores the fashion world and shows that in her work as a seamstress, but she prefers to keep a distance from the often twisted mechanisms through which it functions: her geographic identity, maintained in the way she speaks, accompanies the bluntness in her behavior. Such bluntness and the firm decision to remain herself draw her to Betty from the pilot episode, along with a few other out-of-place women — whom Marc calls "A Bizarro version of *Sex and the City*."³

Henry, on the other hand, is neither perfectly integrated nor completely extraneous to *Mode,* in the sense that his work as an accountant for Meade Publications makes him a functional (albeit not irreplaceable) element, but his not working at *Mode* renders him harmless in the eyes of the integrated. These characters perceive him to be far less of a threat than Betty, who, on the contrary, is a system anomaly that many try to eliminate. Henry gets close to Betty almost right away, and their affinity is aesthetic, cognitive and emotional, from their glasses and clothes, out-of-style yet vividly colored, to certain cultural predilections and a passion for trivia (in Henry's words, "It's just something I know").

Despite being outsiders, Christina and Henry escape the polarization between Manhattan and Queens, which remains strictly linked to a contrapuntal logic of city versus suburbs, although the two boroughs have equal administrative status within New York City. Betty uses these characters' experience to dampen the impact of city life, and as a refuge (sometimes physical, in the case of the Closet, where Christina works) in moments when the world of *Mode* seems to make no sense at all.

The second anomaly in *Ugly Betty* is the introduction of telenovela as a theme in the utterance, and as a parameter distinguishing different planes of reality. The television set in the Suarez home is often on, and usually tuned to a (fictional) Mexican telenovela, *Vidas de fuego*. The story behind this show is not really known, but its themes and figures are recognizable as typical of the genre: housemaids and rich ladies, a Catholicism that is used as a façade to disorderly lives, with pregnant nuns (but are they really pregnant, or even actual nuns?) and murderous priests, as well as guns, chandeliers, soccer balls, and so forth. Ignacio watches this telenovela with the mix of interest and detachment with which many men might follow the genre in empiric reality. His reactions, often nonverbal, comprised of raised brows and gestures of intolerance, confirm his distance from a genre that does not seem to represent any reality with which he might be familiar. Justin, too, in the first episode, watching a scene from *Vidas de fuego*, says, "I hate telenovelas. I wanna watch Fashion TV."[4]

It could be argued that in the world of telenovelas telenovela does not exist. The inclusion within a certain text of a metasemiotic, metatextual and partly self-referential reference to a text of the same genre creates a sense of awareness that could harm the main text's reality effect. The same could be said about American soap opera, in which television is, at most, a means to obtaining news, and not really to enjoy fictional stories — to the extent that television sets rarely appear in rooms' décor. On the contrary, the inclusion of television and telenovela as thematic elements and the inclusion of television sets as one of the show's main figurative elements in *Ugly Betty* lead to a sort of hyperrealism that clashes with the story's thematic and narrative foundation.

It is, however, a selective hyperrealism, in that the presence and the use of television sets does reflect empiric-world behaviors, but such use is limited only to two genres, or two types of texts: telenovela (only and always the same show) and Fashion Buzz (only and always the fashion newscast, and only when it reports news about *Mode* and the Meade family). What occurs is a phenomenon that one would not find in the original genres, that is the *en-abyme* replication of elements from the primary utterance: on the one hand, in the sense of a genre reference to telenovela, on the other, as a sort of re-appropriation of parts of *Ugly Betty*'s main story by the media. This double face of uttered television mirrors the text's double nature and contradictions — always intentional — at different levels.

The use of Fashion Buzz often extends beyond a simple hyperthematization of the fashion world seen through the eyes of television. Through the face and voice of Suzuki St. Pierre (Alec Mapa), it often performs a very clear metatextual function, recapitulating previous episodes when an explicit paratextual introduction (as the typical "Previously on *Ugly Betty*..." section at the beginning of an episode) is missing.

The simultaneous presence of thematic elements stemming from different textual genres — although akin to one another in terms of social function and enunciative modalities — might reveal a sort of schizophrenia on the part of the enunciative device, which would be dealing with continuous changes in register. *Ugly Betty* solves this possible problem by avoiding it, that is by enacting enunciative practices that are unusual in the genres of reference, and which affect the text's manifestation level and, consequently, its discursive syntax — particularly for what concerns space and time organization and aspectualization.

The relationship between utterative and enunciative times is exemplary: whereas in telenovela (and even more so in soap opera) time is dilated to the point of making it difficult to have a precise understanding of its passage, and each scene can be fractured into a high number of alternating sequences supported by an extreme discursive redundancy, in *Ugly Betty* the opposite is true. The enunciative practices are borrowed directly from contemporary drama, while time is punctuated by ellipses and superpositions that make the utterance highly compact and dense. A single episode of *Ugly Betty* contains enough narrative material to feed weeks of any soap opera's daily episodes.

Betty in the Middle

Considering that the story's perspective is largely based on Betty — which is not surprising, as she gives the show its title, although the point of view inscribed in the title is most definitely that of her opponents — it would make sense to assume the polemic structure were also centered on her. Thus, the subjects of narrative programs clashing with Betty's would become, by definition, anti-subjects. Although Wilhelmina Slater can often be sympathized with, especially in moments of unexpected vulnerability, her discourses almost always carry negative connotations in regard to Betty. Wilhelmina, as well as the world she represents and controls, is the source of the possible obstacles Betty has to face in her job.

Of course, this is the basis for the polemic structure as uttered by the main enunciative device, not what can be derived from each character's behavior and discourses. Betty's role as subject is defined and modalized not only by her intrinsic qualities, but also by other characters' narrative behaviors. One of Wilhelmina's mistakes, so to speak, is to underestimate Betty's abilities from the start, thus deeming her as lacking power. As I will better consider in the next section, this flaw that various characters exhibit when evaluating Betty stems from a series of prejudices that, in a way, blind her opponents, so much so that they keep underestimating her even when it becomes clear — and it does within very few episodes — that her abilities are far broader than expected.

Perhaps, the responsibility of this error is largely due to Wilhelmina's failure to understand the nature of power. To her, power is an acquired state of being, almost permanent and unquestionable. It is first and foremost a political attribute. She does not acknowledge Betty's know-how as a possible source of power — in itself less a political quality and more strictly understandable as a narrative modality. Paradoxically, the more Betty is modalized as a subject of power (being able to achieve her narrative programs), the more Wilhelmina loses her own narrative power, even as she maintains it politically. Betty's know-how also achieves realization when she is able to correctly measure her visibility in the eye of her opponents. Upon closer inspection, however, one might question whether this trait of hers is actually know-how or, rather, a *not being able not to be*. It might be inevitable for Betty to be repeatedly underestimated and considered an easily overcome obstacle, and perhaps she eventually learns to use this quality (or inevitable fate) as a weapon to her advantage — or at least as a defense mechanism.

A recurring element in *Ugly Betty* is different subjects' need to assume as temporary helpers characters that normally function toward them as opponents or even anti-subjects. These "forced" helpers are thus modalized by a *not wanting* associated with a *not being able not to*, which determines the necessity of their behavior.

The characters most often affected by this sort of inevitability are Amanda and Marc, who repeatedly find themselves involved in situations that require Betty's personal and social competence. Although far less frequently, even Wilhelmina tries to convert Betty into a helper, in "Trust, Lust and Must" (106) and "Filing for the Enemy" (302). In 106,

5. Ugly Betty

Betty needs money to pay a lawyer who will assist Ignacio in his immigration case, and Wilhelmina offers her a check. Accepting the offer poses a serious moral dilemma: on the one hand, it would solve all of Betty's problems, but on the other it would imply the possibility for her to betray Daniel's trust at any given time. In the end, Betty preserves her integrity and returns the check, while Wilhelmina, who is also having family trouble and is therefore almost transparent in her emotions for once, says she understands Betty's reasons. In 302, Wilhelmina is in charge of *Mode* as editor-in-chief, after Alexis has transferred Daniel to *Player,* a magazine she deems more in tune with his personality. Wilhelmina offers Betty an assistant position because she thinks having Betty on her side will help her get rid of Daniel once and for all. Marc, annoyed at the idea that Betty may be getting ahead of him in currying favor with Wilhelmina, provides Betty with vital information that will ultimately lead to Daniel being restored as *Mode*'s editor-in-chief and Wilhelmina being demoted to her former position as creative director.

The most striking case of modal, as well as thematic, ambiguity is that of Alexis Meade, whose affiliation changes quickly in the course of just a few episodes, and keeps shifting until the character leaves the show in season three. From her loyalty to Wilhelmina — largely sincere — she attempts to move closer to Daniel, until she establishes herself as an individual subject. All this happens against the backdrop of an unchanging main narrative program, through which she wants to take revenge on Bradford and gain control of the publishing empire. Such modal shifts are partly due to her progressive acquisition of knowledge: when Alexis was nothing more than an unnamed masked woman, the only information she received concerning her family came from the news and Wilhelmina — definitely not unbiased sources. After revealing her new identity, Alexis can finally learn her family's feelings toward her, while leaving unchanged the mutual incomprehension — hatred, even — between her and her father. The exchange of knowledge is mutual, of course, as the rest of the family — at least those who *want to* become closer to Alexis (Claire at first, and then, more cautiously, Daniel) — acquires a progressive knowledge in her regard. However, every shift in knowledge corresponds to new maskings and new shifts in character alliances. Because at *Mode* nothing is as it appears.

Looking It to Be It

In the world of *Mode,* the imperative is "look it to be it." Seeming and being are not, consequently, simple veridictive components whose conjunction leads to a condition of *truth.* They constitute, rather, a logic and a normative passage, a requirement imposed by the social environment that acts as a sender not only to Betty, but to everyone else. "You gotta look it to be it," Hilda tells Betty, not without a reason, in "Queens for a Day" (103).

But since Betty cannot and does not want to appear as something she is not (and when she tries to do so, she fails), appearance's reach broadens from a purely aesthetic, visual level — which might seem predominant in the fashion world — to a more cognitive and pragmatic one that includes her work competences, acquired and acquirable. Betty openly violates the rule, which does not prevent her from being successful from the first episode, thus winning the trust and appreciation of her superiors — Daniel above all, but also Bradford and Claire Meade.

Betty's opponents rarely confess to feeling anything close to appreciation for her, yet they cannot but admit that she is both able and honest. Even Wilhelmina shows some degree of appreciation toward Betty, which she can't fully realize, but tries to express by stating how, no matter how different they seem to be, the two of them share some core qualities: "You are young, Betty, but you're a career girl just like me. You'll see," she tells Betty in "Things Fall Apart" (316).

While everyone says, with more or less sincere regret, that "looking it to be it" is the rule at *Mode,* Betty's opponents not only use this as their motto but also as a means to justify their behavior. Even when they cannot do without Betty and end up positively sanctioning her actions, often by saying things along the lines of, "This doesn't mean that I like you," with a dysphoric moralization that seems to contrast with the positive sanction.

The seemingly negative moralization becomes a way to save face, in order to stick to the general rule: by stating that they do not like Betty, that is what it *seems,* and consequently what it *is.* In the end, the more strongly Betty is despised for how she looks, and even more so for the fact that she does not look like she *should,* the more sincerely she is

5. Ugly Betty

appreciated for what she is — or, at least, the more sincerely her behavior is positively sanctioned.

Wilhelmina is sincere when Betty returns the check in "Trust, Lust and Must": Betty says she cannot accept it and Wilhelmina understands, and comments, "Of course you can't," with resignation and with no hint of irony in her tone.

Amanda is sincere in "In or Out" (113) when she returns the position of Daniel's only assistant to Betty, as she realizes that both want what is best for him. Amanda, despite being an opponent, shows the ambiguity of her character every time Daniel is involved, to such an extent that she is never able to damage him when she tries to do so on purpose. Amanda is, besides Daniel in the pilot episode, the character who actually makes the widest shift in attitude toward Betty. This shift begins in season three, when Betty helps her get back on her feet after she is evicted, and culminates at the point of their becoming roommates. Despite Amanda's flaws and frequent lack of consideration for the rest of the world, the two become friends — which, once again, does not mean that Amanda will not be forced to act like a *Mode* girl, at times.

In a similar way, Marc is sincere in "Don't ask, don't tell" (118), when he tells Betty, "You'll always be my little chimichanga," which in this case is intended as an affectionate nickname. He then corrects himself by saying, "This doesn't mean that I like you." All this topped by mutual smiles, while Betty accepts, yet again, Marc's self-distancing as an inevitable adhesion to rules no one can change. Betty and Marc are able to work together productively on several occasions — even at the start of season four, after Betty gets promoted to junior editor, despite Marc's hatred and disappointment.

The fact that the reactions to Betty's behavior follow such a double standard — the positive sanctions of what she *is* versus the dysphoric moralizations of what she *looks like*— does not imply a general tension toward a reversion of the rule. On the contrary, this opposition stands to confirm that the *Mode* rule is unchangeable, which reveals that Betty's lack — her *not looking the way she should*—will never be completely reversed. This lack is a condition necessary to the story's serial development. Betty, above everyone else, feels no need or desire to change, thus preferring to show what she *is* and *can become* instead of showing something she is not. Contrary to the main character in *Betty la fea*, Betty almost never addresses the issue of her looks, nor does she explicitly mention her supposed ugliness as being an obstacle to fulfillment in her life. "I'm fine with who I am. I know I'm not beautiful," says Betty in "Crush'd" (307). But *non-beauty* and *ugliness* are not the same, and the evolution of the character shows how the latter is, after all, an external construct that Betty never once applies to herself. This is proven by the failure of all her attempts to conform to, or at least become aesthetically closer to, this world of which she is, nevertheless, able to be an essential component.

"Looking it to be it" becomes the line that separates the rich from the poor, the powerful from the subordinates, the town cars from the subway, Manhattan from Queens. In Manhattan, the relationships between people are based exactly on this, often to the point of creating triangular character combinations. One example is the relationship between Bradford Meade and his children, based on the illusion (offered to the world, and first of all to Daniel) that Alex had been the favorite son, possessed of a special relationship with his father — later revealed as untrue when Alex returns as Alexis. Second, we find the triangle between Bradford, Claire and Fey Sommers, built on false appearances, or forced ostentation — until the extreme consequence of Fey's death. Even Betty often finds herself in triangular situations, particularly when they involve (more or less intentional) misunderstandings between Walter and Henry, Henry and Charlie, Daniel and Sofia Reyes, Henry and Gio, Matt and Henry, and, above all and repeatedly, between Daniel and Wilhelmina. Although the players and the values involved might change, trust is what is ultimately at stake in all these relationships.

The environment of Queens is marked by a strong disillusion and a certain idea that if one was born east of the East River, she will never be nor look like someone from Manhattan. The accents, the clothes, the common sense, the bluntness, the simplicity will always be distinctive elements — normally euphorically connoted by the people of Queens, including Walter above all, but also Hilda, and the wife of Walter's boss. The only one from Queens who would like to adhere to Manhattan's ideology is, naturally, Justin, who often shows himself more competent than Betty when it comes to fashion, but also more interested in the fashion world. Unfortunately, his young age does not allow him to have more than sporadic encounters, albeit highly satisfactory, with the people of *Mode*.

Family as Process

If the opposition and logic relation between seeming and being is central in the construction of the *work life* macro-theme, another thematic category, that of *family ties,* pervades the entire text. Its categoric nature can be seen in the fact that both the presence and the lack of family ties, and the strength thereof, are pertinent to the definition of characters, the interactions among them and the show's narrative development.

The three main characters at the beginning of the show — Betty, Daniel and Wilhelmina — have very distinct family situations. The Suarezes' nuclear family is held together by very strong emotional bonds between its members. The loss of Betty's mother Rosa a few years earlier has, if anything, increased the positive tension of such bonds. Everyone's qualities are encouraged, their limitations accepted, while fights are normally ascribed to everyday family management and resolved within the arc of one episode, rarely longer. They are a family of *being* and *seeming,* defined by the wholesomeness of the relationships that bind them.

In Manhattan, the Meades are a family in the legal sense of the term, since Bradford and Claire are bound by marriage, while Daniel's relationship with his father is chiefly work-related, from the point he is hired to replace Fey Sommers as editor-in-chief of *Mode*. The Meade family has also suffered the loss of one of its members, Alex, the older son. The remaining family members always remember Alex's positive qualities, both personal and professional, in opposition to Daniel's negative ones as an underachieving womanizer. The opposition in value between the two sons seems to be a product of Bradford's discourses: as the head of the family, his judgment has become a part of the very definition of the Meade family, so much so that even Daniel repeatedly seems to have internalized this judgment. Given their broken emotional bonds and opportunistic relationships, the Meades are a family of *seeming* and *not being*.

Wilhelmina Slater seems to have no family at all, which, along with other thematic elements that define her character, makes her almost a *figura mythologica,* whose essence is defined exclusively by the functional, timeless role it covers in the story. However, soon enough it is revealed she has a father, whom she usually calls *the Senator,* a daughter, Nico, and a sister, Renée. Wilhelmina's relationship with her father is reminiscent of the one between Daniel and Bradford, wherein the emotional bond is replaced by businesslike behaviors and values. Her fifteen-year-old daughter, Nico (played by Jowharah Jones, then by Yaya DaCosta in season four), whose father remains unknown, does everything she can to gain Wilhelmina's attention, often with the effect of pissing her off and accelerating the outcome she wants to avoid: being sent to boarding school. The relationship with Renée (Gabrielle Union), who has an obscure past involving arson and possibly murder, is purely based on lies and mutual threats, a situation that is exacerbated when Renée decides to date Daniel Meade. The consequences are, predictably, disastrous. The Slater family is based on the repression of any emotional tension, whether positive or negative, making it a family of *not being* as well as *not seeming*. The only reason for a member to intervene in favor of another is to prevent or minimize the fallout that any misbehavior creates.

Nonetheless, the thematic and axiologic construction of these core families is far from stereotypical, as the backstories of each are revealed, and more so once they develop at the narrative level. The stronger the bonds among members, the less likely it is for a family to reveal core-shaking information about its past; however, the stronger the bonds, the higher the surprise and the impact of unexpected information. Family is anything but a monolith; it is, rather, a process, even in the short run.

At first, the relevant process is what leads to the understanding of the current state of a family: the reasons why certain links are broken, the mechanisms by which others survive despite an apparent hopelessness, even the story behind the family's existence. As I have shown, the intensity of a family's bond and the overall legality of its members' current behaviors constitute no guarantee of a clean past: the Meades are, legally, a family unit, whose recent past includes deceit, murder and faking one's own death; even the hard-working, perfect father Ignacio Suarez confesses to being an illegal immigrant, and to having murdered his late wife's previous husband (who actually happens to be still alive, thus clearing Ignacio of all moral charges).

On the other hand, family that seems completely disconnected, like the Slaters, follows surprisingly similar patterns of behavior. Both Wilhelmina and Renée are revealed to be what could be called butterfly personas, real-life characters they have built out of Wanda and Rhonda (their actual birth names). In their efforts to establish themselves in opposition to their family's decisions and to nature's constraints, they are ultimately not too different from Alexis Meade.

At the end of season three, another family enters the scene of *Ugly Betty*—the Hartleys, very rich and very powerful. Betty is romantically involved with Matt Hartley, until a bad breakup, after which he becomes her boss at *Mode*. Betty has not fully experienced class differences until she meets Victoria (Christine Baranski), Matt's mother, and does not really know the meaning of compromise until she meets his father Cal (David Rasche)—who has Daniel dress up as an Easter bunny before deciding to do business with him. As Matt declares in "Rabbit Test" (320), "My mom is like an Easter egg [...]. Dad is more like ... Satan."

Perfectly in tune with *Ugly Betty*'s mission statement of generating several possible new story lines as soon as one is closed, the entrance of this new family makes everything more complicated. The Hartleys are a family of *not being,* given that Cal and Victoria are divorced and that Matt tries to live his own life as much as he can, but they ultimately *seem* more compact and single-minded than expected. A past affair between Cal and Claire Meade will trouble the waters even further.

Ultimately, family construction — and destruction — is a process that can never be taken for granted or assumed as complete, no matter how constant and wholesome a family may seem. Wholesomeness relates to consistency and trust, the trust that binds family members to one another, and the trustworthiness of the family in relationship to the world.

6

Genre Dynamics

My intention is neither to discuss and undermine the concept of *genre* in regard to televisual production,[1] nor to propose new classifications or taxonomies. Considering the current state of the matter and the textual analyses just conducted, I will accept the double nature of the concept of genre, which is at once textual and technical. Situation comedy itself, as I noted, takes its name from properly semiotic features of texts to which the expression is applied, but is better defined through technical traits of textual production, which avoid the tautologies hidden in any definition of comedy.

I have shown how the series I have analyzed distance themselves, at least from the point of view of their enunciative structures, from traditional sitcom. I have thus established from the start that these shows should be excluded from the realm of sitcom, whose most evident and best-known technical traits are the use of more than one camera for filming, a soundstage used as a stable set and the existence of a laugh track within the soundtrack, normally a recording of the live audience present when the episodes are being filmed. I decided to reduce the technical definition to these three features because their absence marks a clear distinction from a historically solid and widely recognized televisual format — which makes sitcom an ideal benchmark for the goals of this analysis. However, considering that both the audience and the producers keep referring to such shows as *Scrubs* or *The Office* as sitcoms, I have decided in several cases to use the term traditional or classic sitcom, in order to avoid any possible misunderstanding of the object of my discourse.

There is no doubt of the strictly technical nature of this definition, which relates it not to the texts' intrinsic features, but rather to their productive conditions, usually external to the semiotic field of inquiry. The only exception would be the laugh track, which calls into play a pragmatic aspect of the utterance, which will be better considered in the final chapter. Nonetheless, the very concept of situation comedy implies two

6. Genre Dynamics

elements that are far from technical: first of all the comic component, and second the character of situation, which seems to go hand in hand with the utterance's overtly fictional nature.

The Relationship with Sitcom

Denying Sitcom in Scrubs

From the first episode, *Scrubs* enacts a strategy aimed at marking a distinction between itself and sitcom, one that extends beyond the simple technical differences, which are not always obvious to an inexpert eye. In a very short fantasy sequence, JD is sitting in the doctors' lounge and "sees" on television a glimpse on his future life with Elliot (who in a previous sequence has agreed to have dinner with him). This vision has the clear marks of sitcom, from the audience's laughter to the blond child with whom JD and Elliot exchange humorous lines while seated, unavoidably, on the couch in their home. Dr. Cox entering the scene (both in JD's fantasy and in "real life") abruptly puts an end to the show.

However, it is only in season four that the non-sitcom status of *Scrubs* is affirmed in a more distinct way, with the episode "My Life in Four Cameras" (417). The episode begins in JD and Turk's apartment, where JD has set up a sort of quiz show in order to test his compatibility with Kylie, the woman he is dating. When JD asks her to name three spin-offs of the sitcom *Happy Days*, she answers correctly with *Mork & Mindy*, *Laverne & Shirley* and *Joanie Loves Chachi*. Turk intervenes, loudly urging JD to "marry her now!"

It is not unusual for a television series to make references or direct quotes to past shows, as happens in the cited example. It is also similarly possible for a show to reference other contemporary ones. In season six of *Will & Grace* ("No Sex 'N' the City," 619), Karen is sad because *Sex and the City*, one of her favorite shows, has recently come to an end, but she is relieved at the idea that "at least I still have my *Frasier* and my *Friends*." She is then taken aback and slaps Jack in the face when he informs her that both *Frasier* and *Friends* are also in their final season that year.[2] It is important to see how in this case two of the referenced shows were broadcast by NBC, the same network on which *Will & Grace* aired, while one aired on cable-channel HBO.

Such a direct reference to competition should not sound strange. First of all, following the parameters mentioned above, *Sex and the City* is not a sitcom, although it is usually classified, for example for television awards, simply as *comedy*. Second, this show started airing in the summer schedule of 1998, while *Will & Grace* started in the fall schedule of the same year, and, while having different target audiences, the thematic coverage of the two shows shared at least one border, if they weren't partly overlapping.[3]

Karen's line reveals itself as a sort of intrusion into the enunciation, which, through a disengagement, is able to give the audience the news that *Will & Grace* will have more seasons to live — as if its longevity could be an index of success compared to HBO's program. The reference to two other, much longer NBC shows not only provides information on the network's programming, but also aims at highlighting NBC productions' success rate over HBO's. Such comparison is all but theoretical, however, as HBO, being a cable channel, cannot but have a much more limited audience base than those of national networks. The exchange of lines between Karen and Jack is nothing more than a textualization of the rivalry between competing networks, halfway between homage and playful spite.

This strategy makes sure the enunciation does not need to show itself more overtly, but can still communicate information — one show's self-promotion, and cross-promotion with shows from the same network — without having to make its voice be heard, which would happen if paratextual elements were used, such as graphic overlays or voice-overs. Instead, a smart and subtle disengagement delegates this task to the utterance's actors, leaving the device undetected.

The aforementioned *Scrubs* episode goes well beyond the simple, "casual" reference to classic sitcom. A multitude of patients overflow the hospital because of an ill-considered announcement in newscasts about possible E. coli infections. JD discovers that one of his potential patients was, in the past, a writer on *Cheers*,[4] and pretends this patient needs a surgical consult so that he can introduce him to Turk and they can both spend more time with the man (who in turn, looks quite annoyed).

6. Genre Dynamics

JD then realizes that the patient is, in fact, sick with lung cancer, and has very little time left to live. When JD and Elliot inform the patient of his condition, JD's voice-over intervenes to comment on the scene:

> (417. *JD and Elliot at the patient's bedside.*)
> JD (*voice-over*): There are moments when we all wish life was more like a sitcom.
> ELLIOT: I'm so sorry.

Suddenly, the lighting changes from a cut from the right to a diffusion that shows bright colors in the room, while the patient responds in a very cheerful manner:

> MR. JAMES: Well, the good news is I won't have to eat my wife's cooking anymore, right?

Elliot responds to this line with a hysterical laughter, followed, very unexpectedly, by the laughter of an audience. JD looks confused, and the next shot shows cameras within the room, which has become a soundstage set. JD's voice-over announces the commercial break:

> JD (*voice-over*): JD's sitcom fantasy will be back after these messages.
> (*Commercial break, introduced and followed by musical cues.*)
> JD (*voice-over*): JD's sitcom fantasy is filmed in front of a live studio audience.

Although this is Zach Braff's voice, it is not technically JD's voice, simply because it lies at a different enunciative level. The level on which it operates is the same as that of the network's graphic overlays, which function as paratext to the episode. In terms of linguistic function, this voice's two instances are, yet again, different from one another. The one before the break serves as a phatic reminder, and textualizes — at least implicitly, referring to a context that is heterogeneous to the episode's fictional content — certain enunciative circumstances. It also implies, even without direct interpolation, the presence of the audience at home, which is kindly reminded not to leave the network during the commercial break.

The instance of Zach Braff's voice after the break, on the other hand, provides information on the episode's technical background, with no references to the context. It changes the voice's communicative function from phatic to metatextual. This functional shift can be confirmed via a simple simulation that changes the enunciative circumstances from "televisual flow" to "DVD edition": the voice's phatic instance would cease to make sense, because of the change in communication channel, while the metatextual one would maintain its function and meaning unaltered.[5]

During the almost ten minutes that follow this event, all of the episode's narrative lines (even those about which JD cannot have any knowledge) are solved, in JD's fantasy, as they would be solved in a sitcom, thanks to happy outside interventions and unexpected revelations. Even Charles James's cancer is revealed to be a mistake, due to his chart being swapped with that of one James Charles — whose fate, in typical sitcom style, does not seem to be anyone's concern:

> ELLIOT: (*Noticing the patient's chart*) Wait a second! This chart isn't for Charles James, it's for James Charles! He's the one who has cancer, not you!
> JD: And who cares about him! He's anti–Semitic!
> (*Audience's laughter.*)

Nonetheless, the patient collapses, and the environment regains its original lighting, while the soundtrack features the beginning notes of "Where Everybody Knows Your Name," the famous theme song from *Cheers*— not in the original version, but as performed by Colin Hay, a frequent musical guest in *Scrubs* (who also took part in the taping of this episode by providing musical entertainment for the audience during breaks).

> JD (*voice-over*): Unfortunately, around here things don't always end as neat and tidy as they do in sitcoms.
> (*Unable to help Elliot and the nurses, JD exits.*)

Just as the patient was actually ill, the other story lines also feature a dysphoric conclusion: Turk and Carla are forced to deal with their problems as a couple, Dr. Cox must fire a cafeteria worker, while JD, disheartened, goes home.

In the very short final sequence of the episode, JD is sitting on his couch watching television, chuckling quietly along with the laugh track. JD as narrator comments on how comforting it is to know that "there's always one thing that can pick your spirits up."

In this episode, *Scrubs* decides to show *one* enunciative device — not its actual device, for sure, but its negation. During the sitcom portion of the episode, even JD's voice-over is suppressed. Affirming the opposition between represented reality and JD's fantasy, it also underscores the distance between situation comedy, its genre of reference, and its own nature. It is a kind of programmatic episode that works backwards, where the idea of non-sitcom is more clearly developed. It is not only a technical affirmation, in which the device reveals — albeit in a negative way — its own productive origin, but also a statement of narrative purpose. It is the enunciation's way of claiming that comedy is not necessarily a world in which everything always ends well, where in the end an element of surprise arrives to give relief to the audience. Comedy is, rather, a spirit with which one can deal with reality, the same spirit JD needs (as others do) to overcome the difficulties of his everyday life.

Involuntary Comedy in The Office

The Office makes few direct reference to specific sitcoms, one of which Michael Scott uses as an example of the way he believes the office environment to be — mostly thanks to himself:

> (*202. Cut to Michael's interview in his office.*)
> MICHAEL: It's how I like to do business. Everybody joking around. We're like *Friends*. I am Chandler, and Joey. And, uh, Pam is Rachel. And Dwight, is — Kramer.

Michael's inability to find direct correspondences, that is, a way to make the two worlds superposable, confirms that this reference to *Friends* is forced and unnatural. He goes as far as to make himself correspond to not one but two sitcom characters (the funny one and the sexy one). Not only that, but in order to assign a character to Dwight, he uses the neurotic Kramer, who belongs to the world of *Seinfeld*. This difficulty stands as a testimony to the impossibility of reducing the world's complexity to a single sitcom model.

Documentary is surely not in charge of describing the whole world of each person involved — on the contrary, its task is to grasp a well-defined portion of reality, including whoever may walk through it. Nonetheless, the portion of his world Michael chooses to map with the fictional world of sitcom reveals itself to be, at least in regard to his attempts at redefining it, more complex even than *Friends*—which is itself based on a broad narrative model, considering it included six main characters, all at the same hierarchic level.

One of the main focal points in Michael Scott's discourse is not sitcom, but a broader idea of comedy. As my analysis shows, comedy as a tool to make others feel at ease is an object of value to Michael, who exploits his own (self-declared) knowledge of American comedy to create for himself an image of great entertainer.

While in *Scrubs* the enunciation deals with genre relationships compared to sitcom, and in *The Comeback* the enunciation shows the act of producing a sitcom, it seems that *The Office* tends to avoid any links to the most classic form of comedy on television. This is even more evident in season one, where it also tends to avoid the most common models of American comedy, thanks to a strict relationship with the original British series, using its timing, taking up both its situations and its jokes. Paradoxically, the goal seems to be that of showing the lack of humor, the absence of euphoric effects in Michael Scott's forced comedy. In a way, it sounds like a goal opposite to that of *Scrubs,* where the comedic effects are developed through a consistent collaboration between enunciation and utterance, but actively aimed at a detachment from consolidated narrative and communicative models — while still affirming their validity and historic importance. In *The Office,* the enunciation takes the opposite path, starting from completely different premises, that is the discursivization of a televisual genre that is not only non-comic, but by definition nonfictional, thus revealing comedy's dysfunctions, with a certain touch of cruelty.

Michael Scott *wants to be* a great comedian — he even *believes himself to be* it, and as such, he wants to impose his comedy on others. The idea of comedy is not only nested within the utterance, as might be the case in *The Comeback,* but it is even confined within the discourse of a single character, whose view of his reality stands in clear contrast with his reality as recorded by the documentary. In a way, it might prove that comedy, and humor in general, needs a consenting and cooperating audience in order to function properly.

In "Sexual Harassment" (202), the company's executives reproach

6. Genre Dynamics

Michael because of the inappropriate e-mail he forwards to the whole office, and in response, he runs to address the employees:

> Michael: Attention everyone. Hello. Ah, yes, I just want you to know, that, ah, this is not my decision, but from here on out, we can no longer be friends. And, when we talk about things here, we must only discuss, ah, work-associated things. And, uh, you can consider this my retirement from comedy. In the future, if I want to say something funny, or witty, or do an impression, I will no longer, ever, do any of those things.

As the serial model opens toward more narrative continuity with the show's evolution in season two, *The Office* tends to assume traits that are more similar to those of sitcom, at least for what concerns the episodes' internal timing and a more predictable rhythm of comedic moments. At the same time, though, it keeps pulling away from sitcom in terms of the tools it uses to produce its comic discourse.

First of all, its complexity tends to increase. On the one hand, sitcom develops its stories as variations to a referenced theme, which — using a musical term — is almost an ostinato: no matter what happens, the characters' thematizations remain anchored to the behavior models established in the very first episodes, and retain memory of events that are often irrelevant, but still confirm a certain thematic investment. In *The Office,* on the other hand, the serial opening entails an expansion of the story lines toward secondary or occasional characters, with consequently more and more need to increase the number of details provided about them. Such need is highlighted also by the conversion of some guest stars — including Melora Hardin — to regulars in season two, and the inclusion of the regulars in the opening credits, right after the main theme. The episodes tend to be shaped more and more like variations on a theme, much as they are in *Scrubs,* whose premises continually shift in new directions.

Thus, while season one focuses more on office-related issues and business relations, only subtly accompanied by allusions to side elements (such as Jim and Pam's sympathy), further developments allow for possibilities previously hidden by an initial lack of definition in certain elements. The secondary actors become not only supporting characters, or a collective straight man to Michael's intended funny man, but also sources of possible narrative evolutions — from Dwight and Angela's secret affair to Meredith's drinking problem, to Kelly's ditzy personality, to the introduction of new characters in season three. Through scenic elements and through the intervention of the protagonists as catalysts, the secondary characters acquire more complexity and, a bit at a time, assume more distinct roles closer to the action's core.

Yet, the episodes' discursive structures also change with the adoption of the cold open, that is, the sudden start of the episode with an introductory sequence before the opening theme, a typical element in sitcom, which is also used by several non-comic shows as "bait," to prevent the audience from fleeing after the opening credits. In most shows, the cold open is followed by a commercial break (this could explain why HBO's shows, not plagued by commercials, do not use the cold open).

Unlike in *Scrubs,* where the introductory sequence may often last longer than four minutes, *The Office* features a very short sequence of about one minute, which does not always introduce the episode's theme, but is always structured as a very long setup for the final joke — which is not always a verbal joke, but can be a gesture, a fragment of action or simply a change of frame, which once again contributes to reaffirming the cardinal role of the enunciative device in the construction of the comic effect.

Lessons of Comedy in The Comeback

The Comeback's initial situation is quite different from that of *Scrubs,* first of all because of the network's approach to the televisual flow (HBO being a cable channel that does not insert commercial breaks within programs), which results in different enunciative circumstances. Second, given the primary enunciative device's transparency, the circumstances themselves are, in a way, overridden by those of the secondary enunciation — made explicit by the introduction screen, which serves as a paratextual marker of their specificity: what will be shown is the rough cut of a reality show, which means that several scenes might contain material the production would not like to reach the audience.

Reality-show actors are always aware of the presence of cameras, which leads to the textualization of an audience's presence — not the

6. Genre Dynamics

empiric one, but the virtual one that will watch the reality show called *The Comeback,* realized within the fictional narrative by the same title. The presence of this audience is at most virtual, because the reality show within the utterance does not air until the last episode of *The Comeback.*

At the same time, the raw-footage expedient reveals what would otherwise be considered taboo in the production of actual reality shows: the "machine" that makes the program work, that is, the crew following Valerie Cherish almost twenty-four hours a day. This accumulation of enunciative levels makes it possible for *The Comeback* to distance itself from both fictional and nonfictional television. On the one hand, bringing onto the screen, in a completely intentional manner on all levels, the productive apparatus of a situation comedy, the show casts a judging eye on a production practice it presents as a laugh factory — not to mention one of scarce success. On the other hand, by "accidentally" showing the way a reality show works, it questions the genuineness of the reality that cameras filter.

Starting with the initial lines of the pilot episode, Valerie Cherish constantly worries about what she says and the way she says it, just as she does when she is on the set of *Room and Bored* (if not even more so). Her effort to make her way again into show business results in a confusion of the planes of existence of "real life" and "fiction," a confusion so thorough that the latter has completely replaced the former. If reality is improvised and natural, Valerie's reality is nothing but a series of double takes, falsely unscripted situations, self-edited moments. Valerie often gives Jane a time-out gesture to indicate where she would like the footage not to be used in the reality show, despite knowing that Jane does not have the authority to turn off the cameras or decide what will or will not be used in the final cut.

With the introduction of the raw-footage level, the resulting enunciative stratification turns *The Comeback* into a fictional narrative about the reality of a reality show, where what happens to Valerie almost never corresponds to the narration she would like to impose on her own life. To Valerie, sitcom is not "something else," but "something real": it is a milieu she works in and allows into her own show. At her level of experience, the role of the sitcom is so overwhelming that she even starts using one of her key lines in *Room and Bored* (an indignant "I don't want to see that!") in everyday life, and never seems to be able to shed the role of the comedian, even when circumstances would require it. This has a doubly negative result: her attempts at joking in real life are never understood, and on the set of the sitcom, she never succeeds in being taken seriously.

Contrary to the sanctioning that takes place in *Scrubs,* the confusion between life and fiction is never openly sanctioned in *The Comeback*: usually, cameras just catch glimpses of other characters looking puzzled or upset or disgusted at things Valerie says or does. Moreover, she is often the one who sanctions attempts by other people (especially her husband) to make her understand the higher value her personal life should have over the fictional one she is trying to rebuild.

Almost paradoxically, Valerie's personal trajectory is the opposite of the one the enunciation enacts. The reality show and the primary device tend to represent or rebuild the complexity of Valerie's life, attempting to show her different roles and her difficulties in managing them. On the contrary, Valerie's sole objective is to suppress such complexity and adapt all non-conforming sides of herself to fit the image she wants to achieve in her work project. While the sitcom's characters are almost completely void of any differentiation, Valerie struggles continuously against a stratification she would rather not undergo, one she believes cannot be anything but harmful to her image.

The Comeback is a text in which the enunciative device predicates its own distance from a certain televisual genre, constructing such distance in a very sophisticated way while at the same time putting forth a subject of the utterance who molds her own life to fit the parameters of sitcom. Life, however, even Valerie Cherish's "televisually modified" one, can never be reduced to a stereotype, and can never be controlled in every aspect. And above all, and no matter how much effort one puts into it, life is no comedy.

Ugly Betty's *Comic Coating*

Although it resumes some of the premises and themes of a Colombian telenovela, *Ugly Betty* does not anticipate a fairy-tale finale in which the protagonist removes her braces, becomes the prettiest, marries her

6. Genre Dynamics

boss and lives happily ever after. Such an ending would have to be preceded by a long preparation that would incorporate this transformation as one of the character's narrative programs. For it to be so, Betty herself should perceive her "ugliness" as lack, whereas the contrary is quite clear from the start. Moreover, Betty seems to acquire from a very early stage the necessary competence to undertake her narrative trajectory, and, no matter how many obstacles she finds along the way, her life never really comes off as one of hardship and suffering.

Thus *Ugly Betty* is, from the beginning, anomalous in some of its telenovela traits. Still, for lack of an "enunciative cocoon" such as that featured in *The Office* or *The Comeback*, the direct references it makes to this genre turn it, but only partly, into a meta-telenovela.

One more difference between *Ugly Betty* and the other shows I have analyzed here is the absence of references to sitcom — and, more generally, to comic genres. *Ugly Betty* does not want to counterpose itself to classic comedy on an existential plane, but would rather assume some of its discursive models as manifestations of non-comic narrative material.

Among such models is the broad use of physical comedy by almost all characters — and it could be imagined that such abilities were behind the choice of actors that play them. Every character has facial expressions and typical gestures that become trademarks and integrate into each of their thematic apparatus. From the very beginning, Betty herself is often shown tripping, stumbling or walking into things (the glass door from the pilot episode is a classic), but also spitting food into a napkin, embarrassed, when someone addresses her while she's eating — and in this gesture, freeing herself of food, she mirrors the rejection of food that is typical — if not stereotypical — of the fashion world.

One more link with classic comedy can be found in the passion for theater, particularly musical theater, common among several characters in *Ugly Betty*. This passion, almost an obsession, is also typical of sitcom, where references to musicals are very frequent, particularly in shows set in New York, where the influence of Broadway is inevitably strong. *Ugly Betty* seems to appropriate not only the attraction to theater — overtly stated by the characters — but also a certain theatricality in the acting that would be proper in situation comedy, an acting style lighter and less exasperated in nature than that found in telenovelas.

After all, as I have noted, classic sitcom is an archaic genre with deep roots in theatrical performance, and it is the only narrative televisual genre that has preserved this distinct trait. With regard to its historical counterposition to tragedy, which Aristotle deemed a superior theatrical and literary genre, comedy has prevailed, at least on television. In the triangle formed by sitcom, soap opera and drama, which sums up the great categorization of fictional genres in American television, there is no room left for tragedy. Exceptions can be found in shows with almost experimental traits and possibly targeted at niche audiences, such as *Six Feet Under,* aired on HBO in five seasons until 2005. The main characters are a family of undertakers who learn to make room in their lives for death and pain — not only other people's, but their own above all.

Other shows that try to walk this path are generally very new productions, whose tragic vocation is made milder by genre hybridization, which shifts the attention to different levels and makes texts less literal. These include *Dexter* (Showtime: 2006–present), the first-person story of a serial killer, which assumes the traits of forensic drama; *Pushing Daisies,* the everyday life story of a pie maker who has the gift of waking up the dead with the touch of a finger, which follows the path of romantic comedy; and even *Lost* (ABC: 2004–2010), which, thanks to the multiple keys to its understanding and its obsessive attention to enunciative mechanisms, is able to avoid becoming a collective tragedy.

Ugly Betty has a much higher tragic potential than any of the shows here analyzed — even higher than *Scrubs—* but decides not to activate it, opting instead to play with its tragic potential not by concealing it, but by turning it into comedy.

Managing Dysphoria

I have mentioned how traditional sitcom tends to systematically avoid dysphoric episodes, and thus to discursivize situations that are at most non-euphoric, only to solve them always in a positive way. Such feature seems perfectly in tune with any existing definition of the comic genre.

To better understand how new comedy shows deal with the issue of dysphoria, I would like to reconsider Aristotle's definition, which provides three crucial elements: (1) an aesthetic/ethical element (the perception of ugliness, αἶσχος [aîskhos], that is — in the Greek vision — of anomalous qualities, thus inferior, worse, Φαυλότερα [phaulótera], although not contaminated by an intrinsically negative quality, οὐ κατά πᾶσαν κακίαν [u katà pâsan kakían]); (2) a sensorial/thymic element (the absence of physical pain, in the adjective ἀνώδυνος [anódynos]); and (3) an aesthetic/thymic element (the ridiculous, in the adjective γελοῖος [geloîos]). To perform an abstraction from the Greek context and modernize this definition, one might say the necessary condition for generating euphoria is the presence of anomalous elements, without permanent negative consequences. It can be inferred that real pain and absolute ill can never be sources of euphoria, which is consistent with the strategies of pain and/or dysphoria management considered in chapter 1.

However, the cultural specificity of Aristotle's definition must be taken into account. Ancient Greek culture established a sort of logic co-implication between ethics and aesthetics, which made naturally ugly anything that was not considered morally acceptable, and vice versa. This is not necessarily true in contemporary culture — and the contrary can often be experienced. What remains valid of this definition is, consequently, the idea that the comic effect rises from a paradox or the violation of a norm. The norm at hand may be general, thus culturally shared, or specific, thus defined within the boundaries of the text itself. A paradox, on the other hand, can appear either as a contradiction between different enunciative levels (not necessarily boxed one into another) or in the utterance's discursive manifestation, as a conflict between isotopic networks.

Once again, though, the thymic category reenters as a discriminating trait of the comic genre. It is euphoria that defines comedy, or, more precisely, euphoria as generated by anomalous and paradoxical situations. The definition remains anchored to the consequentiality between the utterance's euphoric component and the text's comic effects; although Aristotle does not explicitly refer to an audience, one can still be taken for granted, considering the theatrical nature of Greek comedy.

Paradox and norm deviation lie at the root of the ways in which new American comedy shows tend to treat dysphoria without avoiding it (the latter being the trope of choice in classic comedy). Although these mechanisms often coexist in varying measure, each is more clearly noticeable in some shows than in others.

Dilution

In general, the thymic category works fairly well if applied to texts that fall into the macro-genre of drama, which is by definition non-comic. It is as if these texts, of serious inclination, were imposing on the passions they represent a status of literality necessary to the correct application of the thymic category.

Comedy features an opposition between euphoria and dysphoria — there is no lack of examples, including in the shows here examined, and even in sitcom. What changes in drama is the kind of abstraction the text can perform on those passions. The difference is clear when drama is compared to traditional sitcom. The death of a patient in *ER* is more easily part of a discourse that is both more *passionné* and *passionnant* than what may happen if a character dies, for example, in *Friends*.

In *Scrubs*, death is often directly represented, by showing the event itself, the corpses and the dysphoric results (not too different from death's mode of representation in *ER*), and given this fact, the text's distance from the genre of classic sitcom is quite evident. Nonetheless, the text does reprocess the dysphoria generated by the direct representation of pain — either physical or emotional — although not right away — in favor of non-dysphoric developments.

The use of negation in the term *non-dysphoria* is not casual. In fact, it marks a fundamental distinction. Whereas in *Friends*, the (mostly indirect) representation of death can always have a euphoric effect, in *Scrubs* its impact must be limited. The painful situation is diluted, as if in an attempt to overcome it, even at a distance. When Carla's brother, Marco, is introduced, it is revealed that the reason for his hatred toward Turk goes back to their previous encounter, at Carla's mother's funeral, when Turk mistook him for a valet. The effects of patients' deaths on the doctors' lives are always processed in order to shift the attention onto the generated dysphoria, so that it can be overcome and, possibly, eliminated. When this is not possible, the attempts to overcome these dysphoric moments will themselves instigate subsequent euphorizing episodes.

This dilution strategy puts the dysphoric episodes into perspective and performs meta-thymic operations that elaborate the pain at the exact moment in which it is or should be represented. At the utterative level, pain becomes the object of the characters' discourses, which filter its dysphoric charge and allow its reevaluation, even, potentially, in euphoric terms.

Detachment

The mechanisms for managing dysphoria in *The Office* and *The Comeback* are, in part, different from *Scrubs*'s. At the utterative level, we find an abundance of unexpected dysphoric moments in shows that are advertised as comedy. Moreover, almost all the protagonists' euphorizing attempts are in vain, and mostly contain, within the utterance, effects contrary to their intentions.

At play here is the question of the literality of the utterance's content. By *literality*, I mean a lack of consideration for the "container," which in the cases of these two shows is, as seen in the analysis, a complex enunciative structure that cannot and must not be underestimated in order to understand the comic act.

In both of these shows, the *mise en abyme* of a fictional product of reality-based television[6] (that is, a product whose reality status depends on the context in which it is placed) within a real product of fiction (one that exist in the empiric world, but which admits or does not deny that its contents are fictional) openly contrasts with the possibility of reading the utterance as literal. In fact, an accurate reading of the enunciative mechanism provides the key to transforming the dysphoric charge of the utterance into a comic product. The recognition of such artificially augmented distance between enunciation and possible final receiver is necessary in order to the decode, unmask and, ultimately, comprehend the text's comic intent.

Without such distance, that is, if enough space were given to the literality of the utterance, the represented stories would not be other than unfortunate series of events — from Michael Scott's racist jokes during an antiracism seminar he has forced his employees to attend, to Valerie Cherish's continuous yet vain attempts at being liked by the writers of *Room and Bored*.

There is no utterative dilution of dysphoria here, achieved elsewhere through a shift of the text's attention toward the action's context or via the discursivization of disturbances that slow down the action's impact and aim at inverting its thymic value. On the contrary, these texts' adherence to the fictional reality-based discourse sheds even more light onto the their dysphoric mechanisms and serves as launchpad for increasing the distance between the enclosed utterance and the primary enunciation.

This is particularly the case in *The Comeback,* which lacks, until the end credits, any mark of the primary enunciation, which is, up to that point, completely replaced by the device of uttered enunciation. The reality effect aims at being total, as total as the apparent focus on the literality of the utterance. The premise for the success of the series is, in this case, an agreement to *pretend* that the utterance is real, until the end of the episode, when the agreement is made explicit.

On the contrary, the veridictive contract of *The Office* is quite clear from the start, while the uttered-enunciation device sneaks in even more subtly. It does not intend to hide. I have noted how the device's presence is fundamental not only at the enunciative but also at the utterative level, but its revelation of itself only as a reflection, only through other actors' actions is, once again, a simulation of reality. The distances between the various levels are systematically shown as smaller than they actually are, and, as in a successful optical illusion, they are further increased in their results.

Acceptance and Conversion

Contrary to the other three shows here considered, *Ugly Betty* does not possess a complex enunciative structure that might provide the distance necessary to activate any dilution or detachment mechanisms. Thus, the enunciation acts in a different way, generating discursive structures typical of classic comedy from narrative structures with prominent dysphoric traits. At stake here is not simply the literality of the utterance, but also the possibility for it to be related back to the genre of telenovela, to which it refers but does not belong.

Based on such fictitious relation, the text accepts dysphoria as an inevitable, yet not inescapable condition highlighting the link between

Ugly Betty and the macro-genre of drama. In most cases, drama's effect is to remove dysphoria or its causes, often only temporarily and not always successfully (this is typical of forensic drama, such as the *CSI* franchise). In *Ugly Betty*, we find instead a passage toward further states of euphoria. The instability of euphoric positions thus reached acts as a launchpad for the show's narrative evolution.

The movement from acceptance to conversion is even more evident in shows such as *My Name Is Earl* or *Samantha Who?*, where the acceptance of dysphoria is the condition of existence of the protagonists' narrative programs. In *My Name Is Earl*, Earl Hickey (Jason Lee), a typical small-time crook of the American suburbs, realizes after being hit by a car all the bad things he has done and discovers, from a television program, the concept of karma. Believing in karma proves a sort of instantaneous mechanism; he writes down a list of all the people he has hurt in order to make it up to them. In a similar way, Samantha Newly (Christina Applegate), wakes up after an eight-day coma (interestingly enough, she was also hit by a car) with total retrograde amnesia. Whatever she is able to remember makes her realize what a terrible person she used to be, and she spends her days trying to remember who she was so that she can avoid being that person in the future.

The shift from dysphoria to euphoria is encoded into the series' narrative structure, so much so that the conversion process becomes a narrative program of use to Earl, who wants to maintain good karma; to Samantha the conversion is a main narrative program, while recovering her memory becomes only functional to self-improvement.

All such cases work on premises that could form valid bases for drama series, if not for the particular intervention of enunciative structures that mark the deviation between the various thymic states in various ways and create, where it would not be present otherwise, the distance necessary to underscore the utterance's non-literality.

Strategies of Distancing and Rapprochement

In contrast to situation comedy's technical and formal solidity, the newer series' forms are more malleable, and tend not only to pull away from the comic genre, but also to continuously and consciously reposition themselves in relation to it. Although they refuse to *be* sitcom from the outset, none of the new American comedies studied here could really do without it. If *Scrubs* bases its existence on a genre comparison that goes well beyond extratextual references to open an explicit discourse on the nature of comedy, *The Office* and *The Comeback* intend, at least at first glance, to distance themselves from comedy even more; however, they end up depending on it to an even greater extent. The maximum distance seems to be found in *Ugly Betty*, which, in drawing on telenovela, a fictional genre that is at once fabular and revealing of its cultural context, carries some of sitcom's typical traits, reviving it in the process.

While in traditional sitcom the enunciative mechanism is very well consolidated, with rare exception, newer comedies play at testing unusual relationships between enunciative levels, and between these enunciative levels and the utterances they produce. Far from being unreachable, the realm of enunciation becomes present and active within the utterance itself, open to variations distinct from the merely narrative ones sitcom offers, thanks to the texts' serial nature.

These distancing strategies, which might sometimes seem to favor the enunciation's intervention and other times the utterance's, are in fact the product of a dynamic coordination between the two levels. I certainly do not want to make the error of considering the two levels as separate entities: the primary enunciation always remains in charge and aware of what happens within the utterance, but it seems true that by exploiting its ability to become more or less transparent, the primary utterance can continually attain new presence effects.

If the distance from sitcom in *Scrubs* is usually predicated at the level of the utterance — both filmic and verbal — and even more so in the actors' discourses, it is a direct intervention of the enunciation that makes it possible to define this distance more precisely. The device violates its own rules, and not only activates an enunciation other than its own, but creates an actual discourse on the televisual culture to which it belongs. This discourse treats situation comedy, first of all, as genre of reference and, in a way, of origin; second, it treats its own genre, which is never given a name, but which must belong to the realm of comedy (other-

6. Genre Dynamics

wise the *mise en abyme* of a comic enunciation would never be justified and would entail a sort of schizophrenia unseen so far in non-comic genres); finally, this discourse establishes once and for all that, despite its distance from sitcom, the text maintains a relationship with its genre of origin, and it is that relationship which founds the meaning of the show. In the absence of sitcom and textual references to it, *Scrubs* would be just another show about doctors with serious existential issues.

I will explore a different order of questions raised by the shows I have analyzed, in more detail, in the final chapter. These questions concern the texts' relationship with reality. If *Scrubs* focuses on the inverse effects of sitcom on the characters' lives, *The Office* and *The Comeback* offer a more direct look at two genres (reality show and documentary) that are, by definition, charged with representing the empiric world. Just when the difference with sitcom seems to have reached a peak, the genre is exploited by the utterance via forced negation (in *The Office,* which, however ends up assuming some of its narrative models), or thanks to a display of the way it functions, or rather, how it dysfunctions (in *The Comeback*). At the same time, the discourse on nonfictional television tries to shed some light on the limitations of reality-based television and injects the possibility, paradoxical yet not unfounded, that the most lucid gaze onto represented realities — and the clashes between different planes of reality — might ultimately be that of comedy.

7

Comedy, Misplaced

This chapter explores three cases in which series that by definition do not belong to a comic genre employ comic techniques to develop odd episodes. While this is practice is far from uncommon in contemporary television, I have chosen only three of the most striking examples from the past few television seasons. The first example comes from the third season of *Lost,* whose fourteenth episode, "Exposé," provides interesting variations on the show's themes and, at the same time, a remarkable derailment of its core structures. The other two examples come from *CSI: Crime Scene Investigation* (CBS: 2000–present), a series so strongly positioned in the genre of forensic drama that it has contributed to a redefinition of that genre. Despite some exceptions, forensic drama is not usually associated with comedy, nor does it normally bear euphoric connotations. From *CSI*, I will examine the eighth episode of season eight, "You Kill Me," and the twentieth of season nine, "A Space Oddity."

The non-comic quality of these series does not correspond to a complete disregard for humor or a lack of any comedic qualities among their characters and situations. On the contrary, both *Lost* and *CSI* feature humor, irony and sarcasm as some of their characters' prominent traits, thus manifesting these traits in main story lines — and not just as a secondary detour the text employs to lighten up the mood.

It has become a consolidated practice for television shows to use witty titles based on puns and variations on quotes or other cultural references, even when the show is not a comic one per se. *Lost* and *CSI* do not escape this general behavior, but the episodes under examination in this chapter take it one step further by becoming explicitly meta- and intertextual. While "Exposé" is not an immediately recognizable cultural reference, it does name the title of a fictional show that is central in the episode and creates a semantic link with the investigation performed by the characters, becoming an exploration of *Lost*'s enunciative mechanisms. "You Kill Me" has the same title as a criminal-comedy film released just a few months before the episode first aired[1]; thus, it establishes a direct relation with a comic text, hinting at the unusual character of the episode. "A Space Oddity" is a classic wordplay on *2001: A Space Odyssey*,[2] pointing to the episode's unusual qualities. These are only paratextual hints to the extraordinary behaviors these texts exhibit on all structural levels.

"Exposé"

"Exposé" is widely considered one of the lowest points of the whole series of *Lost*. While it does constitute a notable anomaly — and does so in different realms — a closer look will reveal it as a sort of programmatic episode, similar to what "My Life in Four Cameras" is to *Scrubs*.

Fans often refer to "Exposé" as "the Nikki and Paulo episode," after the names of the two characters whose story line it follows. The most evident anomaly lies in the fact that for the first and only time in the series, the episode does not focus on one or more of the show's main characters, who, consequently, assume supporting roles or simply remain in the background.

The second anomaly, related in part to the previous one, is the absence of three major characters, Jack, Kate and Locke, from the present timeline. The narrative reason is that they are still at the Others' village, whether voluntarily or not. "Exposé" is actually sandwiched between a Locke episode, "The Man from Tallahassee," and a Kate episode, "Left Behind," which are both rich in information and revelations about their relevant characters. Therefore, one might experience the lack of substantial action involving the main cast in "Exposé" as a surprise or understand it as a technique used to delay any further elements of suspense, if not both.

Nikki and Paulo are two passengers of Flight 815 who have emerged from the indistinct background of nameless characters in the previous several episodes. The first scene of "Exposé" shows Nikki (Kiele Sanchez) approaching Sawyer and Hurley, but she can't reach them before dropping to the ground, muttering words the two men cannot understand, and — as far as they can tell — dying in front of them. Sawyer thinks she said "plywood," while Hurley hears "power lines," or "Paulo lies." This last interpretation leads them to investigate further and look for Paulo, whom they will find dead in the jungle. It turns out both characters are under the effect of spider venom, which has paralyzed them (as Nikki was trying to say) and slowed down their heartbeat to the point of making them seem dead.

The first flashback reveals that Nikki is a somewhat famous television actress, who was in Australia to shoot, as a guest star, an episode of a fictional mystery show, *Exposé,* in which her character is killed. She is then seen having a romantic relationship with the director of the show, much older than she is, who employs Paulo (Rodrigo Santoro), a Brazilian man, as his personal chef. The flashback reveals that Nikki and Paulo already knew each other and had conspired to kill the director and steal diamonds from his safe. After succeeding in their mission, they fly back to Los Angeles. (Or at least they try.)

The present timeline concerns the investigation into Nikki and Paulo's apparent deaths, which involves Sawyer (Josh Holloway), Hurley (Jorge Garcia), Charlie (Dominic Monaghan) and Sun (Yunjin Kim). The main story line would not progress at all, if not for Charlie revealing to Sun that he, not the Others, was responsible for attacking her — one full season before, in "The Long Con" (213). While Sun is obviously deeply upset at the news, this revelation does not seem to have long-lasting effects in the following episodes, except for increasing Charlie's willingness to become a better person and help instead of hurting others, an arc that will lead to his sacrifice in the season-three finale.

By going back to the time before the plane took off from Sydney, this episode's flashbacks bring back — albeit only for a moment — characters that died in the previous seasons such as Shannon (Maggie Grace) and Boone (Ian Somerhalder), whom Nikki and Paulo run into and interact with at the Sydney airport. The episode is a sort of pretext to recapitulate the main points of the whole show through reenactment. Technically, the production has gone so far as to digitally insert the new characters into two-year-old scenes or to recreate original sets — including parts of the crash site from the pilot episode — in order to fit them into the story or into scenes and dialogs in which they were not originally present. If this sounds like a little too much for a secondary,

7. Comedy, Misplaced

content-poor episode, it is because "Exposé" offers a lot more than meets the eye.

The story of Nikki and Paulo is one of deception and betrayal. They steal the diamonds and lose the suitcase in which they were carrying them. Paulo finds it but pretends he did not, and when Nikki realizes that he did, Paulo tells her it was only because he had seen how those diamonds were driving them apart. No one will ever know if that was true, since Nikki uses a spider to poison Paulo, and in so doing attracts other spiders, which in turn poison her.

Eventually, the main characters, always zealous when it comes to tending the dead, find the diamonds, realize that Nikki and Paulo were the wrong kind of Romeo and Juliet, and bury them, but not before scattering the diamonds — useless on the island — over their bodies. In macabre symmetry with the open eyes of awakening that were typical of many season-one episodes, Nikki's eyes open suddenly just as her face gets covered with dirt, but she is still unable to speak or move. Next, Sawyer and Hurley are seen leaving the burial site, while the orchestra soundtrack imitates a scream that the buried alive could obviously not produce.

One might wonder why the creators would construct a self-contained and quite unanticipated narrative (although it does have some appropriate anticipations in previous episodes), featuring characters who are immediately killed off, and whose story neither influences the show's main narrative nor evidences any effects on subsequent episodes. One hint at the functional role of "Exposé" can be found in the episode's opening, within the first flashback, right after Nikki's character is killed off in the show in which she is guest starring, after the director — her lover, whose death she has been planning — suggests that she might be resuscitated in a following episode. Her answer is very matter-of-fact: "I'm just a guest star, and we all know what happens to guest stars." In case it had not been clear from the anomaly of the flashback itself, this is an explicit indication that the whole episode will be one of a different kind.

The anomaly in this first flashback — the only one in this episode that does not bear a superimposed time indication (a rare occurrence in *Lost*, which usually leaves time relations undefined) — lies in Nikki's role as an actress on a television shoot not being evident until her character starts interacting with others (with very poor lines and quite bad acting).

The layering of planes of reality and of enunciative levels is impressive for being achieved in such a short time: Nikki, played by a guest star in *Lost*, plays a guest star in a fictional show (which ends titling the episode), whose villain is played by another, more important guest star (Billy Dee Williams), who is actually called by his real name in the fiction. It could hardly get more complicated than this. Nikki's key line appears to be a metasemiotic remark, which in turn becomes a metatextual one: we know what *usually* happens to guest stars (they leave, or get killed), hence we know what *will* happen to guest stars in this episode.

Moreover, the first flashback and the shooting of *Exposé* constitute more than just an embedding of enunciative layers. They form a *mise en abyme,* which anticipates the episode's main themes and dynamics — which are, in turn, a concentrated reminder of the themes and dynamics of the whole series: deception, betrayal and death. Or, better yet: death-related ambiguity: faked, apparent, then ultimately, actual.

Another important theme is that of the withdrawal of information, which permeates *Lost* at both the utterative and the enunciative levels. If the characters are, in themselves, reticent to divulge facts about their past — or even their present, for that matter — the whole show plays with the information it provides to the audience. On the one hand, it withholds important details or provides misleading information about the characters; on the other, it gives the viewers a false sense of omniscience via the abundant use of frequent redundancy and flashbacks (as well as, from the end of season three, flash-forwards).

As I have shown in previous chapters, layering mechanisms such as this one, which provide metatextual insight, are quite typical in televisual comedy. In fact, the way the text of *Lost* deploys these mechanisms in this episode reveals a slight (albeit temporary) shift in the show's semiotic practices toward those of comedy. This is not to say that *Lost* becomes comedy, except maybe for those brief moments in the first flashback during which the acting quality and the scenario within the embedded show are so unlikely that they seem built directly upon Aristotle's definition of comedy. Yet, the text's comic mechanisms are employed to create a sudden distancing effect in a show that has been, since its inception, extremely involving, very much intent in establishing the literality of its own utterance and, ultimately, establishing the verisimilitude of the world it has constructed.

The layering technique does not stop at the embedded *Exposé,* but is carried on throughout the episode, with hints of—and winks at—forensic drama, when the main cast is trying to figure out what "killed" Nikki and Paulo. (Eventually, poison is mentioned, but since no one there is either a forensic scientist or a doctor, they will never get to the truth.) The use of anomaly, of which enunciative layering is only one example, continues into the utterance itself, in the form of irony. The most brilliant example is in Sawyer's failure to know, recognize or acknowledge Nikki and Paulo, in both the present timeline (by saying, "Who the hell is Nikki?" right after she has dropped to the ground and Hurley has mentioned her name, unequivocally referring to her) and in flashbacks ("And who the hell are you?" yelled at Nikki after a heated argument). Sawyer's lines cannot but highlight, once more, the anomaly of the sudden emergence of two previously irrelevant characters as the main focus of the episode.

One further kind of anomaly lies more on the productive side, but has a fundamental impact on the narrative structure, namely the re-creation of scenes from previous episodes — even previous seasons — aimed at inserting these anomalous characters into the past story of *Lost.* Such re-creation can be seen as a form of self-layering or self-remixing through which the enunciative device shows its potential, and, at the same time, reestablishes the boundaries between reality and fiction.

"You Kill Me"

The main story line of this episode of *CSI* is almost entirely occupied by the secondary characters, led by David Hodges (Wallace Langham)—who is a series regular, despite his thematic role as a "lab geek," hence imaginably lower than the field agents in the narrative hierarchy. During the whole episode, Hodges stages a "thought experiment," as he calls it, with which his lab colleagues will try to solve the different murder scenarios he creates.

The episode starts with a conversation in the hallways between Gil Grissom (William Petersen) and Jim Brass (Paul Guilfoyle) about events that occurred in previous episodes—specifically, Sara Sidle's departure of from the lab and its impact on her relationship with Grissom. The scene moves to one of the labs, where Archie Johnson (Archie Kao) gets killed in the explosion of a brick of cocaine he was logging. Hodges enters the lab and cannot control a burst of evil laughter, which is carried on after the cut to the next scene, where he is sitting at a desk facing Wendy Simms (Liz Vassey).

The transition reveals the previous sequence to have been a product of Hodges's imagination, part of the game he is playing with Wendy, who, albeit skeptical at first, eventually becomes more involved with the game. During the episode, Hodges stages four scenarios in which a different member of the lab is killed by a colleague. The last case is the only exception, in which Hodges himself is both the victim and the perpetrator, an expedient he uses to frame Bobby Dawson, the "gun guy," target of a running gag in all scenarios.

Hodges eventually reveals that he is designing a board game called Lab Rats: The Game of Science and Murder, similar to *Clue*, centered on the daily work of the *CSI* lab team. The details of every single scenario are not pertinent to this analysis, and can be left to the enjoyment of the viewers. What matters most is to highlight the specific ways in which this episode constitutes a break from the regular *CSI* format, while still connecting to the rest of the series, and how this break presents some of the typical traits of contemporary televisual comedy.

The first anomaly lies in the whole episode being set in the *CSI* offices, labs and morgue, without a single outside scene. It is the first constraint of Hodges's game, due to the small number of possible characters and the narratives he creates being restricted to predefined spaces. For the same reasons, victims and perpetrators must be chosen from the same small pool of characters.

As I mentioned, by centering the perspective on the lab team, the episode subverts the regular hierarchy of characters. However, each scenario is structured very much like a regular *CSI* episode, with the field agents in charge of the investigations. Because the scenarios are seen from Hodges's point of view, the field agents excessively thematize the importance of trace analysis: "Trace. Is there anything you *can't* do?" says Catherine Willows (Marg Helgenberger), with a dreamy expression, in the second scenario.

On the temporal level, there is no relationship between the primary and secondary narratives, which possess, in fact, a completely atemporal quality. Nonetheless, all utterances are linked by the constancy of themes and the ideal continuity of the alternate realities they stage. This connectivity results in the consistency between the world in which the characters live (within the main utterance) and the fictional ones created and developed by Hodges and his colleagues in each instance of the game.

The thematic continuity between the various uttered worlds is rendered by the primary enunciation via a substantial lack of boundary definition between them, especially when new scenarios are introduced. Most hallway scenes, particularly those not related to the single-serving murder cases, can easily pertain to either the world of *CSI* or Hodges's secondary utterance. Most striking is the repeated interference between the two enunciative levels, which allows the secondary utterances to be remarkably different from regular episodes.

The fact that dead bodies can speak is only the most immediate comic effect. What is more important is that the characters in the secondary utterances are allowed to gaze into the camera and even interact with it. This interaction is a simulacrum of the interaction between Hodges and whomever he is talking to in each case. Despite being in charge of an investigation, hence supposedly not knowing certain information, the character who looks at the camera is already sharing with Hodges indispensable information for the resolution of the case. Consequently, the camera—the enunciative device—assumes the cognitive position of whichever character is trying to solve the murder. This constitutes nothing unusual in *CSI*, which is normally based on a device that, by assuming the cognitive position of an external observer (ultimately the audience's), is less than omniscient; what is unusual, however, is the device finding itself face-to-face with characters who seem to already know how to solve the investigation.

As seen in the analysis of *Scrubs,* a speaking character cannot possibly perform an enunciative disengagement to produce a filmic utterance, due to formal constraints. Thus, the main enunciative device translates the dialogs between Hodges and his colleagues (which can be assumed to have a verbal form even when they are not directly heard) to the filmic form, thus eliminating the need to discursivize most of the actual dialog. At the same time, though, the device turns these secondary utterances into meta-discourses in which the voices from the primary utterance can not only still be heard, but in which they can also interact, in part, with the action and be aware of the images as they are presented.

Just as an example, the third scenario begins with the camera panning over a dead female body from feet to head. When the victim's face is shown as that of Wendy — who has just told Hodges that she is interested in taking the CSI field test, to which he has responded evasively, as if he were hurt by it — her voice is heard saying, "That's a little passive-aggressive, don't you think?" This happens in open violation of the integrity and isolation of the primary utterance, and it is an instance in which the enunciative device plays at losing its transparency — hence becoming, in a certain way, visible.

As clearly stated by dead Archie in the first scenario, the goal of Hodges's experiment is to answer two questions: "Whodunnit? And how?" Wendy is skeptical because the whole exercise forgets to investigate the motives behind the murders, so in the end they appear pointless, and, until Hodges reveals that he is working on a board game, so does the experiment. The lack of motives is another element that makes the scenarios seem odd compared to the typical *CSI* investigation.

On the one hand, Hodges's experiment is an attempt at understanding the narrative mechanisms of crime construction. But there is no crime without a motive, no narrative without intentionality. When Hodges admits to the completely random nature of the crimes he has envisioned, compared to the complex construction of the weapons, Wendy cannot help but ask, "Who was the killer, Wile E. Coyote?"

By removing motivations from the investigative narrative, "You Kill Me" empties the secondary utterances of their intended meaning, which is left for other elements to make. The theme that is consistently made relevant at all levels — besides the standard forensic theme — is that of romantic involvement, which is manifested on the one hand through discourses involving or relating to Grissom and his relationship with Sara, and, on the other, Hodges's attraction to Wendy. Oddly, all appearances of Grissom and people's attempts at talking to him about his romantic situation seem to either be part of Hodges's scenarios or fade into them, all except one, when Hodges explicitly asks Grissom about it. His interest in Grissom's story is more than incidental: by understanding the logic behind it, Hodges seems to be trying to find explanations and preventive motivations to his own actions. Ultimately, Hodges, like a sloppy criminal, makes that one mistake that prevents him from bringing his feelings for Wendy to fruition, leaving the door open for the romance theme's development in future episodes.

"A Space Oddity"

The twentieth episode of *CSI*'s season nine presents itself, at first glance, as a tribute to science fiction television, particularly focused on, but not limited to, *Star Trek*. The episode begins showing David Hodges attending a convention that revolves around a vintage television show, *Astro Quest*, where he finds Wendy Simms dressed up in a costume from the show. Shortly after, Jonathan Danson (Reg Rogers), a filmmaker and *Astro Quest* fan who has produced a sequel to the show called *Astro Quest Redux*, is found dead.

The regular field agents take over the investigation, while Hodges and Simms are sent back to the lab, where they can be more helpful. The suspects include the woman who financed the project, who is revealed to have had a sexual relationship with the victim; a group of *Astro Quest* fans who normally live their lives as if they were actually *in* the show (to the point of re-creating the inside of a spaceship in the attic where one of them lives); and Dr. Penelope Russell, a college professor in media studies who was filming a documentary about the victim's project. Ultimately, the investigation will find the professor guilty of the murder.

The regular forensic themes of the show are accompanied, more prominently than in "You Kill Me," by the intrusion of the love theme, which becomes predominant throughout the episode. Hodges's attraction to Wendy is played out in a series of fantasy sequences in which he imagines himself and Wendy — and occasionally other characters — in episodes of *Astro Quest,* to the point that the science fiction world becomes, to Hodges, an allegory of his work in the lab. The hierarchy, the duties and the impossibility of his dealing with his feelings for Wendy are transferred to this fictional plane, while in the meantime, his fantasy episodes start interfering with his efficiency on the job. Ultimately, his knowledge of the show will allow his discovery of the detail that leads to the murderer. Despite his ability to be fairly explicit with Wendy this time, he backs off once again because a relationship on the job will mean that one of them has to be moved to a different shift (not that this had ever been an issue for Grissom and Sara Sidle in the past), which would make it virtually impossible for them to actually spend time together.

The elements of this episode that are relevant in the analysis include the unusual enunciative structure, the subversion of actorial hierarchy, the richness in extratextual links, and the metatextual and self-referential character of the text. All these elements considered together reveal an underlying comic strategy, which plays out in spite of the fact that "A Space Oddity" — contrary to "You Kill Me" — partly follows *CSI*'s narrative canon, in that an actual investigation is undertaken in the main utterance.

Like "You Kill Me," this episode features prominent — albeit not as extensive — fantasy sequences that disrupt the enunciative structure normally found in *CSI,* but with the notable difference that only one subject (Hodges) is in charge of them; therefore, any collective construction of these scenes is completely involuntary. In other words, the only reason other characters may enter these fantasies and, consequently, shape them is that Hodges is effectively daydreaming, hence still cognitively immersed in the real world around him.

By showing Hodges's fantasy sequences, *CSI*'s enunciative device introduces a secondary enunciation linked to a specific character's subjectivity, and yet it produces an utterance that does not aim to fulfill the show's normal task. Moreover, by spreading the fragments of this anomalous utterance uniformly across the episode, it not only establishes Hodges's story as dominant over the crime story, but it reframes most of the main utterance within his perspective and, often, within his point of view. *CSI* ceases to be a forensic drama and becomes something else, but an analysis of the enunciative structure alone is not enough to explain exactly what.

Even in its most unusual moments, *CSI*'s theme deployment is focused on the job of solving crimes by collecting evidence, analyzing it and understanding suspects' potential motives. The interference of odd themes such as love and romance — the ones relevant to this analysis — is usually still confined within a strict relationship with the forensic job. The characters' decisions to be CSIs are usually motivated by some past experience that makes the job a vocation; their behaviors in their personal lives are also conditioned to what they do for a living. Relationships, when there are any, seem to be built on the same idea, and if they interfere with the job, it is not because of incompatible schedules, but because the intellectual activity required by forensic work is so overwhelming that it overflows into other aspects of the characters' lives.

However, "A Space Oddity" shows an external side of romance. Hodges and Wendy do work together, and that is most definitely the reason they met and got to know each other, the basis, in other words, for their possible compatibility. But the episode also states their compatibility's transcendence: they meet at the convention purely as a coincidence, and, despite how geeky the occasion may be, their presence there is motivated by a personal inclination that does not necessarily have to do with their jobs as scientists. If there were a correlation between being a scientist and being a science fiction fan, Hodges would not have an argument with Mandy — who is also a scientist in the lab — over the difference between science fiction and fantasy, on which they have completely opposite points of view — although Mandy may be arguing for argument's sake, or to annoy him.

While Mandy's intentions are ultimately not relevant, the argument is anything but futile, because it brings to the table the themes of the definition of a genre and the link between reality and fiction — even more importantly, that between the empiric world and televisual worlds. As I have shown in the main analyses of this book, when a television show does this sort of thing, it is not by chance.

One more oddity in the episode is the subversion of the actorial hierarchy, that is the relevance of the characters as elements of the utterance. This subversion is not a matter of thematic hierarchy (who the boss is, who the lab rats are) or of productive hierarchy (main cast, regulars, guest stars, etc.). (These two kinds of hierarchies do not necessarily coincide, incidentally, or Laurence Fishburne would not be the first credited actor on the show, since his character has only recently joined the team as a level-one CSI.) It is, instead, a matter of actantial hierarchy, which ultimately depends on the perspective given to the narrative: whose story are we following? No matter what the results, whose is the main narrative program in the utterance? In "A Space Oddity," the usual perspective shifts, not only making Hodges the main subject, but pointing the spotlight to secondary characters, specifically Wendy Simms.

This shift in perspective does not go unnoticed, and its acknowledgment is textualized as a sort of cognitive dissonance between the level of the utterance and that of the enunciation—specifically, by the characters' knowledge about one another and the knowledge the text assumes its audience to have. When Hodges calls Jim Brass about the dead man at the convention, Brass does not recognize Hodges or seem to know who he is; annoyed, Brass asks Hodges why he has his number. In just a few lines, two out of the three possible kinds of hierarchy clash together: the thematic pecking order, according to which Hodges should not be allowed to have access to Brass's number; and the productive one, which sees Wallace Langham (playing Hodges) appear before Paul Guilfoyle (playing Brass) in the opening credits. This clash makes it suddenly clear that these two characters, with whom the audience is very well acquainted, do not normally interact, and that such interaction constitutes a violation of long-standing rules.

If Brass not recognizing Hodges can easily be or become a *CSI* inside joke, the episode offers much more than that, at different levels of access. At the productive level, which remains strictly extratextual but which can still provide relevant information, it should be noted that one of the episode's writers, Naren Shankar (who also cowrote "You Kill Me"), used to be a writer and producer of *Star Trek: The Next Generation,* along with Ronald D. Moore, who codeveloped the 2004–2009 series *Battlestar Galactica* (Moore plays the first person to shout angrily, "You suck!" after watching the preview of *Astro Quest Redux*). Also, "A Space Oddity" cowriters Bradley Thompson and David Weddle, along with director Michael Nankin, previously worked on *Battlestar Galactica.* Further-

7. Comedy, Misplaced

more, Wallace Langham and Liz Vassey had guest-starring roles on *Star Trek: Voyager*, and the role of Dr. Penelope Russell, the murderer, is a cameo by *Battlestar Galactica* star Kate Vernon.

While this sort of information may expand the text's reach and provide an enriched experience to a prepared audience, this refined level of extratextual knowledge is not indispensable to an understanding of the text. Thus, the production level becomes a sort of idiolect, one that only a fraction of the audience — no matter how large — might understand. No matter how solid the extratextual links or how rich the viewers' encyclopedia, the episode opens from the start a discourse on television that continues until the end, at the moment of discovering the reasons for the murder (which is revealed to be little more than an accident).

This episode is not only a game that may appeal to fans (or anger them, depending on their sense of humor): it also summons aspects of television that are normally not openly considered in the communication between a text and its viewer. With the introduction of a media-theory professor among the characters, "A Space Oddity" necessarily expands the discourse to include the existence of other meta-discourses on television, thus assuming an ulterior layer of complexity. I think this is a particularly clever way of introducing a comic device: the text is able to mock, at once, itself (by way of a surrogate, and by subverting its own rules), its genre (as *CSI* is often considered partly science fiction), and any possible non-televisual discourses *on* itself.

What makes a semiotician jump from his chair is Dr. Russell's explicit mention of semiotics while talking to Jim Brass — something actually not new in *CSI*. Dr. Russell was angry at Jonathan Danson for not acknowledging her after using her research to create *Astro Quest Redux*, as the show was meant to be a deconstructionist operation based on the original show. When Danson tells her she has wasted her life on something useless (media theory), she pushes him, and he hits his head on the control panel of the spaceship model. She tells Brass, "He was killed by one of the signifiers he sought to subvert."

Suddenly, a text that is usually about mundane, concrete things — crime, addiction, death, the human body — discovers and unveils the abstraction of its own existence, revealing the extraordinary quality of this event by marking certain elements of its discourse in a way they would not otherwise be marked. Jim Brass is the last one to be marked, when he catches Dr. Russell's reference to Jacques Derrida. This is unexpected to her, and more generally, something Jim Brass would not normally be talking about — as it's most likely not in inscribed his character's thematic investment.

"A Space Oddity" does not deconstruct its foundation, and it certainly does not reveal, by denying them, its mechanisms to show the instability of their structure. The episode is a game, a poke in the ribs that is more or less subtle depending on the level at which it is enjoyed. By marking itself as odd — even in its title — it redefines what the show's standard should be. Brass's last line, "Epistemological dichotomy — I just call that second-degree murder," becomes, in retrospect, both a fuller explanation of the episode and the end of its oddity, as it verbalizes a return to normality, saying, in essence, "This one has been about television, but now it is once again all about the murders."

Deconstructing, Reconstructing

As seen in the shows in this book's core analyses, the act of putting televisual texts in perspective, in other words, the fact that a text is willing to talk about the mechanisms by which it exists, is an indication of the text's ability to take a step back from itself, keep its distance, discuss itself using the only language it knows and lose — even for just a moment — its seriousness, without losing its integrity.

These series do not become comedy. The do not want to be funny or humorous in a traditional or ingenuous way. They assume traits and mechanisms from comedy to create awareness, to make meaning out of difference (a very structuralist action). They put into perspective the relationship between their utterance and reality, making their utterance a discourse about the world. But it's not necessarily — or ever at all — the empiric world they deal with. The final chapter will explore what television does when it deals with reality, and what kind of reality this might actually be.

8

Comedy and Reality

Critique of Veridiction

A common misconception regarding comedy is that the excess of euphoric effects produces a perceptive detachment from what is commonly considered reality, which would give the comic genre a lesser ability to describe the empiric world. Although this is no place for delving into the depths of a broader discussion of non-comic genres, I would like to extend the field enough to place the analysis of comic series into the context of American televisual fiction.

Not only comedy, but televisual narrative genres in general have been underestimated as forms of expression, due to their intrinsic quality of invention. Despite its permeating the shared culture in ways that no other medium has been able to match (at least until the mass diffusion of Internet-based media, whose consolidation is still in progress), the public considers the production of televisual narratives largely as pure entertainment, and more traditional academia has historically confined it to the realm of popular culture — a politically correct expression to define all that is not "high" culture, or in other words, deemed worth being known and discussed. Although this has not slowed down the development of academic discourses on the subject, television is still in search of legitimation.

After more than half a century of history, television still suffers from a sort of discrimination that does not seem to hit other media, no matter how young. It certainly does not affect cinema, usually enjoyed more for its fictional genres than for nonfictional ones. Definitely, it does not afflict literature, where fictional stories are so common that the term *literature* has become a synonym of the more appropriate *literary fiction*. While it is common knowledge that the veridiction criteria of a literary or cinematic text should be considered valid only within the boundaries of the text itself, this does not always happen for television. It is as if television, whether or not willingly, were charged with a task of faithful representation of reality, leaving in the background anything that breaks this rule.

However, televisual fiction's maintenance of a dominant role in hours with higher viewership is quite remarkable. In Italy, prime time[1] is the ideal placement for feature films (borrowed from cinema, thanks to the semiotic affinity between the two media), but also for successful series. In the United States, it is the home of quality fiction, not only drama but in large measure, also comedy.

This is not the place to change the world, to free the spectators from the sin of watching televisual fiction — and academics in the field of television studies from their suspicion of dealing with cultural products whose aesthetic and cultural values are lower than those of the products of other media. Nonetheless, I will try to correct, with another paradox, the tendency to consider television as the realm of the representation of reality.

Nothing (on Television) Is Real

If the idea that nothing is real might seem radical, one must consider that even newscasts are real only to the extent that the so-called reality they represent is selected, discursivized and given a narrative structure (one not always coherent with the facts). However, the audience does not know "the facts," and *cannot but accept* the veridictive status of the news, that of an enunciative instance committed to a *making believe* related to verifiable narratives — not personally and empirically verifiable, but verified through the cooperation of other texts.[2]

I must underscore, nonetheless, that the production of news discourses is other than an unbiased account of reality, and the facts do not manifest themselves directly through the news — if it were so, there would be no actual need for several news programs and channels. Accepting without reservation the news enunciation's *doing* as a *true-saying* would be like insisting on studying the structure of a language by way of such decontextualized sentences as, "The cat is on the chair." It is the kind of ingenuity that does not stand the test of basic semiotics courses, and which can definitely not work at this analytical level.

8. Comedy and Reality

The audience knows that news programs represent reality in a way that is anything but transparent (in the United States, the constant debate over Fox News's transparency is a perfect example), but still cannot do without the discourses they generate, or perhaps it is a lack of information about the world they cannot do without. Consequently, in either case, the representation creates reality to the extent that, without this level, the real (that large portion of the empiric world that would not be seized by an individual's direct experience) would be rendered inaccessible.

Television's veridictive status *must* be taken for granted, no matter how regretfully, and its confirmation or confutation left to intertextual relations. This is necessary in order to at least believe in a certain level of access to the real, even in those cases wherein the meaning of the real is almost inaccessible, and the narrative machine of news-making is not always able to accurately describe it.[3]

This level is, in a way, as close as possible to reality, and the only one for whose veridictive status any meaningful considerations can be made. Nonetheless, when we talk about reality television, we are using a broad term that covers several phenomena, yet not those genres — such as newscasts, inquiry and documentary — that take portions of the empiric world as objects of their discourses.

During the past twenty-five years, and particularly since the 1990s, the most distinct televisual formats have been produced and sold to the viewers in the name of televisual neorealism.

> The term "reality-based" is bandied about as a description for everything from video compilations to made-for-TV spectacles, newsmagazines, and game shows. Although these programs share a few characteristics such as participants who are not actors, minimal scripting, and drama or narrative created through structure and editing, none of these shows represent real events as they occur.[4]

According to these considerations, while fiction still holds a clear place in the world, less clear is that of reality-based television. Its function would be to provide spectators with an experience similar to, but with fewer certainties than the experience fiction provides. The idea of having variables that could get out of the producers' control could possibly make reality-based television even more interesting than fiction. New comedy attacks this kinds of televisual texts on this front and, acting precisely according to its own plan, works to uncover reality television's limitations and presumptions.

We could pretend just for a moment that reality-based television were an unequivocal class of objects. We could consider it, on the one hand, in its relationship with the kind of programming whose declared aim is to provide an actual representation of reality and, on the other, with fiction, which tends to reproduce and recreate reality. The impact of scripting can be minimal, the absence of professional actors can be total, but the influence of the production's narrative hand is such that these genres end up bearing strong affinities with fictional narratives.

Reality show is normally defined by a class of televisual formats that present a few common traits: the presence of characters that are not acting professionals and who consequently play themselves; the existence of a form of competition; the participants' awareness and acceptance of the presence of the cameras, hence of being included in an enunciative act of higher level. Reality show wasn't born — we should remember that — with *Big Brother* and its derivatives. Observing the everyday life of groups of people was already popular in the early '90s, in programs such as MTV's *The Real World*. The success of that format was due to both its novelty and its peculiarities: "gather an ensemble of young and attractive people, place them in an enclosed living or travel space, document them on small format video, and watch as they disclose things about themselves that 'professional actors' never would or could."[5]

The Italian version of *Big Brother* was received with diffused indignation, due to its voyeuristic quality, the brutal exploitation of ordinary people, often ridiculed in front of the cameras, and the broadcasting of images that were not always edifying (but still nothing severe compared to versions of *Big Brother* produced in some other countries). If *The Real World* was self-contradictory because it selected those who gave the illusion of being ordinary people and made them live together in unusual situations, without concealing a forceful direction of narrative mechanisms, *Big Brother* felt too crude and too real right from the start.

Here is a new paradox: reality shows were negatively judged for reasons that were the opposite of those used to judge fiction, which can be considered not realistic enough. Once again, veridiction comes into play:

8. Comedy and Reality

while *The Real World* was sincere about its mechanisms, not hiding the fact that it did not necessarily tell the truth, the *Big Brother* of the genre's beginnings was surrounded by a halo of innocence that, consequently, turned it into a sort of televisual fish tank.

Big Brother's tendency to voyeurism can naturally be reconnected to its putative parent, the successful film *The Truman Show*.[6] Such a pairing — both natural and definitely wanted by the producers — horrified part of the public, namely critics and institutions, and gave an impression that *Big Brother* was somewhat truer than *The Real World*. Not taking into account the participants' wills — a distinctive trait from *The Truman Show*, where the protagonist was an unknowing victim of a veritable enunciative machine — leads to overestimating the show's ethical aspects and giving the wrong relevance to the issue of veridiction.

What happens in *Big Brother* is real to the extent that the interaction between actors is real. And such interaction is real only if considered from the point of view of its premise, which is artificial by definition — possibly even more so than that of *The Real World,* whose participants were at least allowed out of the house, an indispensable condition to the show's narrative development. When it became clear that *Big Brother* did not lack an elementary form of scripting, and that the participants received forbidden communications from the writers (who do exist for a reason), a new scandal seemed to rise because the program was not as real as it had proposed itself to be.

Once again, veridiction is used as a criterion. *Big Brother* presents itself as a reality show, hence affirming a certain degree of adhesion to reality. The public (in the broad sense of whoever is not part of the production) accepts such statement of sincerity, even though it may not approve of it on an ethical level, then feels betrayed when it discovers that the rules have been broken. Plot twist? Not really. The initial error was to consider the "reality" in reality show as an element external to the text, and any rules as if they were imposed onto the text from the outside. This kind of text, on the contrary, is largely composed of the rules themselves, which are totally included in it, under the control of the enunciative device. Another error was a faulty estimation of the text's extension. *Big Brother* is anything but a closed text[7]: it evolves continuously; it is remodeled; and, due to its interactive nature, it feeds off apparently extraneous elements including the vote from home, indispensable to the narrative development, and also all discourses *on* the text, which in some cases becomes an integral part *of* it. This is to say, in brief, that believing the news of rule violations as indiscretions gone out of the production's control means failing to see the big picture: not only are the violations part of the text, but so are the news leaks on the subject.

Big Brother cannot be evaluated without understanding and recognizing that the veridictive criteria remain, once again, strictly textual: there is no "outside reality" to which the text is referring (its possible existence is not decisive to textual construction). The notorious house where the participants live exists only because of *Big Brother,* and so do the interactions among the participants. It is not a matter of reality but of engineered realism[8]: all possible squabbles, conflicts, refusals of the rules by participants, and at the same time the supposed excess of voyeuristic pleasure on the audience's and on the media's part are not attempts at "going beyond the rules of the game,"[9] but behaviors that are predictable — and undoubtedly predicted, when not even intentionally provoked by the production —*given* certain rules of the game.

A more detailed investigation on the reality show genre should not underestimate another aspect of the text, namely its often extreme nature of commercial product, which makes it subject not only to an aesthetic examination, but also to an analysis according to the principles of semiotics of objects. It would become easier to see and explain how the audience is inscribed into the text not only as the receiver of an act of communication, but also as an active subject, able to modify the text within encoded limits.

In the end, reality show does not seem that different from fiction, and, just like in good fiction, the secret to success lies in keeping some of the rules duly concealed.

Substitution of Reality

Reality show reveals itself as a *presumption* of reality, where the object of *making believe* is not, as in news programs, something empirically or intertextually verifiable, but a textual construction for the enjoyment of which one must suspend any veridictive judgment. Likewise, such suspension is necessary for dealing with a properly fictional category of texts which constitute the macro-genre of drama. This term is normally used to cover all televisual fiction except situation comedy and soap opera. Conventionally in the United States, drama also differentiates itself from comedy in terms of the different duration of the episodes — about forty minutes versus comedy's twenty.

Without necessarily establishing any kind of link to reality, apart from the fact of being similar to it to different degrees — the mimetic principle applies also in this case — drama stages worlds that may or may not represent a portion of the real. Even when there is a lower degree of similitude, from a thematic and figurative point of view, such as in science fiction series, or in those that feature paranormal or supernatural elements in an otherwise "normal" world, drama tends to reproduce models of behavior coherent with those of the empiric world. The operation it performs is a sort of substitution of experienced reality with its representation: once one suspends any judgment on the veridicality of the latter, one accepts its internal rules, or lack thereof (which in turn constitutes a rule). Contrary to both reality show and comedy, in drama the literality of the utterance in relation to the world it creates within itself is enough to give the text meaning. On the other hand, I consider the reality show's utterance to be non-literal, since the action in which actors are involved finds an ulterior purpose in the competition that sustains the show, so much that if the text's veridictive status is not in question (because it is not pertinent), that of the utterance definitely is. The survival (at different levels) of the participants is only metaphorical (that is, no one really expects anyone to die on *Survivor*'s island), and metaphorical *cannot but* be the friendships and alliances created within the group. Reality show is "real" only to the extent that the results of all the uttered performances will affect the world outside the text, in terms of recognition, fame, money, and so forth.

Crime shows are exemplary of this fractioning of reality. Series such as *Law & Order,* but also *CSI,* are interested in nothing more than restoring the order they themselves disrupted. Solving mysteries is their only goal, one so all-consuming that, from a rhythmic point of view, they never fail. They continuously exhibit the rules upon which they are built, and the existence of the represented world is not challenged by similarities with the empiric world. Although James Friedman places some of them, particularly *Law & Order* (NBC: 1990–present) and *NYPD Blue* (ABC: 1993–2005), in the category of reality-based television, their detachment from reality is an indispensable condition. At the end of each episode of *Law & Order,* right before the closing credits, a card explicitly states that the story just told was a work of fiction — although Dick Wolf, producer of the series, states that his "bible" is "[t]he front page of the *New York Post.*"[10] All fictional productions must include similar notices, for legal reasons, but they usually are a small print at the end of the closing credits, in a temporal area that American networks usually brutalize with framed commercials or other shows' promos. In this case, instead, the detachment from reality is sharp and voluntary. If any part of the text may be subject to veridictive judgment, perhaps it is this one.

The sense of drama is not much that of *making believe* in the story it tells, but perhaps, paradoxically, in *showing to believe* in it, even though the order it establishes and breaks is anything but structured. In *Lost,* one of the cult shows of the last few years, not only is the initial order completely unclear (which makes the final order unforeseeable), but the text features a systematic destruction of any intermediate orders established along the way. The text *shows to believe* in its utterance in an exemplary way: it creates a value system that is not, ultimately, an actual system, in which contradiction — in facts, in interactions and even as self-contradiction — is the only constant rule. *Lost* plays at continuously debating its own realism, projecting into the utterance any possible objections to the text's veridictive status, and leaving it to the characters to do the cognitive work necessary to comprehend both the events and the whole textual framework.

One current drama that deserves particular attention for gaining momentum in the past few years is that kind involving a revival of supernatural themes. The point of view with which these current shows tackle their topic lacks the intrinsic insolubility of *Twin Peaks* (ABC: 1990–1991), or the internal conflict between belief and skepticism of *The X-*

Files (Fox: 1993–2002), or the acceptance of a parallel world, bordering between religiosity and mysticism, of *Charmed* (The WB: 1998–2006). The newer shows involve the integration of actors who are totally human, yet possess uncommon abilities in a world that, otherwise, seems to completely reflect the empiric one. Examples of this type include Tru Davies, protagonist of *Tru Calling* (Fox: 2003–2005), able to relive one single day in order to save people from death; the tormented Allison Dubois, of *Medium* (NBC: 2005–2009. CBS: 2009–present), a working mom who helps the district attorney with otherwise unsolvable mysteries; Melinda Gordon, the title character in *Ghost Whisperer* (CBS: 2005–present), who helps the dead find peace, and often reconciles with the living they have left behind.

Within the supernatural genre, the element of death is a given, although not always inevitable. The so-called gifts these women possess are widely accepted as real and substantial by characters within the primary utterance, although these gifts often cause the women conflict, both internal and with their loved ones, but they are always used for good. These series, nonetheless, accurately avoid going "outside the text" and forcing any hypotheses by which their realities would be representations of the natural world. Once again, they only *show to believe*—an act necessary for the text to function properly. They show a portion of a possible world, whose origins or complex value systems are mostly left unknown: what is known is the minimum indispensable to accept and appreciate the letter of the utterance.

Newer yet short-lived shows such as *Pushing Daisies* and *Reaper* (The CW: 2007–2009) pick up the experiences of the series just considered, but converge into a new tendency to steer drama toward forms akin to comedy. *Pushing Daisies* is particular in this sense, narrated as it is by a British-accented voice that often makes puns and rhymes and, consequently, sets itself apart from the cultural context of the show. But what pushes it even further from more regular drama is the tendency to mix different genres, even non-televisual ones (fairy tale, comics), to establish intertextual relations (including a strong relation with *Amélie*,[11] at various levels) and to introduce apparently absurd thematic elements, which expand on the surrealism of the initial conditions.

Real Discourses, Discourses on the Real

The preceding digression on how different televisual genres approach reality is necessary in order to understand how new comedy sets itself apart from them, and also to notice a certain progression in the modalities of representation of the real. This progression moves from representations that present themselves as transparent, but actually have very strong manipulatory features, to others, such as sitcom (as seen in chapter 1), which not only have no manipulatory intentions but go so far as to install certain mechanisms into the text to distance themselves from the represented reality.

With this study, I claim neither sitcom's ideologic innocence nor a lack of commitment on its part. The ideologic level pertains to a different plane from what has been considered here, and it is a fact that, often enough, American sitcom has been a carrier of discourses on very sensitive cultural and social matters: from racism to war, from intergenerational clashes to sexual identity. Even some less conspicuous shows may have had relevant roles as pressure valves, as fields of debate, as sources of inspiration. The public's mere need for laughter could not explain the success of a genre that remained for decades, if not unchanged, at least firmly anchored to its own productive principles.

After the end-of-century signs of change, the will to experiment is becoming more and more an evolutionary step, which can be explained with the need of comic genres to grow, overcoming their own stereotypes. The series I have analyzed show a capacity to move away from consolidated genres, while still linking back to them in peculiar ways — a reason that backs my choice — yet I am under no illusion that they form part of a homogeneous movement.

The Office and *The Comeback* show clear signs of a direct evolution in sitcom's narrative forms. Whereas sitcom embedded into a properly televisual enunciation an expressive form typical of a different medium, these two newer series stage the representation of properly televisual genres such as documentary and reality show.[12] Thus, while drama is generally a discourse on a certain kind of reality (whether or not coherent with the natural world), comedy continues to be a discourse on a representation of a certain reality. This is also true for *Scrubs,* although, as

8. Comedy and Reality

has been seen, its two enunciations are not subordinated to one another, but rather establish a freer relationship, often entangling their paths.

Freed from the link with the theatrical set and from the audience's projection into the text, comedy is able to enhance its expressive potential. There are more examples of comedy-oriented shows that tackled such a special relation with reality, yet with premises and outcomes quite different from those presented here. One of the best known and most successful cases is that of *Curb Your Enthusiasm*. Larry David plays himself as the main character in a world that borders between reality and fiction: the other characters, apart from several cameos, are all played by human actors. In each episode, David finds himself dealing with the consequences of misunderstandings he himself causes, and cannot — or largely does not want to — correct, challenging all his relationships, from his relationship with his wife (played by actress Cheryl Hines), to those with friends and colleagues.

It is not even necessary to ask the question of the reality or verisimilitude of the stories, or to know whether the empiric Larry David actually is an insensitive troublemaker. *Curb Your Enthusiasm* is not and does it want to be a biography. It will suffice to know that the basic premise of the show, which is the idea itself that the Larry David in the utterance will get confused with the Larry David who is part of the enunciative device, while on the other hand the former will set himself apart from the latter thanks to his placement into a largely fictional environment. Such a link to reality allows for a detachment and, once again, a non-literal understanding of uttered events, with modalities that are the opposite of those recognizable, for example, in reality show: while in the latter real actions take place in mostly fictitious (or artificial) settings, but with real effects, in *Curb Your Enthusiasm* fictional actions take place in conditions that are partly congruent with elements of the empiric world, with all but fictional results.

In the end, this case is different from those of the four shows examined in this book, because here it is a matter of reality lending a piece of itself to fiction, without creating embedded layers of enunciation. *Curb Your Enthusiasm* does not normally feature cameras in the utterance (whether visible or hidden), there are no narrating voices and the only element extraneous to the canon of televisual fiction is the raw quality of digital video. While the realistic elements of the show may hint to a strategy of *making believe,* the purely fictional elements reveal a higher-level strategy and declare the rules of the game.

Whereas traditional sitcom bases its own operation on the laugh track, an excellent admission of being fictional, which unveils the existence of an audience, a stage, a *mise en scène,* the new series move toward a different kind of reality effect. They shift their own boundaries with the world even as they navigate a broader shift of television production in general. Classic American televisual comedy is, as its name suggests, a comedy of *situations,* where the utterance itself provides solutions to the problems it creates. Once such solution is found, the curtain is drawn and the show can start again. Any references to an empiric context only serve the purpose of fueling the number of possible situations, but they have no existential effects on the show itself. Sitcom is a solid format, and the success of a single series does not depend on its audience understanding the way it functions.

On the other hand, new comedy engages in an open conflict — or at least in open interaction — with both this older model and the more general landscape of contemporary television. The emergence of reality-based television is the kind of phenomenon that comedy could not ignore. These new comedy series challenge and dismantle the very definition of reality-based television, and consequently find themselves in opposition to not only their serious counterparts, but also any kinds of productions that claim to be more realistic than fiction, but are actually less reliable than reality. On the one hand, classic drama stages possible worlds, which may or may not bear resemblance to the empiric one, but still tend to substitute it and not overlap with its realm. On the other, reality-based television pretends to be real, but is not real in either premise or fact. Comedy completes this triangle, admitting — or at least not denying — its fictional status.

Whether through a laugh track, or through the distancing mechanisms already considered, comedy seems to assume a higher point of view. I do not want to assert comedy's moral or aesthetic superiority, which, as any other televisual and artistic genre, may suffer from its own productive conditions, but the analysis thus far conducted gives a clear idea of a genre, or a macro-genre, that *is able to* or *cannot but have* a more lucid gaze on its cultural and media context.

Meta-Comedy, Anti-Comedy

What I have considered in regard to sitcom has led me to conclude that what the text of a sitcom does is to show the staging of a comedy. This entails not only a multiplication of enunciative levels, but also a splitting of the roles (actantial and thematic) attributed to the characters in the utterance. An analysis of sitcom should not underestimate the fact that characters are involved in both an interaction among themselves (within the secondary utterance) and, as part of the device of the uttered enunciation, in an interaction with the audience. The possibility for the action to be modified according to the audience's reactions should not be considered as an imperfection of the text, that is, an exception to the transparency of the enunciative devices (assuming, but not granted that such transparency be the norm), but rather an important marker of their complexity. From a semiotic point of view, such presumed imperfection is a distinctive trait of this textual genre, which thus overtly shows its own nature. This does not exclude the possibility of still enjoying sitcom in a naïve or superficial way. One might have a perfectly satisfying experience considering the acting and the story as the only possible utterance within the text. Yet, structural complexity guarantees the potential for different kinds of enjoyment. While this analysis does not directly focus on the different modalities in which texts are enjoyed, it can definitely take into account the different possibilities envisioned by the texts themselves.

This does not work with newer series. As I suggested in chapter 6, concerning genre relationships, these shows address the issue of comedy in quite different ways. Sitcom shows a comic device without necessarily constituting a discourse *on* comedy. Any references to comic shows from the past serve as back-links to a shared culture, and are actually used more often by more recent series. When the genre was younger, such intertextual references were made to different portions of culture — not only mass culture, as cinema could do. Remarkable are the frequent references to classic mythology made in series such as *Bewitched*.[13] But while sitcom represented a world that was comic by definition, and whose theatricality it openly admitted, the newer shows prefer providing a comic version of a certain reality. Better yet, they show certain portions of reality (not unlike what happens in drama, but with different enunciative structures) highlighting their ridiculous—yet not necessarily euphoric—aspects.

Such perspective on reality exists thanks to the application of the considered enunciative mechanisms, which thus assume a different relevance from those adopted by sitcom. In *Scrubs*, JD's voice may not be responsible for the filmic enunciation, but its presence gives the filmic utterance meaning effects it would not otherwise possess. The filmic utterance is modified *according to* the verbal enunciation. The fantasy inserts acquire a large part of their meaning thanks to JD's voice. The knowledge JD provides about himself and the world in his monologs justifies the constant shift away from a naturalistic representation of the reality he experiences.

Paradoxically, JD's voice makes the fantasy sequences, although objectively surreal, almost more realistic than reality itself, or at least representative of a level of access to reality normally not practicable. The comic aspect of such reality emerges not so much because of the peculiar tone of the footage, but because of the verbal enunciation's comedic activity, which is, however, far from being a fact. JD's obsession with comedy is not a need to entertain (as is Michael Scott's), but a tension toward the integration of comedy into everyday life, where comedy would otherwise be confined to a purely fictional plane. JD *sees* his own reality through the lens his passion for comedy provides him, and *cannot but show* his reality through the same lens.

Hence, in *Scrubs*, represented reality and comedy are fused together, and become each other's condition of existence. Reality exists (or, in a way, it can be sustained and survived) thanks to the lens of comedy, which in turn is an aspect of reality itself: not only a way to represent and understand it, but a way to live it.

In the cases of *The Office* and *The Comeback*, despite several distinctive elements, the texts discursivize not a representation of reality but one of a second discursive device, which in turn represents one reality. Unlike in sitcom, whose uttered enunciation was a properly fictional device (the staged action), these two shows' secondary enunciations have another kind of relationship with the reality to which they refer. As seen, also the link to comedy changes in regard to *Scrubs,* and particularly so

8. Comedy and Reality

in *The Comeback,* where comedy (and specifically sitcom) is a job, a way to earn one's living, a possible path to success.

Comedy in *The Office* has a very different role from the one it plays in *Scrubs.* Michael Scott does not recognize comedy's existential role, but considers it an instrument of self-recognition. From a thematic point of view, the character of Michael Scott is the opposite of that of JD, both with regard to his hierarchical position (which, at least at the beginnings of *Scrubs,* makes JD more likable the more he is mistreated by his superiors) and because the comedic abilities he attributes to himself are nothing but a denial of his current life conditions. As much as Michael considers comedy a form of entertainment, he administers it to others almost like a punishment, undermining its foundations and inverting its meaning.

The Office might become, consequently, a form of anti-comedy, such as *Curb Your Enthusiasm* might also be, if not for the peculiar way in which the camera crosses the boundaries between enunciation and utterance, entering the narrative structure as more than just a simple observing subject, but also as an interlocutor (voiceless, formally invisible, but nonetheless capable of acts of communication), ultimately responsible for the transformation of meaning. It is important to differentiate between the camera as an actor (hence the montage as a realized mode of its action) from the enunciative device, which in turn remains always a logical entity. The camera's proper filmic act, joined with the declaration of its presence within the utterance, highlights the show's peculiarity as opposed not only to sitcom but also to the other shows considered here: this act is not a camera caught in the act of filming, as it may be in *The Comeback,* but rather the camera is an instrument of the enunciative act.

The paradox created here lies in the presumed transparency of the device (flattened in favor of the utterance), in the mistaken impression of its ontological unity, which, while allowing once again a multi-level fruition, plays on the possible equivocations. The comic effect stems from the awareness of the illusory character of such transparency, and from the need to shift the focalization one step back.

The Comeback deploys a similar kind of transparency, but its referenced reality is largely a self-reflection. The camera is, in this case, not an actor, but an instrument; it does not directly take part in the enunciation, if not in the form of a display of the device, at once wanted (by the enunciation) and undesired (in the utterance). Hence, the object of representation is not the filmic act but the conditions of its production. At the same time, though, a correspondence is established between Valerie Cherish's struggle for the realization of her own narrative programs and the discursivization of the text's possible modes of existence — in this case, those of the reality show as a fictional text.

The flattening, in this case, is not in favor of a realized text, but rather of its actualization, whose role in the represented world is unclear. No one knows who the receiver of the raw footage is: certainly not a regular television audience (given the scarcity of the paratext and the presence of undesired elements) and barely someone involved in the production (someone who, in turn, might not even need the introduction screen). This hints at the possibility that this phase of the reality show is only a syntagmatic hypothesis, never actually realized in the uttered world.

Ugly Betty stages yet another world, where comedy might indeed be a lens through which reality can be observed, but this reality has already been filtered through an adhesion to a different textual genre. The genre of telenovela has, from the start, access to certain cultural contexts and their systems of values, and is given precise textual boundaries — those that soap opera lacks. The comic coating *Ugly Betty* adds to telenovela highlights even more the exaggeration of some of the genre's typical traits, without necessarily devaluing its ability to represent portions of the world.

And the mark of the empiric world, in *Ugly Betty,* lies not in the likelihood of certain events (which, if taken singularly, might even be plausible), but rather in the possibility of recognizing certain narrative mechanisms, in terms of deep semantic oppositions. Comedy is the glue that allows the series — anything but an accumulation of situations, but rather one single narrative progression — to sustain the full load of such oppositions, no matter how extreme such a load might become.

Hypothesis of an Evolution

In the end, new American comedy shows a clear fracture with other forms of televisual narratives, both past and contemporary. On the one

8. Comedy and Reality

hand, drama follows a few communication precepts that could be linked back to classic forms of film, where the enunciative device was intentionally hidden, masked, to give the illusion of its absence. In classic film, revealing the device — which, as Metz warns, is seldom a genuine act and more often a way to show *one* device, not *the* device — is by definition an extraordinary event, a violation of the rules of the game and of the *making believe* that sustains such genres in film and television.

On the contrary, new comedy does not fear exposing its own device, but rather confirms its existence over and over through its multiplication. It is true, however, that even in this case, the devices shown produce not the primary text, but rather those it embeds, which end up coinciding with the main text to the extent that they occupy its entire space and time of representation. Comedy becomes then a gaze onto reality — *one* chosen reality, or several hierarchical reality levels, among which, not last in importance, lies the reality of television production itself. Although in different forms, the series here analyzed acquire a metadiscursive attitude that is anything but occasional, as opposed to certain nonstandard episodes of shows such as *ER* (NBC: 1994–2009) or *M*A*S*H* (CBS: 1972–1983).

John Caldwell refers to an episode of *M*A*S*H* where a (naturally fictitious) crew is shooting a documentary in the field hospital in which the show is set, and to an *ER* episode shot and broadcast entirely live, once again through the documentary expedient.[14] Rather than incursions of television into reality, these are incursions of television into television, not too different from episode 417 of *Scrubs*. The difference, substantial in the case of *ER*, is that such episodes are completely exceptional: while they do challenge each show's modal investment, they never really undermine its premise. On the contrary, "My Life in Four Cameras" falls right into the communication perspective typical of *Scrubs,* and exists thanks to the development of discursive and narrative traits consolidated throughout the previous seasons.

If reality-based television discursivizes a *squared reality,* reality as hyper-represented by new comedy gains one extra dimension and becomes almost a *cubed reality.*[15]

Traditional televisual narratives — including sitcom, due to the fossilization of its expressive form and to the progressive loss of value of its being a represented representation — show a cancellation of the distance between signifier and signified, so much so that the only meaning of what can be seen *is* what is shown. New comedy reopens this divide, overtly signaling it, but does anything but create a conflict: the meaning of what is shown must be found in the act itself of showing, which turns the gaze *of* the device *onto* the device in a critical act and necessary condition of the existence of the audience's critical gaze.

Far from denying all semiotic devices, all this confirms and reinforces the text's central role in providing a semiotic definition of televisual communication. Communication, that is interaction whose receiver is eventually called to reconstruct the text's production and signification processes — particularly so in the case of a medium whose production and reception acts, while not perfectly coinciding, bear a strong resemblance, since the spectator sees what has already been seen.

I must underscore and affirm, once again, the text's self-awareness, which must not be confused with the presumed awareness of the actors in the utterance about textual mechanisms. The latter is largely artificial, partly a simulacrum of textual awareness, its discursivization, a rhetorical game that confirms the fluidity of the relationship between enunciation and utterance, historically meant as simple presupposition of the former by the latter.

By revealing the centrality of the role of enunciative mechanisms in the development of the comic process, I have aimed to demonstrate that such relationship is in fact often more complex than one might foresee, and should not be taken for granted. Texts, as well as discursive and narrative forms, show that numerous and largely unforeseen possibilities for evolution still exist, and that it is necessary — inevitable, even — for semiotic theory to evolve with them.

Glossary

actant. *See* narrative program.

actor. Strictly speaking, an actor is defined as the union of at least one actantial role (*See also* narrative program) and at least one thematic role (a culturally defined, stereotypical role), which are susceptible to transformation within a text. Actors also possess individual qualities that make them unique, such as proper names and specific physical and psychological features.

The concept of *actor* only partly overlaps with that of *character,* and has a wider scope than the latter. This may create misunderstandings when applying semiotic analysis to the performing arts, where actors are the empiric people who play a certain character, which is why in many cases throughout this book the term *character* has been used instead of the more semiotically accurate *actor.*

actorialization. *See* discursivization.

aspect. The syntactic components of the discursive levels (actors, space and time) are normally described in their *aspect,* that is their quality as processes, as detected by an observer actant. Temporal aspect can be articulated among several categories, such as *inchoativity/terminativity* (the initial or final phase of a process), *punctuality/durativity* (an instantaneous action or a process in development), *singularity/iterativity* (a once-only event or a series), *perfectivity/imperfectivity* (a process being accomplished or not).

The aspectual categories of space (such as *perspective, direction, high/low*) and actors (the most conspicuous of which is *individual/collective*) clearly depend on the presence of an observer.

The process by which the enunciation applies such qualities to the elements of discourse is called *aspectualization.*

axiology. *See* thymia.

character. *See* actor.

discursivization. The procedure by which, through operations of disengagement and engagement, the enunciation moves from the semio-narrative structures to the discursive structures of a text. Its components are *actorialization, spatialization* and *temporalization*.

disengagement. The mechanism by which an enunciative device or instance (*See also* enunciation) installs, within the utterance it produces, subjects other than itself, as well as spaces and times different from those in which it operates. Such installations are cases of actantial, spatial and temporal disengagement. The inverse process, by which the enunciation denies an utterative instance and resumes its original actantial, temporal and spatial position is called *engagement*.

Verbal semiotics makes a distinction between *enunciative* and *utterative* disengagement. The former occurs when simulacrums of the enunciation are installed within the discourse, such as in the case of first-person speech. The latter occurs when the actors of the utterance are different from those of the enunciation, such as in third-person speech.

Things are more complicated in cases of non-verbal or syncretic semiotic systems, such as audiovisual media, where the enunciation is, by definition, largely impersonal. However, when a text makes it pertinent, it is possible to highlight a distinction between enunciative and utterative disengagements, despite the lack of pronominal deixis. Examples can be found in chapters 3 and 4 of this book.

dysphoria. *See* thymia.

engagement. *See* disengagement.

enunciation. In structural semiotics, enunciation is not the pragmatic, empiric act by which a subject produces an utterance, but the traces of such production within a text, as logically presupposed by an utterance. It is the logic instance of an abstract I/here/now that disengages (*See* disengagement) all possible subjects, spaces and times within the text.

While the concept dates back to a theory of semiotics strictly bound to linguistics and focused on the study of aesthetic verbal texts — thus implying a certain degree of the enunciation's personalization and psychological characterization. The expansion of the theory to non-verbal and non-aesthetic texts, as well as to syncretic systems, has made a revision necessary.

Christian Metz's (1995) formulation of the concepts of impersonal enunciation and enunciative device (according to which there is, in some cases, no "I," hence no "subject" of enunciation) can be seen, in this regard, not as an introduction of a special case, limited to cinematic and audiovisual texts, but as a more general approach to the theory of enunciation, of which the classic theory is but a subset.

euphoria. *See* thymia.

generative trajectory of meaning. The theoretical construct that describes the immanent conditions of meaning, independent of a text's level of manifestation — that is, the semiotic system in which it is expressed. Meaning generates from a more abstract layer called semio-narrative structures, further divided into a deep and a superficial level. The enunciative device is in charge of transposing the semio-narrative structures to the more concrete layer of the discursive structures. *See also* discursivization.

isotopy. The redundancy and repetition of minimal elements of meaning that allow for a homogeneous and univocal reading of a certain text. The possibility for a text to carry out several contrasting isotopic networks (which may generate effects of deceit) is one of the basic semiotic devices available to humor and comedy.

modalization. The attribution to subjects of basic semantic determinations, called *modalities*. There are modalities of *being* and modalities of *doing*. Subjects can be modalized by *wanting, having to (do or be), knowing* and *being able to (do or be)*. Modalities of doing affect action programs, while modalities of being affect subjects' passions and states.

narrative program. The abstract description of the logic operations underlying a certain narrative and the relationship among the subjects involved. These subjects operate toward the fulfillment of goals, called *objects of value*. Narrative programs exist, in the generative process of meaning, at the surface level of semio-narrative structures. The subjects involved are abstractions of the actors, which are entities involved at the discursive level. Such abstractions are called *actants*. The actant charged with a certain narrative program is the *subject,* while the *sender* and the *receiver* are, respectively, the actant who charges the subject with a certain program and the ultimate beneficiary (intended or actual) of the subject's actions. *Helper* and *opponent* are two more kinds of actantial roles.

A single actor can cover multiple actantial roles (for example, subject and receiver; this is a case of actantial syncretism); multiple actors can cover a single actantial role (for example, there can be several helpers, or even several subjects).

narrative schema. All narrative programs can be articulated in four stages that together constitute the narrative schema. These stages are: *manipulation,* in which a sender invests a subject with a certain narrative program; *competence,* in which the subject is modalized (*See also* modalization) as the narrative program requires; *performance,* in which the subject operates transformations on the state of things; and *sanction,* in which the sender judges the subject's performance according to the contract inscribed in the manipulation stage. The narrative schema is often called *canonical* because it can be generalized to all narrative texts.

narrative trajectory. The logical organization of narrative programs (*See* narrative program), chained together in hypotactic relationships, so that every narrative program presupposes or is presupposed by another.

sanction. See narrative schema.

syncretic system. A syncretic system is one in which several semiotic systems operate at the level of manifestation. Television and cinema are the two examples most pertinent to this book. Performing arts in general are often manifested by syncretic systems, such as theater and opera. Even oral communication is not limited to verbal components, but "also includes paralinguistic elements (such as gestures and proxemics), as well as sociolinguistic ones, etc." ("Syncrétisme," Greimas and Courtés).

thymia. The thymic category is articulated in the opposition between/ *euphoria* and *dysphoria,* a fundamental step in the development of axiologies from semantic micro-universes. By connoting certain semantic elements as euphoric and connoting as dysphoric those pertaining to the opposite deixis (obtained by contrariety and denial), a text "attributes positive and/or negative values to each term of the elementary structure of meaning" ("Thymique," Greimas and Courtés).

value. *See* narrative program, thymia.

Glossary

utterance. The resulting state of an enunciative act, regardless of its length or its nature in terms of substance of expression.

veridiction. The veridictive category is the correlation between the oppositions *being/not being* and *seeming/not seeming,* used to express judgments about the relationship between an utterance and its referent. In classic theory, the conjunctions between different states of the veridictive category produce statements of *truth* (*being* and *seeming*), *secret* (*being* and *not seeming*), *lie* (*seeming* and *not being*) and *falsehood* (*not seeming* and *not being*).

Chapter Notes

Introduction

1. John Hartley, "Textual Analysis," *Television Studies*, ed. Toby Miller (London: British Film Institute, 2002) 30.
2. Maria Pia Pozzato, introduction, *Variazioni semiotiche. Analisi, interpretazioni, metodi a confronto*, by Guido Ferraro, Valentina Pisanty and Maria Pia Pozzato (Roma: Carocci, 2007) 9–16.
3. Umberto Eco, *Lector in fabula* (Milano: Bompiani, 1979) 24–25.
4. Maria Pia Pozzato, *Semiotica del testo* (Roma: Carocci, 2001) 283. The author dedicates a whole chapter to semiotics and television that is not aimed at the analysis of fictional texts. She explicitly mentions the lack of semiotic approaches to such texts and cites only one "pioneer study" on the subject, dating back to the previous decade: Pier Luigi Basso, Omar Calabrese, Francesco Marsciani and Orsola Mattioli, *Le passioni nel serial TV* (Torino: Nuova ERI, 1994).
5. Gianfranco Marrone, *Estetica del telegiornale. Identità di testata e stili comunicativi* (Roma: Meltemi, 1998); Maria Pia Pozzato, ed., *Linea a Belgrado. La comunicazione giornalistica in tv durante la guerra per il Kosovo* (Roma: RAI-ERI, 2000); Cristina Demaria, Luisa Grosso and Lucio Spaziante, *Reality TV. La televisione ai confini della realtà* (Roma: RAI-ERI, 2002); Antonio Savorelli, "CNN Breaking News: 11 settembre 2001," *Leader, oracoli, assassini. Analisi semiotica dell'informazione*, ed. Maria Pia Pozzato (Roma: Carocci, 2004) 169–187.
6. Maria Pia Pozzato and Giorgio Grignaffini, eds., *Mondi Seriali. Percorsi semiotici nella fiction* (Milano: RTI, 2008).
7. Giovanna Cosenza, "Perché *The O.C.* non ha funzionato? Trionfi e cadute della fiction per adolescenti," in Pozzato and Grignaffini 277–291.
8. Isabella Pezzini, "Uno sguardo trasversale sulla fiction italiana. Il caso *Boris*," in Pozzato and Grignaffini 187–196.
9. Pezzini 187.
10. "Forme (Form)," "Matière (Purport)," "Substance," Algirdas Julien Greimas and Joseph Courtés, *Sémiotique. Dictionnaire raisonné de la théorie du langage* (Paris: Hachette, 1979).
11. "Acteur (Actor)," "Personnage (Character)," Greimas and Courtés.
12. *Sex and the City* was, indeed, based on the articles of a real-life sex columnist, eventually collected into a book: Candace Bushnell, *Sex and the City* (New York: Warner, 1996).

Chapter 1

1. *The American Heritage Dictionary*, 1994 ed.
2. "Situation comedy," *Encyclopædia Britannica Online*, 2009. Encyclopædia Britannica, 1 Nov. 2009 <http://www.britannica.com/EBchecked/topic/667010/situation-comedy>.
3. Brett Mills, *Television Sitcom* (London: British Film Institute, 2005) 50.
4. Aristotle, *Poetics* 1.5.1. The translation is mine.
5. "Comedy," *The American Heritage Dictionary*.
6. As will be shown, it is a reality effect and not the actual reality of production, which is far from improvised.
7. Disagreements between Suzanne Somers, production, and co-stars led, at first, to the marginalization of the character Chrissy Snow, then ultimately to her removal from the show.
8. Not remembering details of Chandler's personality, such as what his job is or whether he wears glasses, is a running gag

Chapter Notes

in *Friends*, where Chandler's predilection for nervous humor serves both as a defense mechanism and as a way to stand out in a world that tends not to notice him. This also constitutes an element of self-awareness, which places *Friends* at a more mature stage of sitcom evolution, in tune with newer shows.

9. The grandmother, whose death has already been called, wakes up for a few seconds, then "dies again" — hence the title of the episode, "The One Where Nana Dies Twice" (*Friends*, 108).

10. Joanne Morreale, "Sitcoms Say Good-bye: the Cultural Spectacle of *Seinfeld*'s Last Episode," *Critiquing Sitcom*, ed. Joanne Morreale (Syracuse: Syracuse University Press, 2003) 274–285.

11. This is a properly semiotic distance, different from the more cognitive, perceptive distance Brett Mills sees in sitcom, where "characters [...] don't know they're being watched" (an arguable statement, considering that the live performance has an impact on the characters' behaviors, which a semiotic approach cannot fail to consider), as opposed to newer series like *The Office* (the British original in Mills's example), which "presents us with laughable characters without distancing us from their actions" (Mills 64). As I will discuss in chapter 4, *The Office* (the British and the American versions both function in a similar way in this respect) maintains, from a strictly semiotic point of view, a form of distance between utterance and intended receiver — only, implemented in a very different way from sitcom's at the discursive level and for what concerns the structure of enunciation.

12. NBC used this slogan for more than twenty years, starting in 1982, to indicate its Thursday-night comedy schedule, but then extended it to some of its non-comic programming.

Chapter 2

1. Dr. Kelso had forbidden this wish being granted, considering that a heavy-metal song would clash with the hospital's decorum. The title of the episode, although containing an improper usage as a noun of the verb *meddle*, makes a homophone of the American pronunciation of *heavy metal*.

2. The four members are, in real life, an actual a cappella group called The Blanks. In the show, their appearances are sources of various references to American television culture. For example, in "My Hero" (123) the group sings cartoon themes, while in a later episode Ted announces they have moved to themes from prime-time shows — which in the United States can also mean sitcoms.

3. The DVDs do show titles for episodes used as special features, namely those with audio commentary by actors or by the series creator, Bill Lawrence. In such cases, the DVD submenu indicates the exact titles, while the main menus identify episodes only by their progressive numbers.

4. Not to forget, of course, that the title of the reality show is, in turn, a reference to George Orwell's *1984*. However, it must be noted that Dan Dorian, JD's big brother, is no Big Brother — thus the connection may be lost in favor of a more general wordplay.

5. *O Brother, Where Art Thou?*, dir. Joel and Ethan Coen, perf. George Clooney, John Turturro, Tim Blake Nelson, John Goodman, Holly Hunter, and Charles Durning, Touchstone Pictures, 2000.

6. *My Best Friend's Wedding*, dir. P.J. Hogan, perf. Julia Roberts, Dermot Mulroney, Cameron Diaz, Rupert Everett, and Philip Bosco, TriStar Pictures, 1997.

7. Such appearances are usually cameos played by distinguished television and film actors who create a tight network of intertextual links: Dr. Kevin Casey was played by Michael J. Fox; Julie Keaton by Heather Locklear, Fox's costar in *Spin City*, which, like *Scrubs*, was created by Bill Lawrence; Neena Broderick was played by Julianna Margulies, who also played nurse Carol Hathaway in *ER*; Ben Sullivan by Brendan Fraser; Harvey Corman by Richard Kind, another *Spin City* star. Examples abound, as usual.

8. Although traditional sitcom can present this trait, the most extreme example of a certain "short memory" of details can be found in animated series like *Tom and Jerry*,

where the effects of a given action are almost always erased by the next sequence, and the final results of any episode (including the "death" of a character) have no influence on the next. In fact, such animated series lack the concept of a next episode, since each of them exists in a time and space that is limited, enclosed and completely autonomous.

9. Qtd. in Christian Metz, *L'énonciation impersonnelle, ou le site du film* (Paris: Klincksieck, 1991) 45.

10. Metz, *L'énonciation* 47.

Chapter 3

1. An appropriate example would be *Extras*, one of Gervais and Merchant's creations, whose first season was imported to the United States culturally "untranslated" in 2005, and whose second season was co-produced by HBO.

2. Christian Metz, *Essais sur la signification au cinéma (Tome II)* (Paris: Klincksieck, 1972).

3. Metz, *Essais* 117.

4. This shot does not seem to come from any specific episode, but is likely to be taken from the deleted scenes for episode 201, "The Dundies." The title of the episode refers to the trophies Michael awards his employees every year. With this event, he would like to hold a homemade version of the Oscars ceremony, of which he always ends up being the undisputed protagonist.

Chapter 4

1. Metz, *L'énonciation* 95–97.

2. James Friedman, ed., *Reality Squared: Televisual Discourse on the Real* (New Brunswick: Rutgers University Press, 2002).

3. James Burrows has directed several television shows, including episodes of *The Mary Tyler Moore Show* and *Laverne & Shirley* (ABC: 1976–1983); 237 of the 269 episodes of *Cheers*; several episodes of *Frasier*; the pilot episode (among others) of *Friends*; and also 163 of the 186 episodes of *Will & Grace*, among them the series finale.

4. Not irrelevant is an incident that casts a very bad light on the sitcom's writers: upon learning that the writers stay up until late to rewrite scenes, one night Valerie decides to bake cookies and bring them to the studios, as a sign of appreciation. When she arrives, through the windows she sees Paulie G. miming sexual intercourse with one of the assistant writers, who is wearing a red T-shirt on his head, which stands for Valerie's red hair. Despite being visibly shocked, Valerie decides she will not take offense and to consider it a way for the writers to joke around to blow off some steam (episode 6).

Chapter 5

1. *The Devil Wears Prada*, dir. David Frankel, perf. Anne Hathaway, Meryl Streep, Emily Blunt, Stanley Tucci, Simon Baker, Adrian Grenier and Daniel Sunjata, 20th Century–Fox, 2006.

2. In some countries, Italy among them, "Swag" was aired as originally produced and in the intended order, thus without the flashback mechanism and all scenes from the modified version. As such, its structure is nothing too different from that of all regular episodes.

3. Bizarro is Superman's imperfect clone. While trying to emulate his original, his imperfection leads him to commit evil acts. He lives in a sort of inverted-value world; hence, he is often invoked in comedy, as well as in everyday language, in reference to a state of things that is contrary to reality or common sense.

4. What is called Fashion TV early in the show is eventually renamed Fashion Buzz. This is probably due to copyright issues: the DVD edition of *Ugly Betty*'s season one bleeps out any mention of Fashion TV.

Chapter 6

1. An examination of the issues related to the definition of *genre*, with particular attention to televisual texts, can be found in Pier Luigi Basso's "Intorno ai generi mass-mediatici" (Basso *et al.* 25–46).

2. In the 2003-2004 season, *Frasier* and *Friends* (both aired on NBC), were, respectively, in their eleventh and tenth seasons, thus becoming two of the longest and most successful series in the history of American television.

3. This border can be found at the site of sexuality, seen, on the one hand, in *Sex and the City*'s extreme ease in dealing with sexual themes, and, on the other, in the presence of explicitly gay people among the main characters in *Will & Grace,* which declared from the outset this show's commitment to such issues. Along this border we also find *Ellen* (NBC: 1994–1998), *Friends* and, in a way, the more classic sitcom *Three's Company.*

4. The character's name, Charles James, is in itself a homage to *Cheers,* having been derived from the names of the show's creators, Glen and Les Charles and James Burrows.

5. In reality, however, the DVD edition of the fourth season of *Scrubs* does not suppress the first voice, which loses its reason to exist due to the lack of an actual commercial break.

6. I will return later to the issues of what is reality-based and how such a concept assumes different forms not only in regard to the evolution of the televisual medium but also at any specific point in its history.

Chapter 7

1. *You Kill Me,* dir. John Dahl, perf. Ben Kingsley, Téa Leoni, Luke Wilson and Dennis Farina, IFC Films, 2007.

2. *2001: A Space Odyssey,* dir. Stanley Kubrick, perf. Keir Dullea, Gary Lockwood, William Sylvester, Daniel Richter, Leonard Rossiter and Douglas Rain, Metro-Goldwin-Mayer, 1968.

Chapter 8

1. *Prime time* was transposed into Italian television lingo as *prima serata,* which literally means early night. It is an obvious case of mistranslation due to a false friend between the two languages, which loses any reference to the value of the relevant audience and airtime, and consequently to the quality of the programming. Over the years, the start of the Italian *prima serata* has been pushed progressively later; it currently starts at 9:00 or 9:30 P.M.

2. Pozzato, *Leader* 34.

3. Savorelli 176–179.

4. Friedman 7.

5. John Caldwell, "Prime-time fiction theorizes the docu-real," in Friedman 272.

6. *The Truman Show,* dir. Peter Weir, perf. Jim Carrey, Laura Linney, Ed Harris, Noah Emmerich and Natascha McElhone, Paramount Pictures, 1998.

7. This is the case not only because the text is subject to an undefined number of interpretations (Eco, *Lector* 56–69; "Clôture [Closing]," Greimas and Courtés), but also due to the difficulty in ascribing it physical boundaries.

8. Salman Rushdie, *Step Across This Line. Collected Non-Fiction, 1992–2002* (London: Vintage, 2003) 379.

9. Pozzato, *Semiotica* 224.

10. Qtd. in Friedman 6.

11. *Le Fabuleux Destin d'Amélie Poulain,* dir. Jean-Pierre Jeunet, perf. Audrey Tautou, Mathieu Kassovitz, Rufus, Claire Maurier, Isabelle Nanty, Dominique Pinon, Serge Merlin, Jamel Debbouze, Arthus de Pengerne and Maurice Bénichou, UGC, 2001.

12. There certainly exists a cinematic form of documentary, but the expressive modes employed in *The Office*— from the use of very narrow shots to the agility of movements — reference a typically televisual form.

13. These changes in citation sources may be indications of changes in the cultural context and in the audience's shared imagery, rather than the genre's intention to self-legitimize.

14. Caldwell, in Friedman 265, 277.

15. *Reality Squared,* the title of the collection of essays edited by James Friedman, is in fact a reference to the "squaring" of reality as operated by the television screen, but it does create a mathematical pun — as if the televisual eye gave reality a

second dimension of existence. Thus, the idea can be expanded to include a third dimension by which television can look not only at the world, but also at the world *as represented* by some other form of televisual expression.

Bibliography

1. Some episodes are marked with two episode numbers: the first is the airing progression, as used in the text; the second is the production code, which follows the order in which episodes have been produced. The distinction is not relevant for all series.

Bibliography

Works Consulted

Ace, Goodman. "Of Glamour, Grammar and Good Times Gone," *Television Quarterly* 30.2 (Fall 1999): 11–14.

Aristotle. Poetics. "Περὶ Ποιητικῆς." *Wikisource.* 24 Sept. 2009, 13:45 UTC. 9 Nov. 2009. <http://bit.ly/925zSi>.

Aumont, Jacques, and Michel Marie. *L'Analyse des films.* Paris: Editions Nathan, 1988.

Auster, Albert. "Much Ado About Nothing: Some Final Thoughts on Seinfeld," *Television Quarterly* 29.4 (Fall 1998): 24–33.

Basso, Pier Luigi. "Intorno ai generi mass mediatici." Basso *et al.* 25–46.

_____, Omar Calabrese, Francesco Marsciani and Orsola Mattioli. *Le passioni nel serial TV.* Turin: Nuova ERI, 1994.

Brook, Vincent. *Something Ain't Kosher Here: The Rise of the "Jewish" Sitcom.* New Brunswick, N.J.: Rutgers University Press, 2003.

Brunschwig, Jacques and Geoffrey E.R. Lloyd, eds. *Le Savoir grec.* Paris: Flammarion, 1996.

Buonanno, Milly. *Le formule del racconto televisivo. La sovversione del tempo nelle narrative seriali.* Florence: Sansoni, 2004.

Bushnell, Candace. *Sex and the City.* New York: Warner, 1996.

Caldwell, John. "Prime-Time Fiction Theorizes the Docu-real." In Friedman, ed., *Reality Squared*, 259–292.

Campbell, Sean. *The Sitcoms of Norman Lear.* Jefferson, N.C.: McFarland & Company, 2007.

Cardini, Daniela. *La lunga serialità televisiva.* Rome: Carocci, 2004.

Casey, Bernadette, Neil Casey, Ben Calvert, Liam French and Justin Lewis. *Television Studies: The Key Concepts.* 2nd ed. London and New York: Routledge, 2008.

Casetti, Francesco. *Dentro lo sguardo. Il film e il suo spettatore.* Milan: Bompiani, 1986.

_____, and Federico di Chio. *Analisi della televisione. Strumenti, metodi e pratiche di ricerca.* Milan: Bompiani, 1998.

_____, ed. *L'immagine al plurale. Serialità e ripetizione nel cinema e nella televisione.* Venice: Marsilio, 1984.

Ceriani, Giulia. *Il senso del ritmo. Pregnanza e regolazione di un dispositivo fondamentale.* Rome: Meltemi, 2003.

Chion, Michel. *Le Son au cinéma.* Paris: Ed. de l'Etoile—Cahiers du Cinéma, 1985.

"*The Comeback* (2005)." *The Internet Movie Database.* 1 March 2010 <http://www.imdb.com/title/tt0434672/>.

Cosenza, Giovanna. "Perché *The O.C.* non ha funzionato? Trionfi e cadute della fiction per adolescenti." Pozzato and Grignaffini, eds., *Mondi seriali*, 277–291.

Creeber, Glen, Toby Miller and John Tulloch, eds. *The Television Genre Book.* London: British Film Institute, 2001.

"*CSI: Crime Scene Investigation* 'A Space Oddity' (2009)." *The Internet Movie Database.* 1 March 2010 <http://www.imdb.com/title/tt1280103/>.

"*CSI: Crime Scene Investigation* 'You Kill Me' (2007)." *The Internet Movie Database.* 1 March 2010 <http://www.imdb.com/title/tt1143237/>.

Danesi, Marcel. *The Quest for Meaning: A Guide to Semiotic Theory and Practice.*

Bibliography

Toronto: University of Toronto Press, 2007.

Dayan, Daniel, and Elihu Katz. *Media Events: The Live Broadcasting of History*. Cambridge, Mass.: Harvard University Press, 1992.

Demaria, Cristina, Luisa Grosso and Lucio Spaziante. *Reality TV. La televisione ai confini della realtà*. Rome: RAI-ERI, 2002.

The Devil Wears Prada. Dir. David Frankel. Perf. Anne Hathaway, Meryl Streep, Emily Blunt, Stanley Tucci, Simon Baker, Adrian Grenier and Daniel Sunjata. 20th Century–Fox, 2006.

Dusi, Nicola. "Replicabilità audiovisiva." Dusi and Spaziante, eds., *Remix-Remake*, 95–154.

_____, and Lucio Spaziante, eds. *Remix-Remake. Pratiche di replicabilità*. Rome: Meltemi, 2006.

Eco, Umberto. *Kant e l'ornitorinco*. Milan: Bompiani, 1997.

_____. *Lector in fabula*. Milan: Bompiani, 1979.

_____. "Tipologia della ripetizione." Casetti, ed., *L'immagine al plurale*, 19–35.

Eisner, Joel, and David Krinsky. *Television Comedy Series: An Episode Guide to 153 TV Sitcoms in Syndication*. Jefferson, N.C.: McFarland & Company, 1984.

Fabbri, Paolo. *Elogio di Babele*. Rome: Meltemi, 2000.

_____. *La svolta semiotica*. Rome and Bari: Laterza, 1998.

Le Fabuleux Destin d'Amélie Poulain. Dir. Jean-Pierre Jeunet. Perf. Audrey Tautou, Mathieu Kassovitz, Rufus, Claire Maurier, Isabelle Nanty, Dominique Pinon, Serge Merlin, Jamel Debbouze, Arthus de Pengerne and Maurice Bénichou. UGC, 2001.

Ferraro, Guido. "*Matrix*: l'anomalia e il sistema." Dusi and Spaziante, eds., *Remix-Remake*, 279–300.

Ferraro, Guido, Cecilia Gallotti, Laura Rolle and Alessandra Scaglioni. *Uno sguardo in camera. Materiali per l'analisi del linguaggio televisivo*. Milan: Cooperativa Libraria IULM, 2000.

Ferraro, Guido, Valentina Pisanty and Maria Pia Pozzato. *Variazioni semiotiche. Analisi, interpretazioni, metodi a confronto*. Rome: Carocci, 2007.

Feuer, Jane. "Situation comedy, Part 2." Creeber *et al.*, eds., *The Television Genre Book*, 67, 69–70.

Fontanille, Jacques. "Des simulacres de l'énonciation à la praxis énonciative," *Semiotica* 99.1/2 (1994): 185–197.

_____. *Sémiotique du discours*. Limoges: PULIM, 1998.

Friedman, James, ed. *Reality Squared. Televisual Discourse on the Real*. New Brunswick, N.J.: Rutgers University Press, 2002.

Friend, Tad. "The Paper Chase. Office Life in Two Worlds" *The New Yorker*. 11 Dec. 2006. 9 Nov. 2009 <http://www.newyorker.com/archive/2006/12/11/061211crte_television>

"*Friends* (1994) — Episode List." *The Internet Movie Database*. 1 March 2010 <http://www.imdb.com/title/tt0108778/episodes>.

Genette, Gérard. *Figures III*. Paris: Seuil, 1972.

Geninasca, Jacques. *La Parole littéraire*. Paris: PUF, 1997.

Goodman, Nelson. *Languages of Art: An Approach to a Theory of Symbols*. Indianapolis: Bobbs-Merrill, 1968.

Greimas, Algirdas J. *Sémantique structurale. Recherche de méthode*. Paris: Larousse, 1966.

_____, and Joseph Courtés. *Sémiotique. Dictionnaire raisonné de la théorie du langage*. Paris: Hachette, 1979.

_____, and Jacques Fontanille. *Sémiotique des passions. Des états de choses aux états d'âme*. Paris: Seuil, 1991.

Grignaffini, Giorgio. "Eppur si muove. Moti immobili nella soap opera." in Dusi and Spaziante, eds., *Remix-Remake*, 355–366.

Bibliography

———. *I generi televisivi*. Rome: Carocci, 2004.

Hall, Sean. *This Means This, This Means That: A User's Guide to Semiotics*. London: Laurence King, 2007.

Hanot, Muriel. *Télévision. Réalité ou réalisme? Introduction à l'analyse sémiopragmatique des discours télévisuels*. Brussels: De Boeck Université, 2002.

Hartley, John. "Situation comedy, Part 1." Creeber *et al.*, eds. 65–67.

———. "Textual analysis." Miller, ed., *Television Studies*, 29–33.

Jakobson, Roman. *Essais de linguistique générale*. Paris: Editions de Minuit, 1963.

Landowski. Eric. *Présences de l'autre*. Paris: PUF, 1997

Long, Rob. *Set up, Joke, Set up, Joke*. London: Bloomsbury, 2005.

"*Lost* 'Exposé' (2007)." *The Internet Movie Database*. 1 March 2010 <http://www.imdb.com/title/tt0988050/>.

Manovich, Lev. *The Language of New Media*. Cambridge, Mass.: MIT Press, 2002.

Marrone, Gianfranco. *Estetica del telegiornale. Identità di testata e stili comunicativi*. Rome: Meltemi, 1998.

Martin, Bronwen, and Felizitas Ringham. *Key Terms in Semiotics*. London and New York: Continuum, 2006.

Mattioli, Orsola. "Beautiful, o delle passioni verbalizzate." Basso *et al.* 67–84.

McCabe, Janet, and Kim Akass, eds. *Reading Desperate Housewifes: Beyond the White Picket Fence*. London and New York: I.B. Tauris, 2006.

——— and ———, eds. *Reading Sex and the City*. London and New York: I.B. Tauris, 2004.

Metz, Christian. *L'Énonciation impersonnelle, ou le site du film*. Paris: Klincksieck, 1991.

———. *Essais sur la signification au cinéma (Tome II)*. Paris: Klincksieck, 1972.

Miller, Toby. *Anti-Americanism and Popular Culture*. Budapest: Center for Policy Studies, 2005.

———, ed. *Television Studies*. London: British Film Institute, 2002.

Mills, Brett. *Television Sitcom*. London: British Film Institute, 2005.

Mizzau, Marina. *L'ironia. La contraddizione consentita*. Milan: Feltrinelli, 1984.

Monico, Francesco. *Il dramma televisivo. L'autore e l'estetica del mezzo*. Rome: Meltemi, 2006.

Morreale, Joanne. "Sitcoms Say Goodbye: the Cultural Spectacle of *Seinfeld*'s Last Episode." Morreale, ed., *Critiquing Sitcom*, 274–285.

———, ed. *Critiquing Sitcom*. Syracuse, N.Y.: Syracuse University Press, 2003.

My Best Friend's Wedding. Dir. P.J. Hogan Perf. Julia Roberts, Dermot Mulroney, Cameron Diaz, Rupert Everett and Philip Bosco. TriStar Pictures, 1997.

O Brother, Where Art Thou? Dir. Joel and Ethan Coen. Perf. George Clooney, John Turturro, Tim Blake Nelson, John Goodman, Holly Hunter and Charles Durning. Touchstone Pictures, 2000.

"*The Office* (2001)." *The Internet Movie Database*. 1 March 2010 <http://www.imdb.com/title/tt0290978/>.

"*The Office* (2005)." *The Internet Movie Database*. 1 March 2010 <http://www.imdb.com/title/tt0386676/>.

Orwell, George, *1984*. New York: Harcourt Brace Jovanovich, 1949.

Page, Adrian. *Cracking Morse Code: Semiotics and Television Drama*. Luton: University of Luton Press, 2000.

Perrotta, Marta. *Il format televisivo. Caratteristiche, circolazione internazionale, usi e abusi*. Urbino: QuattroVenti, 2007.

Pezzini, Isabella. "Uno sguardo trasversale sulla fiction italiana. Il caso *Boris*." Pozzato and Grignaffini, eds., *Mondi seriali*, 187–196.

Pozzato, Maria Pia. "Come aprire il testo senza gettare la chiave." Ferraro *et al.*, *Variazioni*, 9–16.

———. *Leader, oracoli, assassini. Analisi semiotica dell'informazione*. Rome: Carocci, 2004.

———. *Semiotica del testo. Metodi, autori, esempi.* Rome: Carocci, 2001.
Pozzato, Maria Pia, ed. *Linea a Belgrado. La comunicazione giornalistica in tv durante la guerra per il Kosovo.* Rome: RAI-ERI, 2000.
Pozzato, Maria Pia, and Giorgio Grignaffini, eds. *Mondi seriali. Percorsi semiotici nella fiction.* Milan: RTI, 2008.
Rushdie, Salman. *Step Across This Line: Collected Non-Fiction, 1992–2002.* London: Vintage, 2003.
Sandell, Jillian. "The Personal Is Professional on TV. I'll Be There for You: Friends and the Fantasy of Alternative Families," *American Studies* 39.2 (Summer 1998) 141–155.
Savorelli, Antonio. "CNN Breaking News: 11 settembre 2001." Pozzato, *Leader,* 169–187.
Schleifer, Ronald. *A.J.Greimas and the Nature of Meaning: Linguistics, Semiotics and Discourse Theory.* London and New York: Routledge, 1987.
"Scrubs (2001)." *The Internet Movie Database.* 1 March 2010 <http://www.imdb.com/title/tt0285403/>.
"Situation comedy." *Encyclopædia Britannica Online*, 2009. Encyclopædia Britannica. 1 Nov. 2009 <http://www.britannica.com/EBchecked/topic/667010/situation-comedy>.
"Situation Comedy." *The American Heritage Dictionary.* 1994 ed.
Stark, Steven D. *Glued to the Set: The 60 Television Shows and Events That Made Us Who We Are Today.* New York: Delta, 1997.
Thwaites, Tony, Lloyd Davis and Warwick Mules. *Introducing Cultural and Media Studies: A Semiotic Approach.* Basingstoke: Palgrave, 2002.
The Truman Show. Dir. Peter Weir. Perf. Jim Carrey, Laura Linney, Ed Harris, Noah Emmerich and Natascha McElhone. Paramount Pictures, 1998.
Tueth, Michael V. *Laughter in the Living Room: Television Comedy and the American Home Audience.* New York: Peter Lang, 2005.
2001: A Space Odyssey. Dir. Stanley Kubrick. Perf. Keir Dullea, Gary Lockwood, William Sylvester, Daniel Richter, Leonard Rossiter and Douglas Rain. Metro-Goldwin-Mayer, 1968.
"*Ugly Betty* (2006)." *The Internet Movie Database.* 1 March 2010 <http://www.imdb.com/title/tt0805669/>.
"*Will & Grace* 'No Sex 'N' the City' (2004)." *The Internet Movie Database.* 9 Nov. 2009 <http://www.imdb.com/title/tt0748836/>.
You Kill Me. Dir. John Dahl. Perf. Ben Kingsley, Téa Leoni, Luke Wilson and Dennis Farina. IFC Films, 2007.
Žižek, Slavoj. *Welcome to the Desert of the Real.* New York: Verso, 2002.

Television Shows Cited

Accidentally on Purpose. Mary F. Pols. CBS: 2009–present.
Alice. Robert Getchell. CBS: 1976–1985.
Arrested Development. Mitchell Hurwitz. Fox: 2003–2006.
Batman. Bob Kane and William Dozier. ABC: 1966–1968.
Battlestar Galactica. Glen A. Larson, David Elck and Ronald D. Moore. Sci Fi: 2004–2009.
Bewitched. Sol Saks. ABC: 1964–1972.
The Big Bang Theory. Chuck Lorre and Bill Prady. CBS: 2007–present.
The Bold and the Beautiful. William J. Bell and Lee Phillip Bell. CBS: 1987–present.
Boris (Italy). Luca Manzi and Carlo Mazzotta. Fox: 2007–present.
Carpoolers. Bruce McCulloch. ABC: 2007-2008.
Cavemen. Joe Lawson. ABC: 2007.
Charmed. Constance M. Burge. The WB: 1998–2006.
Cheers. James Burrows, Glen Charles and Les Charles. NBC: 1982–1993.

Bibliography

The Comeback. Lisa Kudrow and Michael Patrick King. HBO: 2005.
Community. Dan Harmon. NBC: 2009–present.
The Cosby Show. Bill Cosby, Ed Weinberger and Michael J. Leeson. NBC: 1984–1992.
CSI: Crime Scene Investigation. Anthony E. Zuiker. CBS: 2000–present.
Curb Your Enthusiasm. Larry David. HBO: 2000–present.
Dawson's Creek. Kevin Williamson. The WB: 1998–2003.
Desperate Housewives. Marc Cherry. ABC: 2004–present.
Dexter. James Manos, Jr. Showtime: 2006–present.
Eli Stone. Greg Berlanti and Marc Guggenheim. ABC: 2008-2009.
Ellen. Carol Black, Neal Marlens and David S. Rosenthal. ABC: 1994–1998.
ER. Michael Crichton. NBC: 1994–2009.
Extras. Ricky Gervais and Stephen Merchant. BBC Two/HBO: 2005–2007.
Frasier. David Angell, Peter Casey and David Lee. NBC: 1993–2004.
Friends. David Crane and Marta Kauffman. NBC: 1994–2004.
Ghost Whisperer. John Gray. CBS: 2005–present.
Happy Days. Garry Marshall. ABC: 1974–1984.
I Dream of Jeannie. Sidney Sheldon. NBC: 1965–1970.
Joanie Loves Chachi. Lowell Ganz. ABC: 1982–1983.
Joey. Shana Goldberg-Meehan and Scott Silveri. NBC: 2004–2006.
Laverne & Shirley. Garry Marshall, Lowell Ganz and Mark Rothman. ABC: 1976–1983.
Law & Order. Dick Wolf. NBC: 1990–present.
Lost. Jeffrey Lieber, J.J. Abrams and Damon Lindelof. ABC: 2004–2010.
The Mary Tyler Moore Show. James L. Brooks and Allan Burns. CBS: 1970–1977.
*M*A*S*H.* Larry Gelbart. CBS: 1972–1983.
Medium. Glenn Gordon Caron. NBC: 2005–2009; CBS: 2009–present.
Mork & Mindy. Garry Marshall. ABC: 1978–1982.
Murphy Brown. Diane English. CBS: 1988–1998.
My Name Is Earl. Greg Garcia. NBC: 2005–2009.
The Nanny. Peter Marc Jacobson and Fran Drescher. CBS: 1993–1999.
NYPD Blue. Steven Bochco and David Milch. ABC: 1993–2005.
The O.C. Josh Schwartz. Fox: 2003–2007.
The Office (UK), Ricky Gervais and Stephen Merchant. BBC: 2001–2003.
The Office (USA), Ricky Gervais and Stephen Merchant. Developed for American television by Greg Daniels. NBC: 2005–present.
Parks and Recreation. Greg Daniels and Michael Schur. NBC: 2009–present.
Pushing Daisies. Bryan Fuller. ABC: 2007–2009.
Reaper. Michele Fazekas and Tara Butters. The CW: 2007–2009.
Samantha Who? Cecelia Ahern and Don Todd. ABC: 2007–2009.
Scrubs. Bill Lawrence. NBC: 2001–2008; ABC: 2009–present.
Seinfeld. Larry David and Jerry Seinfeld. NBC: 1989–1998.
Sex and the City. Darren Star. HBO: 1998–2004.
Six Feet Under. Alan Ball. HBO: 2001–2005.
Spin City. Gary David Goldberg and Bill Lawrence. ABC: 1996–2002.
Star Trek: The Next Generation. Gene Roddenberry. First-run syndication: 1987–2004.
Star Trek: Voyager. Rick Berman, Michael Piller and Jeri Taylor. UPN: 1995–2001.
Suddenly Susan. Clyde Phillips. NBC: 1996–2000.
30 Rock. Tina Fey. NBC: 2006–present.
Three's Company, Don Nicholl, Michael Ross and Bernie West. ABC: 1977–1984.

Tru Calling. Jon Harmon Feldman. Fox: 2003–2005.
24. Joel Surnow and Robert Cochran. Fox: 2001–2010; (possibly) NBC: 2010– .
Twin Peaks. David Lynch & Mark Frost. ABC: 1990–1991.
Two and a Half Men. Chuck Lorre and Lee Aronsohn. CBS: 2003–present.
Ugly Betty. Fernando Gaitán. Developed for American television by Silvio Horta. ABC: 2006–2010.
Will & Grace. David Kohan and Max Mutchnick. NBC: 1998–2006.
The X-Files. Chris Carter. Fox: 1993–2002.

Television Episodes Cited

"The Box and the Bunny." *Ugly Betty* 102. Writ. Silvio Horta. Dir. Sheree Folkson. ABC. 5 Oct. 2006.
"Brothers." *Ugly Betty* 115. Writ. Shelia Lawrence. Dir. Lev L. Spiro. ABC. 8 Feb 2007.
"Christmas Party." *The Office* 210. Writ. Michael Schur. Dir. Charles McDougall. NBC. 6 Dec. 2005.
"The Comeback (Pilot)." *The Comeback* 01. Writ. Lisa Kudrow and Michael Patrick King. Dir. Michael Patrick King. HBO. 5 June 2005.
"Crimes of Fashion." *Ugly Betty* 303. Writ. Henry Alonso Myers. Dir. Victor Nelli, Jr. ABC. 9 Oct. 2008.
"Crush'd." *Ugly Betty* 307. Writ. Tracy Poust & Jon Kinnally. Dir. Victor Nelli, Jr. ABC. 6 Nov. 2008.
"Don't Ask, Don't Tell." *Ugly Betty* 118. Writ. Sarah Kucserka, Veronica Becker and Marco Pennette. Dir. Tricia Brock. ABC. 22 March, 2007.
"The Dundies." *The Office* 201/204. Writ. Mindy Kaling. Dir. Greg Daniels. NBC. 20 Sept. 2005.
"East Side Story." *Ugly Betty* 123. Writ. Silvio Horta and Marco Pennette. Dir. James Hayman. ABC. 17 May 2007.
"Exposé." *Lost* 314. Writ. Edward Kitsis and Adam Horowitz. Dir. Stephen Williams. ABC. 28 March 2007.
"Fey's Sleigh Ride." *Ugly Betty* 104/105. Writ. Sheila Lawrence. Dir. Tricia Block. ABC. 19 Oct. 2006.
"Filing for the Enemy." *Ugly Betty* 302. Writ. Joel Fields. Dir. Michael Spiller. ABC. 2 Oct. 2008.
"Halloween." *The Office* 205/206.[1] Writ. Greg Daniels. Dir. Paul Feig. NBC. 18 Oct. 2005.
"Health Care." *The Office* 103/105. Writ. Paul Lieberstein. Dir. Ken Whittingham. NBC. 5 April 2005.
"Her Story." *Scrubs* 405. Writ. Angela Nissel. Dir. John Inwood. NBC. 28 Sept. 2004.
"Her Story II." *Scrubs* 510. Writ. Mike Schwartz. Dir. Chris Koch. NBC. 7 Feb 2006.
"His Story." *Scrubs* 215. Writ. Bonnie Schneider and Hadley Davis. Dir. Ken Whittingham. NBC. 30 Jan. 2003.
"His Story II." *Scrubs* 318. Writ. Mark Stegemann. Dir. Jason Ensler. NBC. 6 April 2004.
"His Story III." *Scrubs* 519. Writ. Angela Nissel. Dir. John Inwood. NBC. 18 April 2006.
"His Story IV." *Scrubs* 607. Writ. Mike Schwartz. Dir. Linda Mendoza. NBC. 1 Feb. 2007.
"Hot Girl." *The Office* 106/102. Writ. Mindy Kaling. Dir. Amy Heckerling. NBC. 26 April 2005.
"In or Out." *Ugly Betty* 113. Writ. Myra Jo Martino. Dir. Michael Spiller. ABC. 18 Jan. 2007.
"The Last One, Part Two." *Friends* 1018. Writ. Marta Kauffman and David Crane. Dir. Kevin S. Bright. NBC. 6 May 2004.
"Left Behind." *Lost* 315. Writ. Damon Lindelof and Elizabeth Sarnoff. Dir. Karen Gaviola. ABC. 4 April 2007.

"The Long Con." *Lost* 213. Writ. Leonard Dick and Steven Maeda. Dir. Roxann Dawson. ABC. 8 Feb. 2006.

"Lose the Boss." *Ugly Betty* 109/110. Writ. Oliver Goldstick. Dir. Ken Whittingham. ABC. 23 Nov. 2006.

"The Man from Tallahassee." *Lost* 313. Writ. Drew Goddard and Jeff Pinkner. Dir. Jack Bender. ABC. 21 March 2007.

"My Absence." *Scrubs* 809. Writ. Debra Fordham and Andy Schwartz. Dir. John Putch. ABC. 10 Feb. 2009.

"My Bad." *Scrubs* 106. Writ. Gabrielle Allan. Dir. Marc Buckland. NBC. 30 Oct. 2001.

"My Bed Banter & Beyond." *Scrubs* 115. Writ. Gabrielle Allan. Dir. Lawrence Trilling. NBC. 5 Feb. 2002.

"My Best Friend's Wedding." *Scrubs* 322. Writ. Tim Hobert and Eric Weinberg. Dir. Bill Lawrence. NBC. 4 May 2004.

"My Big Bird." *Scrubs* 508. Writ. Debra Fordham. Dir. Rob Greenberg. NBC. 24 Jan. 2006.

"My Big Brother." *Scrubs* 206. Writ. Tim Hobert. Dir. Michael Spiller. NBC. 31 Oct. 2002.

"My Brother, My Keeper." *Scrubs* 214. Writ. Eric Weinberg. Dir. Michael Spiller. NBC. 23 Jan. 2003.

"My Brother, Where Art Thou?" *Scrubs* 306. Writ. Mike Schwartz. Dir. Marc Buckland. NBC. 6 Nov. 2003.

"My Cabbage." *Scrubs* 512. Writ. Ryan A. Levin. Dir. John Inwood. NBC. 28 Feb 2006.

"My Chopped Liver." *Scrubs* 517. Writ. Debra Fordham. Dir. Will Mackenzie. NBC. 4 April 2006.

"My Déjà Vu, My Déjà Vu." *Scrubs* 522. Writ. Mike Schwartz. Dir. Linda Mendoza. NBC. 9 May 2006.

"My Extra Mile." *Scrubs* 515. Writ. Mark Stegemann. Dir. Ken Whittingham. NBC. 21 March 2006.

"My First Day." *Scrubs* 101. Writ. Bill Lawrence. Dir. Adam Bernstein. NBC. 2 Oct. 2001.

"My Full Moon." *Scrubs* 813. Writ. Kevin Biegel. Dir. John Michel. ABC. 1 April 2009.

"My Heavy Meddle." *Scrubs* 116. Writ. Mike Schwartz. Dir. Will Mackenzie. NBC. 26 Feb. 2002.

"My Hero." *Scrubs* 123. Writ. Neil Goldman and Garrett Donovan. Dir. Michael Spiller. NBC. 14 May 2002.

"My Jiggly Ball." *Scrubs* 504. Writ. Tim Hobert. Dir. Rick Blue. NBC. 10 Jan. 2006.

"My Last Day." *Scrubs* 124. Writ. Gabrielle Allan and Mike Schwartz. Dir. Michael Spiller. NBC. 21 May 2002.

"My Life in Four Cameras." *Scrubs* 417. Writ. Debra Fordham. Dir. Adam Bernstein. NBC. 15 Feb. 2005.

"My Lucky Night." *Scrubs* 305. Writ. Neil Goldman and Garrett Donovan. Dir. John Inwood. NBC. 30 Oct. 2003.

"My Malpractical Decision." *Scrubs* 409. Writ. Janae Bakken. Dir. Gail Mancuso. NBC. 9 Nov. 2004.

"My Mentor." *Scrubs* 102. Writ. Bill Lawrence. Dir. Adam Bernstein. NBC. 4 Oct. 2001.

"My Musical." *Scrubs* 606. Writ. Debra Fordham. Dir. Will Mackenzie. NBC. 18 Jan. 2007.

"My New Suit." *Scrubs* 518. Writ. Tim Hobert. Dir. Victor Nelli, Jr. NBC. 11 April 2006.

"My Ocardial Infarction." *Scrubs* 413. Writ. Mark Stegemann. Dir. Ken Whittingham. NBC. 18 Jan 2005.

"My Old Friend's New Friend." *Scrubs* 401. Writ. Eric Weinberg. Dir. Bill Lawrence. NBC. 31 Aug. 2004.

"My Old Lady." *Scrubs* 104. Writ. Matt Tarses. Dir. Marc Buckland. NBC. 16 Oct. 2001.

"My Old Man." *Scrubs* 119. Writ. Matt Tarses. Dir Adam Bernstein. NBC. 9 April 2002.

"My Overkill." *Scrubs* 201. Writ. Bill Lawrence. Dir. Adam Bernstein. NBC. 26 Sept. 2002.

Bibliography

"My Philosophy." *Scrubs* 213. Writ. Bill Lawrence, Matt Tarses and Tim Hobert. Dir. Chris Koch. NBC. 6 Jan 2003.

"My Sex Buddy." *Scrubs* 211. Writ. Neil Goldman and Garrett Donovan. Dir. Will Mackenzie. NBC. 2 Jan. 2003.

"My T.C.W." *Scrubs* 218. Writ. Bill Lawrence. Dir. Adam Bernstein. NBC. 20 March 2003.

"My Two Dads." *Scrubs* 105. Writ. Neil Goldman and Garrett Donovan. Dir. Craig Zisk. NBC. 23 Oct. 2001.

"My Way Home." *Scrubs* 507. Writ. Neil Goldman and Garrett Donovan. Dir. Zach Braff. NBC. 24 Jan. 2006.

"My Way or the Highway." *Scrubs* 120. Writ. Eric Weinberg. Dir. Adam Bernstein. NBC. 16 April 2002.

"No Sex 'n' the City." *Will & Grace* 619. Writ. Steve Gabriel. Dir. James Burrows. NBC. 25 March 2004.

"Odor in the Court." *Ugly Betty* 212. Writ. Bill Wrubel. Dir. Victor Nelli, Jr. ABC. 17 Jan. 2008.

"Office Olympics." *The Office* 203. Writ. Michael Schur. Dir. Paul Feig. 4 Oct. 2005.

"The One Where Nana Dies Twice." *Friends* 108. Writ. Marta Kauffman & David Crane. Dir. James Burrows. 10 Nov. 1994.

Pilot. *The Office* 101/100. Writ. Ricky Gervais, Stephen Merchant and Greg Daniels. Dir. Ken Kwapis. NBC. 24 March 2005.

"Queens for a Day." *Ugly Betty* 103. Writ. Marco Pennette. Dir. James Hayman. ABC. 12 Oct. 2006.

"Rabbit Test." *Ugly Betty* 320. Writ. Chris Black. Dir. Richard Heus. ABC. 30 April 2009.

"Sexual Harassment." *The Office* 202. Writ. Ken Kwapis. Dir. Ken Kwapis. NBC. 27 Sept. 2005.

"Sofia's Choice." *Ugly Betty* 112. Writ. Silvio Horta. Dir. Jeff Melman. ABC. 11 Jan. 2007.

"A Space Oddity." *CSI: Crime Scene Investigation* 920. Writ. Bradley Thompson, David Weddle and Naren Shankar. Dir. Michael Nankin. CBS. 16 April 2009.

"Swag." *Ugly Betty* 111/104. Writ. James D. Parriott. Dir. Tamra Davis. ABC. 4 Jan. 2007.

"Their Story." *Scrubs* 617. Writ. Andy Schwartz. Dir. Richard Alexander Wells. NBC. 19 April 2007.

"Their Story II." *Scrubs* 812. Writ. Andy Schwartz. Dir. Michael McDonald. ABC. 25 March 2009.

"Things Fall Apart." *Ugly Betty* 316. Writ. Henry Alonso Myers. Dir. Tom Verica. ABC. 26 Feb. 2009.

"Trust, Lust, and Must." *Ugly Betty* 106/107. Writ. Cameron Litvack. Dir. Jamie Babbit. ABC. 2 Nov. 2006.

"Valentine's Day." *The Office* 216. Writ. Michael Schur. Dir. Greg Daniels. NBC. 9 Feb. 2006.

"Valerie Does Another Classic *Leno*." *The Comeback* 13. Writ. Michael Patrick King. Dir. Michael Patrick King. HBO. 4 Sept. 2005.

"Valerie Saves the Show." *The Comeback* 06. Writ. Michael Schur. Dir. Greg Mottola. HBO. 17 July 2005.

"Valerie Shines Under Stress." *The Comeback* 12. Writ. Heather Morgan. Dir. David Steinberg. HBO. 28 Aug. 2005.

"Valerie Triumphs at the Upfronts." *The Comeback* 02. Writ. Lisa Kudrow and Michael Patrick King. Dir. Michael Patrick King. HBO. 12 June 2005.

"You Kill Me." *CSI: Crime Scene Investigation* 808. Writ. Sarah Goldfinger, Douglas Petrie and Naren Shankar. Dir. Paris Barclay. CBS. 22 Nov. 2007.

Index

ABC 8, 12, 14, 24, 31, 33, 35, 40, 107, 174
Accidentally on Purpose 34
According to Jim 33
actant: actantial model 73, 76–77; actantial role 75, 77, 82, 100, 179; helper 41, 78, 81, 100, 103–104, 120, 124; opponent 81, 100, 103, 120, 123–124, 126–127; receiver 3, 30, 32, 55, 61, 63–64, 77–78, 82, 84, 147, 182, 184; sender 63, 78–79, 97–102; *see also* actor (semiotics); modality; narrative program; object; subject
actor (person) 12, 15, 24, 27, 43, 46–47, 54, 66, 70, 89, 139, 143, 156, 170, 182
actor (semiotics) 12, 41, 52, 62, 77, 81–82, 90, 96–97, 134, 184; *see also* character
actorialization 12, 21, 63, 109, 111
adaptation 12–13, 65
aesthetics 119–120, 126, 128, 145, 168, 172, 178
Åkerman, Malin 93
Alejandro, Kevin 109
Alice 23
alienation effect 57, 71; *see also* reality effect
Amélie 175, 194n11
The American Heritage Dictionary 21
Applegate, Christina 149
archetype 57
Aristotle 22, 32, 144–145, 156
Arrested Development 15
aspect, aspectualization 123; durative 49, 71, 95–96; inchoative 25, 96; iterative 49, 96, 112; terminative 25, 96
aspect ratio (television screen) 43
audience 3, 8, 22–23, 27, 29–31, 55, 72, 78, 96, 98, 132–135, 137–138, 140, 145, 156, 168, 178–179, 182, 184; live studio audience 21, 25, 30, 132, 177
Australia 154
autobiographic lie 50, 63; *see also* biography; narration: first-person
axiology *see* value; value system

Bagnell, Robert 93
Baio, Scott 15
Baker, Leslie David 75
Banks, Elizabeth 44
Barber, Lance 93
Battlestar Galactica 164–165
Baumgartner, Brian 75
BBC 12, 65
Belushi, James 33
Bewitched 179
The Big Bang Theory 33
Big Brother 170–172
biography 6–7, 177
bloopers 43
Blue, David 112
The Bold and the Beautiful 115
Boris 8
Bowler, Grant 112
Braff, Zach 43, 135
Bratton, Creed 76
Burrows, James 93

California 35
camera 23, 25, 31, 35–36, 53–55, 65, 67–69, 72, 77–78, 81–85, 88–90, 93, 96–97, 102, 104–105, 140, 142, 160, 170, 177, 181; as actor 68, 78, 81–84, 92, 181; fixed 84–85, 88, 94; gazing into 65, 67, 82, 92, 97, 159; movements 71, 82–84; multiple 25, 83, 132, 135
Camilleri, Andrea 7
canned applause, laughter *see* laugh track
Carell, Steve 68
Carpoolers 33
Cavemen 33
CBS 23, 26, 33, 152, 175
Chalke, Sarah 44
channel (communication) 64, 136
characters 12, 21, 25–27, 29, 35, 43–47, 49–50, 52, 62, 65, 67–68, 71, 73–76, 80, 82, 84–85, 88, 90, 95–97, 106–112, 114, 124–125, 127–128, 130–131, 139–140, 142–143, 147, 153, 155, 157–158,

205

Index

162, 164, 179; collective 75, 92; hierarchy among 68–70, 75, 108, 115, 138, 158, 162–164
Charmed 175
Cheers 23–24, 33, 134, 136
Cibrian, Eddie 112
cinema 9, 10, 12–13, 28, 87, 167–168, 179
cinematography 89, 135–136
citation 15, 32
cliffhanger 18, 107, 113
Coen, Ethan 42–43
Coen, Joel 42–43
cold open 35, 66, 72, 140
Colombia 12, 107, 111, 142
The Comeback 12–13, 16, 17, 26, 85–106, 114, 138, 140–142, 147–148, 150–151, 176, 180–181
comedy (definition) 5, 22, 144–145, 156
comic effect 9, 22, 30, 32, 140, 145, 181
comic foil 139
commercial break 14, 25, 88, 107, 135, 140
communication 3–4, 13–14, 61, 63, 97–98, 103, 138, 165, 172, 181, 183–184
Community 33
competition 85, 170, 173
conflict 21, 58, 62, 77, 85, 97, 103, 105–106, 118
Connecticut 44, 76
context 71, 135, 150, 178
The Cosby Show 24, 33
couch (use in comedy) 23–24, 29, 53, 133, 136
credits: end 43, 90–91; opening 35, 42, 69–70, 139
CSI: Crime Scene Investigation 149, 152, 157–166, 173
culture 4–5, 7–8, 12, 30, 42, 65, 117, 150, 152, 167–168, 176, 179
Curb Your Enthusiasm 15–16, 177, 181
The CW 175

DaCosta, Yaya 130
Dale, Alan 110
David, Larry 15–16, 177
Dawson's Creek 8
death 28, 117, 146, 154–156, 175
deconstructionism 165–166
déjà vu 26; *see also* repetition
Del Amitri (band) 37
Derrida, Jacques 166
Desperate Housewives 31, 33
detachment 29–30, 63, 167, 174, 177

The Devil Wears Prada 107–108
Dexter 144
diegesis *see* narration, soundtrack
diegetic implication 68
digital video 89, 177
discourse 9, 16–17, 61–63, 71, 77–78, 81, 84, 87, 95–96, 98, 101, 123, 132, 138–139, 147, 150–151, 161, 165–166, 169, 172, 176, 179
discursive structures 10, 12–13, 15, 17–18, 34, 55, 67, 87, 107, 140, 143, 148, 183–184; discursive syntax 123; *see also* actor (semiotics); figurative level; plastic level; space; thematic level; time
discursivization 17, 26, 40, 52, 64, 77, 81, 83–84, 87, 95, 115, 138, 144, 160, 168, 180, 182, 184
disengagement 40, 51–52, 54, 71, 76, 81, 87, 134; enunciative 40, 76, 83, 91, 159; temporal 113; utterative 84; *see also* engagement
distance 32, 51, 142, 147–151, 156, 166, 178, 184
documentary 7, 16, 65, 67, 71, 76–77, 81–83, 87, 137–138, 151, 169, 176, 183
Dominican Republic 45
drama 19, 30, 107, 123, 144, 146, 149, 173–176, 178, 183
dubbing 5
DVD 14, 42, 136
dysphoria 19, 28–30, 77–80, 98, 126, 136, 144–149; acceptance, conversion 148–149; detachment 147–148; dilution 146–147; *see also* euphoria; thymia

Eco, Umberto 4
Eli Stone 40
embedding 16, 40, 84, 135, 156; of genres 65, 83; *see also* enunciation: uttered; *mise en abyme*
empiric world 6, 26, 31–32, 34, 85, 93, 95, 119–120, 122, 147, 151, 163, 166–167, 169, 173–178, 182
Encyclopædia Britannica 21
engagement 52, 71, 91; enunciative 63; *see also* disengagement
English language 6, 7, 42, 63
entertainment 167, 181
enunciation 3, 11, 14, 16, 19, 21, 30, 37–38, 48, 50–55, 62, 64, 76–77, 82–83, 86–87, 89, 101, 112–113, 119, 123, 134, 137–138, 142, 148, 156, 159, 164, 168, 170–171, 176–177, 180–182, 184; cir-

Index

cumstances 64–65, 135–136, 140; filmic 54, 62, 64, 86; impersonal 82; theory 9, 11; uttered, secondary 16, 30, 40, 81, 83, 86–88, 91, 97–98, 105–106, 113–114, 140, 148, 162; verbal 51, 54, 180; *see also* utterance
enunciative device 17, 22, 25, 30–31, 37, 55, 64, 71, 76, 81–90, 98–99, 105, 114, 123, 134, 140, 142, 159–160, 162, 177, 179, 181, 183–184; revealing the device 25, 86–87, 90, 137, 140, 182–183
enunciative structure 31–32, 68, 81–82, 85, 132, 144–145, 147–150, 152, 157, 162–163, 179
episode titles 42–43, 52–53, 72–73
ER 146, 183
ethics 9, 145, 171
euphoria 5, 6, 22, 28–29, 61, 79, 104, 145–147, 149, 152, 180; non-euphoria 144; *see also* dysphoria; thymias
event 26–28
existence (semiotics): actualization 77, 79, 182; realization 41, 74, 78–80, 98, 102, 118, 124, 181–182; virtualization 74, 88, 118, 120, 141
experience 49, 141
expression (semiotics) 76, 91

Le Fabuleux Destin d'Amélie Poulain 175, 194*n*11
Faison, Donald 44
fantasy 39
fantasy (genre) 163
fantasy sequence 36, 39–40, 63, 161–162, 180
Fashion TV 122
Ferrera, America 108
fiction 6–7, 9, 16, 32, 64, 76, 81, 85, 87, 89, 106, 122, 133, 135, 141–142, 147–148, 150, 154, 156–157, 162–163, 167–170, 172, 174, 177–178, 180, 182–183
figure, figurative level 28, 68, 107, 115, 121–122, 173
film 7, 10–11, 68, 86, 107, 182; theory 9, 11
filmic language 7, 13, 42, 63
Fischer, Jenna 71
Fishburne, Laurence 164
Flannery, Kate 75
flash-forward 156
flashback 68, 113, 154–157
Flynn, Neil 42, 45
focalization 90, 98, 181
forensic drama 144, 152, 156–157, 162

form (semiotics) 10, 16, 99, 160
fourth wall 23–24; breaking 55, 65; *see also* camera: gazing into
Fox 8, 15, 175
Fox Italia 8
Fox News 169
Frasier 27, 33, 35, 133
Friedman, James 174
Friends 18, 24, 27–29, 33, 35–36, 44, 85, 133, 137–138, 146
fruition 17, 72–73, 181

Garcia, Jorge 154
Gaudet, Ava 111
generative analysis *see* textual analysis
generative approach, model *see* semiotics
generative trajectory 10
Genette, Gérard 50–51
genre 6–9, 12, 17, 19, 28, 31, 34, 66, 89, 121–123, 132–151, 176, 178–179, 182–183; definition 8, 30, 163
Gervais, Ricky 65
Ghost Whisperer 175
Gold, Daniel Eric 111
Golden Girls 33
Gorham, Christopher 111
Grace, Maggie 154
Greece 145; Greek language 32, 145
Greimas, Algirdas Julien 4, 12
Guilfoyle, Paul 158, 164

Happy Days 8, 15, 133
happy ending 6, 22
Hardin, Melora 76, 139
Hay, Colin 38–39, 136
Hayek, Salma 107
HBO 12–13, 15, 85, 88, 134, 140, 144
Helgenberger, Marg 159
Helms, Ed 76
Helvetica (font) 91
high definition 43
Hines, Cheryl 177
Holloway, Josh 154
humor 5, 21, 22, 33, 133, 152, 166
Hurst, Lillian 93

ideology 62, 176
imitation 32, 65–66
Indelicato, Mark 109
intentionality 97–98, 103, 119–120, 122, 141, 160, 176
interlocutor 84, 87, 92, 98–99, 181
Internet 167; *see also* web

207

Index

irony 152, 157
isotopy 28, 73, 101, 145; thematic 74
Italy 5–9, 119–120, 168, 170

Jenkins, Ken 45
Jensen, Ashley 110
Joanie Loves Chachi 133
Joey 24–25
joke 5, 6, 27, 38, 44, 47, 72, 74, 117, 138, 140, 142, 147; inside joke 18, 28
Jones, Jowharah 130

Kaling, Mindy 76
Kao, Archie 158
Kastl, Johnny 47
Kim, Yunjin 154
King, Michael Patrick 85
Kinsey, Angela 75
Krasinski, John 71
Kudrow, Lisa 85, 91

lack 127, 143
Lafleur, Sarah 112
Langham, Wallace 157, 164–165
laugh track 5, 8, 21–23, 30, 35, 87, 132, 136, 178
laughter 6, 22–23, 29, 32, 133, 135, 176
Laverne & Shirley 133
Law & Order 173–174
Lawrence, Bill 41
Lazlo Bane (band) 41
Lee, Jason 149
lexicalization, lexicon 49, 56–57, 73, 119
Lieberstein, Paul 76
Light, Judith 110
literature 6, 7, 11, 13, 51, 144, 167
Lloyd, Sam 47
Lorre, Chuck 34
Los Angeles, California 93, 154
Lost 144, 152–157, 174

Mabius, Eric 108
Macchio, Ralph 112
Mapa, Alec 122
Marano, Vanessa 93
The Mary Tyler Moore Show 23
Maschio, Robert 47
*M*A*S*H* 183
Mays, Jayma 111
McGinley, John C. 44
meaning 11, 42, 53, 57, 62, 136, 151, 166, 173, 180, 181, 184
meaning effect 26, 28, 63, 68, 84, 180

Medium 175
medium, media 7, 9–11, 13–15, 63, 116, 119, 167–168, 184; media studies, theory 161, 165
Men at Work (band) 38
Merchant, Stephen 65
metaphor 21, 173; *see also* utterance: literality
metasemiotic function 14, 16, 17, 122, 156
Metz, Christian 9, 67, 82, 86, 183
Mexico 108, 118, 121
midseason 36
Miller, Christa 44
Mills, Brett 22
mímēsis (ancient Greek: μίμησις) 32, 173; *see also* imitation
mise en abyme (French) 16, 99, 102, 106, 113, 122, 147, 151, 156; *see also* embedding; enunciation: uttered
mockumentary 65
modality, modalization 56–62, 64, 77–80, 97–98, 100, 114, 119, 124–129, 138, 168, 174
Monaghan, Dominic 154
montage 55, 68, 71, 82–84, 88, 96, 181
Moore, Ronald D. 164
moralization 32, 78–79, 126
Mork & Mindy 24, 133
Morreale, Joanne 30
Morris, Robert Michael 92
MTV 170
Murphy Brown 23
music 11, 37, 66, 68, 70, 90; *see also* semiotics: musical; sound; soundtrack
musical theater 39, 143
My Name Is Earl 33, 149

Nankin, Michael 164
The Nanny 26–27
narration 42, 52; extra-heterodiegetic 50; extra-homodiegetic 50; first-person 63; intra-diegetic 51, 55
narrative level *see* semio-narrative structures
narrative program 41, 57–61, 77–81, 96–105, 123–124, 143, 164, 182; main 59, 63, 78–79, 97, 125, 149; of use 58–59, 78, 97, 149
narrative schema: competence 56–58, 60, 79, 97, 115, 124, 126, 143; manipulation, contract 97, 101; performance 57, 59–60, 77–79, 96, 173; sanction 22, 32, 60, 63, 77–78, 116, 126, 142

208

Index

narrative trajectory 55–62, 77, 79–80, 97, 99–100, 142–143; *see also* narrative program
narrativity 3, 17, 68, 99, 106, 122, 136, 138, 155, 160, 169–172, 176, 184; meta-narrativity 78, 98
narrator 13, 43, 48–55, 62–64, 113, 136
NBC 12, 14–15, 18, 23–24, 33, 35, 65–66, 107, 134, 174–175
network 6, 14, 43, 134–135, 140, 174
New York City 70, 76, 95, 120–121, 143; Manhattan 114, 117–121, 128; Queens 108, 114, 118–119, 121, 128
New York Post 174
news, newscast 8, 16, 82, 134, 168–169, 172
Newton, Becki 110
non-comic genres, shows 5, 19, 138, 140, 151–151, 167
nonfiction 6, 7, 89, 138, 141, 151, 167
Novak, B.J. 74
Nuñez, Oscar 75
NYPD Blue 174

object 62, 77, 87, 101; of value 60, 78–79, 81, 138; *see also* value
The O.C. 8
The Office 12–14, 16–18, 25–26, 33, 65–84, 114, 132, 137–140, 147–148, 150–151, 176, 180–181
Ortiz, Ana 109
outtakes 43

Palm Springs, California 95
paratext 9, 22, 40–43, 48, 90–91, 113–114, 122, 134–135, 140, 153, 182
Paris, France 120
Parks and Recreation 33
parody 9
passion (semiotics) 18, 80, 99, 146
perspective 40, 43, 85, 113, 123, 158, 162, 164, 180
pertinence 11, 71
Petersen, William 158
phatic function 83, 135–136
physical comedy 5, 36, 143
pilot episode: *The Comeback* 89, 97, 101; *Lost* 154; *The Office* 65, 68; *Ugly Betty* 110, 127
Plana, Tony 109
plastic level 91
point of view 40, 63, 85, 123, 158, 162
polemic structure 123

power 59, 69, 79, 124
pragmatics 3, 22, 126, 132
process 130
prolepsis 30, 68; *see also* flash-forward; time
proxemics 82
psychology 83, 86
pun 42, 152
Pushing Daisies 33, 144, 175

quotation 15, 32, 152

radio 21, 32
raw footage 86, 88, 90–91, 99, 140–141, 172
real world *see* empiric world
The Real World 170–171
realism 5–6, 30–31, 106, 169, 172, 174, 180; hyperrealism 122
reality 6–7, 32, 39–40, 83, 85–88, 96–105, 122, 137–138, 141, 148, 151, 156–157, 159, 163, 166, 167–184
reality-based television 147–148, 151, 169–170, 174, 178
reality effect 39, 83, 88–89, 122, 148, 178; *see also* alienation effect; meaning effect
reality show 8, 10, 16, 17, 42, 67, 85–89, 95–97, 99–105, 140–142, 151, 170–173, 176–177, 182
Reaper 175
repetition 17, 23, 49–50
Republic of San Marino 8
Reyes, Judy 45
Rodríguez, Freddy 47, 111
Rogers, Reg 161
Roma Fiction Fest 2007 7
Romijn, Rebecca 110
running gag 28, 78

Samantha Who? 33, 149
Sanchez, Kiele 153
Sanders, Harland 46
Santoro, Rodrigo 154
sarcasm 33, 72, 152
satire 9
Schenectady, New York 120
Schwartz, Mike 47
science fiction 161–163, 165, 173
Scotland 110, 120
Scranton, Pennsylvania 65, 69–70, 76
scripting 4, 7, 169–171; *sceneggiato* (Italian) 7; unscripted television 11

Index

Scrubs 12–13, 16–18, 26, 31, 33, 35–64, 113, 132–140, 144, 146–147, 150–151, 153, 159, 176, 180–181, 183
Seinfeld 15, 30, 137
self-referential function 16–17, 30, 78, 86, 122, 162
semio-narrative structures 10, 15, 18, 28, 34, 66, 75, 107, 113, 129–130, 148–149, 157, 181, 183; deep level 10–11, 182
semiotic system 7, 9, 11, 16
semiotics 3–5, 8–10, 12, 23, 51–52, 54, 106, 132, 156, 165–166, 168, 179, 184; generative 10–11; musical 11; of objects 172
Sex and the City 13, 33, 63, 85, 120–121, 133–134
serial model: open 17–18, 36, 86, 112, 139; closed 17, 49
series finale: *The Comeback* 88, 100, 141; *Friends* 29; *Seinfeld* 30; *Ugly Betty* 142; *Will & Grace* 29
Shankar, Naren 164
shot/countershot 68, 83, 88
Showtime 144
signification 184
signifier 4, 165, 184
Silverman, Laura 92
The Simpsons 28, 93
simulacrum 63, 82, 98, 159, 184
sitcom, situation comedy 5, 8, 15–19, 21–36, 48, 62, 85, 87–88, 91, 93, 95–98, 101–103, 132–144, 146, 149–151, 173, 176, 178–179, 181, 183; technical definition 21, 132; technical opposition with new comedy 34
Six Feet Under 47, 144
sketch 43, 109
Smith, Phyllis 75
soap opera 7, 9, 18, 31, 107, 115, 117, 123, 144, 173
Somerhalder, Ian 154
sound 31, 37–40, 49, 68, 90; sound effects 37, 40, 53
soundtrack 37–41, 67, 132; extra-diegetic 37–40, 66, 68, 90–91; (intra-)diegetic 38–40, 68, 90
space 14, 21, 23–27, 36, 47–48, 57, 70, 83, 86, 88, 94–95, 113–115, 123; hierarchy 25, 47–48, 95, 114; of representation 91, 113, 183
speech 68–69; direct/indirect 84; speaking turns 69
spin-off 35

staging 7, 39, 178–180
Stamford, Connecticut 76
stand-up comedy 38
Star Trek 161, 164–165
stereotype 24, 26, 28, 32, 65, 93, 119, 130, 142–143, 176
structural analysis *see* textual analysis
style 65–66, 87–88, 107
subject 12, 26, 36, 41, 56, 59, 61–62, 67, 72, 77–80, 84, 87, 95, 97, 99, 101, 106, 115, 124–125, 172; anti-subject 81, 123–124 ; of the enunciation 31, 52, 63, 83; observer 31, 65, 84, 100, 181; of the utterance 63, 142
subjectivity 86, 162
substance 52, 64
Suddenly Susan 23
surrealism 30, 39, 49, 57, 175, 180
Survivor 173
Sydney, Australia 154
syncretism 11, 51, 87

teen drama 7–8
telenovela 13, 16–17, 107, 115, 117–118, 121–123, 142–143, 148, 150, 182
television production 6, 7, 90, 132, 157, 164–165, 182–183
television studies 3, 9, 168
televisual context 34
televisual flow 13–14, 136, 140
televisual narrative 7–11, 16, 19, 22, 65, 87, 112, 144, 167, 182–183
tension 130
text 3–4, 13–14, 16, 81, 85, 119, 122, 140, 165–166, 168, 171–174, 184; extratextuality 16, 39, 150, 162, 164–165; intertextuality 14–16, 107, 152, 169, 173, 175; metatextuality 14–16, 37, 50, 70, 122, 136, 152, 156, 162; segmentation 9, 67
textual analysis 4, 8, 10–11, 19, 34–131, 138, 163
textual boundaries 4, 16, 87, 145, 167, 171, 182
theater 12, 22–23, 31–32, 143–145, 177, 179
theme (semiotics), thematic level, thematization 9, 13, 15, 21, 26, 28, 40, 42, 49, 52, 68–69, 72–73, 90, 93, 96, 107, 109, 111, 115–118, 120–123, 125, 129–130, 134, 139, 143, 156, 158–161, 163, 166, 173, 175, 181; thematic opposition 55–58; thematic role 57, 157, 177; thematic trajectory 56–57

210

Index

theme (television): opening 9, 40–42, 68–70, 72, 91, 139–140; *see also* credits
30 Rock 33
Thompson, Bradley 164
Three's Company 24, 27
thymia 5, 22, 145–149; *see also* dysphoria; euphoria
time 13, 17, 25, 32, 36, 48–50, 52, 57, 64, 68, 70–73, 86, 91, 94–96, 99, 112–113, 123, 155, 159, 183; calendar 48, 72, 95; diegetic, utterative 48, 95, 112, 114, 123; ellipsis 95–96, 113, 123; empiric 48, 72; enunciative 49, 95, 114, 123
Tom and Jerry 28
Toto (band) 39
tragedy 6, 144
translation 4–5
Tru Calling 175
The Truman Show 171
truth 82, 126, 171
Tucson, Arizona 120
24 114
Twin Peaks 174
Two and a Half Men 33
2001: A Space Odyssey 153

Ugly Betty 12–14, 16–17, 26, 33, 107–131, 142–144, 148–150, 182
Union, Gabrielle 130
United Kingdom 65, 138
Urie, Michael 110
utterance 3, 11–16, 21, 29–30, 32, 37–40, 48–50, 52–53, 56, 62, 64, 77–78, 80–82, 84–85, 87, 90–91, 95, 97–98, 101, 106, 113, 119, 121–122, 132–134, 138, 145, 147–148, 150, 156, 159–160, 162–164, 166, 173–175, 177–182, 184; filmic 31, 37, 49, 51–52, 54–55, 62–64, 113, 150, 159; literality 146–149, 157, 173, 175, 177; verbal 17, 31, 150

value 74, 77, 79, 115–117, 142; *see also* object of value
value system 17, 26, 28, 58–62, 64, 79, 130, 174–175, 182
Vassey, Liz 158, 165
Vélez, Lauren 112
verbal comedy 5
verbal language, text 4, 11, 51, 84, 91
veridiction 5–7, 19, 22, 106, 126–129, 167–174; veridictive pact 6, 148
verisimilitude 111, 157, 177
visual language, text 11, 17, 36–37, 49, 67–68, 88–90
voice-in 54–55
voice-off 69, 87, 90
voice-over 13, 42, 51–52, 55, 62, 64, 69, 134–135, 137

The WB 8, 175
web 14, 42
webisode 14
Weddle, David 164
Will & Grace 24, 27, 29, 33, 35, 133–134
Williams, Billy Dee 156
Williams, Vanessa 108
Wilson, Rainn 73
Winkler, Henry 15
The Wizard of Oz 39
Wolf, Dick 174
workplace comedy 21, 23–24, 27, 55
Wright, Aloma 47
Writers Guild of America strike, 2007–2008 35, 66

The X-Files 174–175

Yo soy Betty, la fea 13, 107, 128
Young, Damian 92

www.ingramcontent.com/pod-product-compliance
Ingram Content Group UK Ltd.
Pitfield, Milton Keynes, MK11 3LW, UK
UKHW042000140426
5217IPUK00015B/905